Miles to Go...

Episodes from a Life Half-Lived

Keith (Kim) Mathias Miles

Copyright © 2021 by Keith Mathias Miles

All rights reserved.

ISBN 978-1-62806-345-5 (print | paperback)
ISBN 978-1-62806-347-9 (print | paperback for distribution)

Library of Congress Control Number 2022901082

Published by Salt Water Media
29 Broad Street, Suite 104
Berlin, MD 21811
www.saltwatermedia.com

Cover image: The Five Miles Farm on Parkers Creek, looking towards the Bay, by Gordon Campbell, AtAltitudeGallery.com and is used with permission.

Interior images provided by the author and/or used with permission of the owner, the newspaper, and/or the media outlet.

Additional copies can be obtained by visiting the publisher's website or by calling the publisher directly at (443) 513-4422.

Dedication

This book is dedicated to my parents, Helen and Keith C. (Abie) Miles, who gave me not just life, but life on The Five Miles Farm, on the Eastern Shore of Virginia, a college education, values that I treasure, and support throughout my life.

Acknowledgements

I thank Miles Barnes, one of the Shore's leading historians, who slogged through the book and gave me valuable advice on how to improve it.

And much appreciation goes to Curtis Badger, a celebrated author in his own right, and who offered me advice about the ins and outs of how to publish.

Finally, and most of all, I thank my wife, Wendy, for putting up with my 5 a.m. writing sessions, who proved a most worthy editor and proofreader, and who helped immensely in making this at least halfway readable.

Contents

Author's Note	i
Early Memories - The 1940s	1
The House on Kerr Street	1
Grandparents	4
Big Momma and Big Daddy	4
Mom Mom and Pop Pop	4
Life on the Farm - The '50s - Early '60s	11
The House on the Farm	11
The Lane	14
The Docks	15
Work on the Farm	16
The Betrayal	18
The Critters	19
Hog Killing	23
The Tree	24
The Woods	25
Leslie	26
The Creek	28
The Heat	32
Hunting	32
Self-Entertainment	34
Hurricanes	35
Sisters	38
Sam	38
Barb	40

PARENTS	44
Mom	44
Dad	54
Sailing	61
THE EARLY 1960S	65
Christmases	65
School	66
Athletics	70
The Break	76
The Trip to Trinity	78
THE TRINITY EXPERIENCE	80
The Wreck and the Draft	86
Boeck's Sarcoidosis	88
The Florida-Bahamas Lark	90
The Sit-In and Takeover	91
Fraternity Impact	96
The Pranks	97
The Rhodes Scholarship Experience	99
NYC and A Night to Remember	104
POST COLLEGE EXPERIENCES - THE EARLY '70S	112
The European Motorcycle Tour	112
Graduate School at Princeton	118
The Ford Foundation - A Night to Forget	120
The New York City Experience	125
Legionnaires Disease, Maybe	125
The Personal Growth Movements	127
The Wandering Months	131
The Governor's Justice Commission	132
The 1976 Bicentennial Voyage	133
Arthur D. Little, Inc.	137

THE WHITE HOUSE YEARS	139
The Inauguration	139
The Executive Office Reorganization	143
Wing And Feather	149
The Reorganization of the Government	154
The Camp David Run	160
THE VOYAGE	163
Drifting	168
THE DEERING EXPERIENCE	172
The Worth of a Homeplace	175
The Group	182
New Hampshire Dartmouth Psychiatric Research Center	184
WHAT WOMEN TAUGHT ME	190
The Longer-Term Relationships	192
The Lessons	205
THE SURPRISE TRIPS	211
The Little Palm Island Escape	211
The Cheerleading Getaway	212
The Cambridge Surprise	215
The San Francisco Caper – The Big Kahuna	216
THE REMOTE CAMPING EXPERIENCES	219
Upper Pierce Pond and Mayor's Island	219
BACK TO THE FIVE MILES FARM	225
The Five Miles Farm Cannonball	226
Life Now In 2021	227
A Night to Remember at Onancock International Films	231

BACK TO THE FIVE MILES FARM (CONTINUED)
    The Library Experience 235
    The Trips 239

WHO IS KEITH MATHIAS MILES? 245
    Naivete 245
    Empathy 247
    To Understand and to Be Understood 253
    A Need for Justice 255
    An Awe of Nature 257
    Introversion and Extroversion 261
    Touch, and Physical Intimacy 262
    Image 264
    Ethics 265

MY VALUES AND HOW THEY DEVELOPED 267
    Respect for and Appreciation of Differences 267
    Political Values and Thought 269
    The Essentials: Beauty, Truth, Love, and Courage 276

WHOSE EXPECTATIONS? WHOSE SUCCESS? 289

MONEY AND ME 293
    The Windfall 297
    Generosity vs Selfishness 300

RELIGION AND SPIRITUALITY 304
    Space, The Universe, and God 308

MORTALITY 310

WHY "A LIFE HALF-LIVED?" 312

ADDENDUM 314

Author's Note

I am writing this as a remembrance of my life, at age 75 years. I have children, grandkids, nieces, and nephews who someday may wish to know more about who this guy was, and from whence he came. Also, who knows how much longer I may be around, and since I now have the time and mental acuity to record episodes in my life, I have done so.

You may find this to be the story of a young American boy's life, coming of age, then living that age. First growing up in rural America in the latter half of the 20th century, and then coming of age in the more troubled and unmoored first two decades of the 21st. Not exactly a model for others, but more a cautionary tale to live life most fully and authentically, moment to moment.

What you will find here is not necessarily the truth, but only the truth as I remember it. Any judgements or opinions I express are my own, reflecting what I believe, seen through my own lens and biases. It is my life as I see and remember it now, from a distance. Others may, and probably will, have somewhat differing memories of events documented here. And I may find my views and memories altered with time. While not a "Tell All" book, it is a "Tell Most" effort, for it reveals much, perhaps too much, of myself and my experiences in life. But for now, it is what it is … necessarily limited in space and inclusiveness. Thank you for considering this, my self-indulgence, written in a succession of early mornings over seven months in the pandemic winter and spring of 2021.

Thank you,
Keith (Kim) Mathias Miles

Early Memories - The 1940s

The House on Kerr Street

Fragments. That's all the memories I have of our first house on Kerr Street in Onancock, and our time living there. Onancock is a small town on the Eastern Shore of Virginia, a little piece of heaven located on the Delmarva peninsula on the eastern side of the Chesapeake Bay. I started writing this book for my family. Thus, this first part is about a little family history, and in some ways starting here is not the most interesting of reads. But it will give some context and a sense of the Miles and Mathias history in this country and my parent's and grandparents' experience on the Shore, before launching into the good stuff. If you're interested in snatches of ancestry, how we came to the Shore, early life in the 1920s, the Mathias stores, and Mom's and Dad's origins and courtship, read on. If not, move on to "Life on the

The Kerr Street House, Onancock

Farm" on page 11. I have included a section on both sets of my grandparents in an addendum following the end of this book.

The house on Kerr Street, our first real house, was my grandparent's house. A. J. and Bessie Mathias, my mother's parents, built the house in the late 1930s on Kerr Street, across from the lot behind Ker Place. (Ker Place is a famous old residence, both the street and home spelled Kerr and pronounced as "cur" back then. Today, after finding the original spelling of the large brick historic home, they dropped one "r" from the name and it is pronounced Ker [car] Place, although folks still refer to the street as "cur street".)

My few memories of the Kerr Street home were collecting my comic books, rushing Daddy in the testicles when he came home from work one day and hurting him, burning my hands badly on the stove playing blind man's bluff, playing with Brenda Parker in the sandbox out back, almost getting run over leading younger sister Sam across the street in front of the house, and playing "show me yours" with our neighbor Jane at ages five and nine respectively in her playhouse behind her house (she was

Brenda Parker and me

my "older woman", much more experienced in these things). And riding my tricycle up and down the sidewalk. Mom, Dad, and the family lived there only until I was five years old.

Grandparents

Big Momma and Big Daddy

My mother, Helen Mathias Miles, was a "come here" arriving on the Shore in 1921 at the age of two. Dad's family were longtime Shore residents having been on the Shore from the 1650s. Upon graduation from Onancock High School, Mom went to Goldey-Beacom College in Wilmington while Dad entered the Coast Guard in 1938. After a long on and off again courtship, one weekend just before Dad left for the Pacific, home on a break from the Coast Guard in 1941, they ran away to Princess Anne, MD, to get married. Sister Barbie was born in 1942, while I was born in '46 and Sam, my younger sister, joined us in 1948. We lived at the Kerr Street house for about 5 years after Dad came home from the war in the Pacific in 1945.

In those early years, our parents had little money and Dad tried several things, raising mink among others, while Mom worked in the family store, Mathias 5 and Dime, on Market Street in Onancock. It was the first 5 and 10 cent store on Virginia's Eastern Shore. It turned out to be one of four such stores that my grandparents, Big Momma (Bessie McPherson Mathias) and Big Daddy (Allison or A. J. Mathias,) owned in Onancock, Pocomoke, Parksley, and Exmore. The Onancock store became known as the first store that began offering "Green Stamps", redeemable 10 for a dollar.

The start of the stores was interesting. Big Momma and Big Daddy and their three children were living in Greenbush, VA about six miles up the road from Onancock. They had moved from Ellicottville, NY, in 1921 when Mom was two. After moving to Greenbush, Big Momma got a catalogue one year (from Butler Bros. in Baltimore, one of the first ones that came out). She started ordering things she needed from it, and selling some as well, originally just to raise some money for the church next door. Then her neighbors started asking her to order more things for them from the catalogue. One story is that soon the collective orders were large enough that the train, which ran right straight down the entire Eastern Shore, and right by the house, started making stops in Greenbush to drop off Big Momma's orders. (Probably fantasy as Greenbush was almost certanly a stop in its own right.)

The Mathias Five and Dime Opens (Image used with permission)

Mathias Five and Dime on Market Street in Onancock, 1937
(Image courtesy of Tom Badger and Curtis Badger)

*The Christmas Candy Giveaways
(Image used with permission)*

After several years of operating this way, the orders were getting out of hand and delivering them took considerable time. Big Momma had the idea of starting a store in Onancock, since by that time she had a good feel for what her neighbors wanted in terms of household goods. In 1929, just before the depression started, they rented a store right in the center of town on Market Street close to Wises' Drugstore on the corner of Market and North Streets and set up shop. It was called the Mathias 5 and Dime.

The store was successful from the start, with the grand opening sell-out providing money to cover the first order and provide funds for the second order. This success was mainly due to the fact that Big Momma priced things so low (with only a small mark up since she did not want to take advantage of her neighbors). Many things were really sold for 5 or 10 cents, and her 9 cent sales were famous. The store, and the Mathiases, were known for being very generous. For instance, each Christmas they gave away 2000 lbs. of candy to kids who came into the store.

They also took things in trade when customers did not have money for the goods (this was the Depression). Big Daddy helped out folks in need anonymously. He had a reputation as being the kindest man around (this being told to me by old codgers and women who had known him way back). The store survived the Depression and thrived. As the store prospered, Big Momma (Bessie) and Big Daddy (Allison) built the new house on Kerr Street, probably in the mid to late 1930's.

My very earliest memory was of pushing through some heavy draperies hung from the ceiling to separate rooms above the store on Market Street. I played there during the day when Mom worked in the store. I could not have been more than three or four as I was born in '46 and the stores were sold not many years after.

Today the Eastern Shore peninsula consisting of the parts of Delaware, Maryland and Virginia lying east of the Chesapeake Bay is called "Delmarva", a term used commonly by everyone. What is largely unknown, is that Allison Mathias, our Big Daddy, helped name the peninsula "Delmarva". There was a contest to name the peninsula put on by a newspaper, *The Peninsula Enterprise*, I think, back in the twenties or thirties. Big Daddy and another fellow submitted the name "Delmarva" and won,

Sugar Purchase Certificate

Dad returns from the war and meets Barbie

Helen and Abie (Keith C.) Miles Mom and Dad

splitting a $10 prize. There was a newspaper clipping about it in one of Mom's scrapbooks. I say "helped" because there are earlier references to the Delmarva Peninsula that have been found so maybe the newspaper was just running the contest to name the peninsula for their own use. Oh well, one for the historians.

In the early years in Onancock, Big Daddy was the brains behind starting and managing the finances of the stores, while Big Momma was the brains behind the merchandising and sales. Big Daddy, and later with his son, Mom's brother Robert, was in charge of managing staff, buying and starting stores in other towns, and generally serving as the managers of the stores. They ran the four Eastern Shore stores, with my mother and Robert, until they sold out. We have no record of how much they sold the four stores for or exactly when or why, most think it was around 1950. Their son, Robert, owned two other stores in the western part of Virginia which he kept into the '50s and another two he kept into the '60s or later.

At one point in the late '50s, Robert started the Dollarama in Onancock, a forerunner to the dollar stores and overstocks today where everything came from either overstocked merchandise or "seconds" of merchandise that could not be sold anywhere else under the original brand name because of a minor flaw. Most things were priced at a dollar, including tax, or two, three, or four for a dollar, etc. so you didn't have to worry about pennies.

Mom worked in the Onancock store, until the store closed around the early 1950s. She loved the work and was a born businesswoman. During the war, before I was born, Mom and Peggy Mathias, Robert's wife, lived with the two children, Barbie and Peggy's daughter Gayle, above one of the stores. During that time, Peggy took care of the children while Mom worked during the day in the store. They endured the shortages and rationing during the war, but the stores continued to prosper. At some point early during the war, Mom, Dad, and Barbie, my older sister, moved into the Kerr Street house with Big Momma and Big Daddy, where Sammie and I were later born.

Dad with the three kids

Dad did not like living with Big Momma and Big Daddy on Kerr St., not due to any dislike of them at all, but a feeling that he should raise his family on his own and live independently in his own home. Understandable. He landed a job at the Chincoteague Naval Base as a carpenter in the late 1940s and began saving his pennies for a house. Somehow, after searching every Saturday and Sunday, in 1950 Dad found an old waterfront house on Parker's Creek off Onancock Creek. It had 35 acres with a third of a mile of waterfront which they bought for $4,000 with a loan. Dad said he never got a wink of sleep until he had paid off the loan in 1957 or '58. The farm played a huge role in my growth and development, and as for real memories, my life started there.

Life on the Farm - The '50s - Early '60s

I credit my life on the farm for my appreciation of nature, my love of hard work, peacefulness, compassion, self-reliance, loyalty, and love of animals and living things. I would not trade it for anything.

We moved down to the farm which Dad christened "The Five Miles Farm" in 1951 when I was five. The farm was five miles from town, with five in the family, and the name was Miles, hence the name "The Five Miles Farm".

The House on the Farm

The house was nothing to speak of. The original house was built (I mean standing) either in 1780 or 1812. We know this because when I returned to the house with my wife Wendy in 2008, I gutted the house, and the contractors found a cannon

The Original House — "The Five Miles Farm"

ball from that era embedded in the rafters of the original section (story later).

Earliest memories of the first two years were of the outhouse, a spider-filled regular outhouse with a big hole and a wooden lid for a toilet seat. We used this when the weather was warm enough (the house did not have a bathroom at the time and the former owner piped the grey water directly into the creek.) We used the outhouse until we dug a cesspool to use, allowing a new bathroom. When the weather was cold, we used a bucket on the porch, or (as my sister, Barb, remembers) slop buckets in each bedroom with a piece of fabric around the edges so it wasn't so cold. Mom would empty them every day. After we got a new bathroom, we used the old outhouse, sans seat, as a shelter from the rain while waiting for the bus at the end of the lane.

That first year or so I remember that we had a stove in the living room and heated with coal which was delivered. We took baths at least every Saturday (probably more often) in a big, galvanized tub in the living room that Mom filled with hot water

Moving the outhouse to the end of the lane

from the stove … last in got the dirtiest water. An electric water heater and shower came later with the new bathroom.

As we entered school, we walked down the lane to the bus each day with a succession of collies, Prince (Barbie's favorite), Queenie (who died at age three months by us running over her on the way to Sunday School), Duchess (my favorite), Duke (Sam's dog), and Joy, the cocker spaniel, our first dog who licked all the after-dinner dishes clean, named after a dish detergent at the time. Each died of heart worms which could not be easily stopped back then.

When I entered first grade at the Onancock High School in 1952, the teacher, Mrs. Jacobs, showed all of us a picture of Lassie, the collie on TV. Since I had never heard of Lassie, not having a TV or seeing any collies other than our Prince, I insisted that the dog was our dog Prince and demanded to know how the teacher had gotten a picture of Prince. And who was this Lassie? Mom straightened me out when I got home.

Going to school was uneventful, though the bus with the older kids could be stressful at times. Coming home was another matter. The collies would meet us at the bus every day and walk up the third of a mile lane with us. I enjoyed draining the potholes after a rain and watching the water run-off into the ditches. I was going to be a dam builder back then.

Dad improved the house gradually over the years, first adding a bathroom in year two, with a shower (God's gift to the human race!), then a central floor furnace (God's second gift), and finally two new rooms off the kitchen (a dining room, formerly a rickety screened-in porch), and a sunroom off the living room. Life was really primitive only for the first year or two.

The Lane

A portion of my woods clearing project and the Shatterhouse Path

Ah, the lane. It was a dirt lane about a third of a mile long without good ditches, causing the road to fill up with mud and potholes so badly that often we had to leave the car at the end of the lane and walk up through the mud, or risk getting stuck for the duration. This continued for many years until Dad was able to get someone to come and carve out ditches with a machine. Keeping the road stable and in good (decent) condition was a constant struggle until then, but today it is in great shape, and a beautiful 1/3 mile walk through now towering pines.

I remember one winter, Dad challenged me to clear about three acres of brush and small trees, leaving any tree over four inches in diameter. I was about 12 and he promised to give me $50 if I finished the job. So, every day after school, I came home, got my small 24-inch ax, perfect for me, and whittled away at this task for about two hours until sunset. This took me two months of solid work, but I didn't cut my foot off, and had those three acres looking beautiful (to what end I don't know to this day, as 60 years later it has all grown up again in 30 foot trees and brush). But I was able to buy an A2000 baseball glove with some of that money.

The Docks

Dad constructed several docks from whatever hose-pumped posts and lumber he could muster, only to see them destroyed by the ice every other winter, pulling up the pilings and leaving a mess for Dad and me to clean up. We went swimming off these docks, tied our sailboats and rowboat up there, and caught crabs clinging to the pilings. This was a great pastime, as we looked for anything to hold our interest in the summer. For some reason we rarely fished off the docks, just used them for other recreation.

One time on a very cold February morning, for some reason Dad said to 12-year-old sister Sam at the breakfast table, "Give you $5 if you go out on that dock and jump over." Whereupon, Sam, not one to walk away from a challenge, and before Dad could stop her, jumped up, ran out on the dock and jumped over, onto and through the skim ice on the creek. Of course, Dad ran after her, thinking she was gonna kill herself. She didn't, and he paid the well-earned $5. That was Sam.

Life on the farm was idyllic for me. Home after school, often to go hunting squirrels with my 22 rifle, which I never hit anything with because 60 years later my cousin Greg Parks (Dad's sister Sis's son with her husband Wimpy) found that the sights were off about two inches at 40 yards and six at 100! Sometimes I went

Ice damage to one of the many docks

hunting with my friend Jack, mostly rabbits as his dad had dogs. Sometimes alone. We had great times and actually brought some game home every once in a while, with my trusty bolt action .410 gauge shotgun. Jack is a wonderful guy. Perhaps the most guileless and good hearted man I've known.

Often after school I would stay in town waiting for Mom to get off from work at Pyrofax Gas as an administrative assistant to the owner, Granville Northam (she pretty much ran the place). I would play touch football with my friends behind the post office until she got off work around five. Mom worked there from when I was about 8 to age 16 or 18 when she joined my father at NASA (which had taken over the Naval Base around 1960 and Dad had gotten a job with them). They traveled the 50 minutes by carpool up and back every day, leaving at about seven a.m., about an hour before we caught the bus for school.

Work on the Farm

Pitching hay into the loft

On weekends and sometimes after school and when needed after Dad got home, I would help him on the farm, running the tractor, shucking corn, cutting and loading and pitching hay into the loft of a beautiful old barn we had. It was hard work, but with Dad it seemed to not be bad at all (except he was not too patient with me when I'd bring the wrong tool or make a mistake ... a trait I unfortunately see in myself all too often also).

One advantage of growing corn was after we had cut all the corn stalks down, we would stack them vertically into individual "fodder shocks" about 20-30 yards apart. These looked like teepees and we would get inside, spread out the base of the stalks and have perfect huts to play in. Couldn't have had better huts. We were always sad when the shocks had to come down and be taken to the barn for feed for the cattle.

Sundays fell into a routine. Dad and Mom picked us up from church in Onancock (Dad and Mom didn't go, as Dad didn't want to and Mom was too shy and class conscious to go alone to the fancy church in Onancock). Then Sunday dinners were the best, and a tradition, as Mom made a full dinner at around two p.m. This usually consisted of a chicken or a roast and "slippery" dumplings, mashed potatoes, macaroni and cheese, collard greens, peas, string beans, carrots and the biggest and best three-part, cloverleaf, really hot, yeast dinner rolls you have ever tasted.

I would be sitting on the rug in the sunroom basking in the sun pouring in through the south window reading the funnies of the *Baltimore Sun*, our Sunday paper, while Dad read the news. Barb would be helping Mom get dinner. My job with Sam was clearing the table after the dinner, while Barb put the extra food away and Dad and Mom shared dishwashing.

Later in the afternoons, we would either go sailing in the summer, or Dad took a nap while we played outside until evening, which we spent devouring leftovers. Every Sunday night Dad would make a cake or a pan of brownies, and he was exceptionally good at both. Warm out of the oven, with milk, neither could be beat. Yes, life was pretty idyllic.

The Betrayal

I was six years old and going to the dentist for the first time. I was scared. I had heard all kinds of stories about how terrible it was to go to the dentist. How it hurt, and all about the drilling. The high whiney noise of the slow dull drill and having to keep your mouth open. And if that wasn't bad enough, I had heard about the needle they used, and how the dentist stuck it into your gums. And how you were in this big chair and couldn't get out. I had heard all these things from my sister, who was four years older and not only knew about these things but reveled in scaring the hell out of me with stories of them.

And what was much, much, worse ... I had heard about having a tooth pulled and that it was very painful and just about the worst thing that you could have done at the dentist. But the most awful thing was that I had a loose baby tooth, one of my last ones. It was just hanging by a small thread in the back of my mouth, and I had been playing with it with my tongue for about a week or so. I told my mother that I didn't want to have the dentist pull that tooth no matter what because I knew it would hurt terribly, because my sister said it would. My mother said that I didn't have to have that tooth pulled because it would just fall out on its own and to just tell the dentist not to pull it.

The dreaded day came, and I went into the dentist's office and my turn came to climb up into the chair. I did. I immediately told the dentist about my hanging tooth and made him promise, really promise, not to pull that tooth no matter what. After looking at it, just hanging there, he promised, and laughed and I felt relieved. Then he started doing his job in my mouth. I can't remember what he did, but I do remember him going into my mouth with a small string with a loop on it, and the next thing I knew he had put the loop around the thread holding my tooth in and closed it and snipped off the tooth. He pulled it out and showed it to me.

I had never been so mad. I was enraged. HE HAD PROMISED!! And he had broken his promise and laughed about it! I had never had anybody break their promise to me, even my sisters, whom I had fought with a good bit. And this dentist was an adult. and he had promised!

I never went back to that dentist.

This taught me a few things. One of course was that often if you dread something a great deal it turns out to not meet your awful expectations. And second, there were some people who while they may think they are doing you a favor, will break a promise without thinking of the consequences to you, and them.

The Critters

We raised all sorts of animals at different times. About 15 to 20 sheep, which had the run of the place (except around the house which we kept fenced in). These we sheared once a year on shearing day, when a team would come in and cut and bag the wool in huge seven-foot-high burlap sacks. Of course, we had favorites among the lambs born, including an all-black one we called Lucky.

And there were the very early years when we had a milk cow, which Mom faithfully milked each morning before work, and though she taught us how to work the teats to get the most milk the quickest, she usually did it, as it was required once a day at least for the cow to be comfortable. We drank the milk after letting the cream separate. We later got our milk from

Sam and me hoeing the garden

Sam, Me, and Gayle with a calf

Stuart, me, Joy, Wade, and Sam
"Jes Chillin"

Henry Custis, the farmer next door, who had a dairy barn with milking machines that made the job easier. I remember those old-fashioned bottles. We also got our collie puppies from Mr. Custis.

We raised chickens not only for the eggs we got each day, if we could find them, and then judge whether they were fresh or had been hidden from us for a week or two. Don't know how Mom did that, but we were never sick from them. We also slaughtered them for chicken dinners. The process was a little gruesome in retrospect, but fun at the time. Mom would take a white basin about five inches deep and maybe 16 inches in diameter and place it over a chicken after catching it (we only raised "free range "chickens at the time, cooping them up at night at feeding time to spare them from the critters, mainly foxes).

Once the chicken was caught under the pan, Mom would reach under and pull the chicken's head out from under the side of the pan, pinning it down with the pan and WHACK! cut its head off with a hatchet. Then the funny part started, as Mom would take the tub away and the chicken would begin running around headless, spouting blood from its neck for anywhere from 10 to 15 seconds until it finally "realized" it was dead.

And there were cattle, not too many, maybe four to six at most, usually two or three. They ate the corn stalks left over after shucking the corn, or the hay we grew. The last stage in harvesting the corn was shelling it with an antique corn sheller with a huge flywheel that you manually turned to shell the corn off the cob. One day after I had been away at college, I came home to find that Dad had given away all the old antique farm implements we had. I told him that they were valuable up north and it was a shame that he had let them go and to please check with me before giving any other things away. I'm afraid I hurt Dad's feelings in saying that.

The hardest job I ever had in my life was to pry out the 12 inches of deep layered cattle crap mixed with hay. It was packed solid in the cattle stall where we would pen a steer up for about three weeks before slaughter to tenderize the meat and to keep them from eating wild onions and spoiling the meat. Each time I did this (took about three weeks of ridiculously hard work to pry it up and spread it on the garden) I would break about three pitchfork handles and Dad would have to fashion new ones.

One time Dad tried to kill and slaughter one steer himself. He led him into the garage with my uncle Kenny Miles (Dad's brother) and my great uncle Harry Miles. Dad led him into the garage and shot him between the eyes with my .410 shotgun … to absolutely no effect … as the pellets bounced off the forehead. So, Dad got his 12 gauge out with a deer slug and put him down on the floor of the garage, planning to string him up by the rafters and gut, skin, and carve him up there. HOWEVER, he had forgotten that the rafters were two by fours and a 800 lb. steer would bring the entire garage down, so he had to drag the steer out to the woods with the tractor, find a tree and hoist him up there to finish the job. Dad was a might bit embarrassed about that.

A particularly sad and startling event happened one night in the late 1950s when I was about 12 or 13. I awoke upstairs, in the middle of the night, to find a bright light flashing in my window in the bedroom. I arose and looked out the window and saw that the house across the creek was on fire and fully ablaze. I ran downstairs to find Dad on the phone with the fire department, who had already been alerted. The department was all volunteer and 15 minutes away even after the men assembled from their homes. There was little chance of saving the house. For us it was a four-mile trip to get around and across the creek to the house from our house so all we could do was sit and watch as the rest of the house burned to the ground. A new family had just moved in after Elizabeth Rue had died.

The fire engines arrived soon after, but we learned on the national news the next morning that a wife and four young kids had died in the fire. The father had climbed out of the upstairs window while the mother went back to get the kids to throw down to him. She never came back to the window as the house was full of fire and smoke. A real tragedy.

Hog Killing

My friend Jack's dad raised hogs and would have a hog-killing night every year that was absolutely magical for a boy. We looked forward to it every year. Just think of it. A cool dark October or November night, shots fired over in the field as darkness fell, tractors dragging the hogs one by one from the far field, around the corner into the barn area. The whole place lit by huge fires, with tubs of scalding water boiling over the fires, smoke rising everywhere. The teams of skilled men and women were ready to clean, gut, skin, and carve up the hog into hams, bacon, pork loins, and sausage, using special knives and instruments to scrape the skin and carve the hog. It seemed nothing was wasted, even the feet.

The fires glowing all night, smoke rising everywhere, the smokehouse where the hams would be stored gradually filling, shots fired from afar, it was mystical for two 12-year-olds. It would last all night and in the morning we would stuff ourselves with the best sausage ever made. Doesn't get much more exciting than that for a 12-year-old free to roam around all night watching the various operations of the skilled team, who were brought in from away, going from farm to farm to expertly do their thing. A totally magical night.

But mainly my life at home on weekends was working with Dad on the farm. Raising whatever crops he thought might help with the finances (but we barely broke even I'd guess most years, even with me and sometimes my sister Sam's help). Barbie was four years older and too "smart" for field work, and she was needed by Mom in the house though she preferred to be out roaming the fields and woods with us. Barb took care of us in the mornings with breakfast after Mom and Dad had left for work.

The Tree

We had a huge eastern cottonwood tree at the end of the house with several incredibly long limbs parallel to the ground, where we hung trapezes and pretended to be circus performers.

We gave performances of all our tricks on a Sunday once a summer for the parents and relatives. We would time ourselves to see who could run down the limb the fastest from the trunk to the end, about 50 feet. I usually won as I was pretty nimble and athletic. Sam wasn't far behind. Barb, being four years older, was more sophisticated and restricted herself to the trapezes. The tree must have been six or seven feet in diameter and was a huge shade tree. One time coming home from college I learned that Dad had had the tree cut down, leaving only a 7 x 14-foot trunk standing. The man doing the trimming evidently wanted an extra "surprise" $700 to remove the stump as well. Dad, ticked off greatly, refused to give it to him and the stump, sprouting leaves, stood for years, looking like a huge phallic symbol in the yard.

    I was very mad at Dad for cutting down that tree, as it gave great shade and held fond memories. His story was that once or twice a year he and Mom had the entire church over for a lunch on the lawn and the members parked their cars under the tree. Dad was afraid that a limb would fall on the cars, as during storms, some limbs did usually come off the old tree. I told Dad that they only held the party when it would be a sunny calm day and no branch was likely to fall then, but the damage was done. I'm afraid I gave Dad too much grief for that … shouldn't have.

The Woods

    I loved the woods and we all played there. We built numerous "shatter houses" which were really lean-tos made from downed limbs, with pine needles (shatters) placed on top. We would clear paths and name them … the Shatterhouse Path, the Wagon Trail, the Secret Rabbit Path, we had a ball. And then there was the Indian Burial Grounds. Barbie named that ... a spot not far off the road where there were about six or eight mysterious (to us) mounds of earth covered in years of pine needles (shats). We were convinced they were Indian burial sites. There was also a special place which had a ten-foot ring of beautiful lady slipper flowers, right in the middle of the woods, rimming a small depression in the ground. We speculated that a very small asteroid or comet had fallen and brought the seeds and made the depression. Great for our imaginations.

Lots of times after school, I would just go to the woods and sit under a tree, waiting for the squirrels to come home to their nests. I knew every inch of those 25 acres of woods including the Sunday tree. This was where the whole family one Sunday took a blanket and picnic and had a lunch under a tree. Dad hammered spikes into the tree so we could climb up. I wouldn't climb it, as even then I was suffering from a decent case of acrophobia. However, Sam scrambled right up. I was embarrassed and ashamed in front of Dad, but not enough to get me to climb it. Barb was above doing silly things like that, being four years older.

To this day I still go out two or three times a week and sit quietly on a chair in the woods silently watching the trees, the deer, the birds and animals, whatever is around. I marvel at the growth over time, though the seasons. It's my meditation time and I can't think of a better way.

Leslie

I had a friend, Leslie Murray, who stayed with us several summers around the age of 10 to 12 as his mother wanted him away from the "big city" of Onancock. Les and I would play all summer, one game being to stand across the field about 200 yards apart and shoot arrows to each other ... long sharp 28" target arrows which would have easily killed us if we had been hit. We fastened whistles to the end of the arrows and hid behind a tree and then yelled for the other to "let 'er rip!" as we'd wait for the "missile" to come whistling by, then go pick it up and fire it back, with warning of course, as we were not stupid ... well, not too stupid.

Leslie and I must have spent three or four summers playing in the woods, crabbing on the creek, sailing, whatever looked interesting. I remember that one beautiful summer day, Leslie and I lay down in the woods after picking blueberries to watch the clouds drift by, naming each one after whatever it looked like. Two days later we had a terrible case of the chiggers. He had 112 and I had 115 or something like that. It was the most awful two weeks I had experienced at that time, itching terribly. I remember my testicles were swollen with chigger bites. Nothing would stop the itching. To this day, I rarely venture into the

Leslie and me sailing about age 8

woods during the summer months, even though chiggers don't seem to be as much of a problem as they once were for some reason.

One summer Leslie and I got the idea to cut a canal through a narrow spit of land which jutted out about 150 yards into the creek, almost cutting it off. It served as a form of breakwater in the creek but also meant we had to go around it to go down the creek with our boat. So build a canal we did, cutting slabs of marsh grass and moving them away so the water could run through. Little did we know that the remaining 75-yard island tip of the land would erode over the years, leaving the creek open to storms sweeping up the creek and further eroding the land on our opposite shore. Oh well, unintended consequences.

The Creek

It wasn't just any creek because it was OUR creek. OK, not really ours as several other houses were on the creek: Charlie Dye's (the artist) about 1000 yards down the creek from us on the eastern side like us, and Elizabeth Rue, who ran a restaurant in Onley, lived up the creek across on the western side, as did old Henry Custis (another Henry Custis) in another ramshackle house right across from us. It fell down after he died in the '50s. Judge Northam and his sons Ralph and Tom and wife Nancy also lived around the bend on our side as well. Ralph is Virginia's Governor now.

Other neighbors were Emma White, who lived in the house directly across from our lane, on Finney's Creek, and the Shillings in a house at the end of Mimosa Lane, directly across from our lane and where Sonda and Beman Dawes lived much later. This small lane now has about seven more houses on it, and I thank Dad for not dividing up our 35 acres into house lots, which he could have done to make money for sure. And back then we needed it.

Dad bought on the water because he loved it and was a sailor all his life. It was a shallow creek not much more than five to six feet deep at its deepest at high tide, though 200 years ago supposedly larger boats would come up the creek to load crops to go to market. It was the only way to get harvests to market without trains or decent roads or cars and trucks back then.

How we played on that creek, catching crabs (doublers – two attached crabs shedding or pealing their shells), a little fishing (without too much luck) and jumping off the end of the dock up to four or five times a day in the heat of the summer (before air conditioning) just to cool off.

And we skated on the creek every winter after the ice became hard enough (Dad tested it for us). Had a ton of fun on used skates, none of which fit any of us very well. And Dad and the collies skated with us. Had a ball! I remember also skating at nighttime parties on Nelson Pond halfway to Onancock. The adults would build a big bonfire on the ice and we kids, ages 10 to 16 usually, would skate around and flirt with our girlfriends and boyfriends with the fire glowing and places marked off where we could not skate (too thin). Those were magical nights as well, a much different kind of magical from the hog killings nights I described, much more romantic. Nowadays, the creek rarely freezes thick enough to skate on, just skim ice for a day or two.

The many moods of the water fascinated me and still do. The quiet mornings when the creek was like glass as the sun came up, and some evenings too when the breeze died down (Wendy's and my favorite time to go kayaking, which we now do very often). Then the raging nor'easters which brought white caps and surges bringing high tides. The days when a steady light breeze meant good sailing. And watching the shifts in wind as the fronts moved through with dark-edged clouds leading the way. The many varieties of waterfowl we spotted on the creek were always a wonder, as fall and spring migrations were underway.

Yes, Parker's Creek gave us many pleasures, not the least of which now is to sit out near the edge of the water in our Adirondack chairs watching the sunsets, feeding the gulls. Facing west, we have some beautiful sunsets, particularly in late fall and early winter. And the pleasure, as kids, of being able to just jump in the water to momentarily escape the heat which was indescribable (not so needed now with air conditioning).

Of course, the sea nettles (now called jellyfish, a term we applied only to those sea nettles without nettles) were meddlesome, causing stinging for an hour or so. Vinegar was said to help ... but not much. I do remember climbing up on one

A creek sunset on a calm evening

of the big pilings to dive, and as I headed down into the water, was headed for the biggest sea nettle I had ever seen! That hurt a while and I was lucky I wasn't blinded.

Speaking of blinded, in about the fourth grade at age 10 or 11, I went to get my eyes checked as a teacher noticed I was squinting to see. Turns out I was severely near sighted, meaning I could not see far away at all. Dr. Wescott checked my eyes and sure enough I needed glasses badly. He ordered a pair and asked me to put them on. He then asked me to look out the window and tell him what I saw. It was magical. For the first time I could make out individual leaves on a tree 40 yards away, formerly just a blur of green. And I could see the white mortar between the bricks of a building at the same distance! I was astounded! It profoundly changed my life as I no longer had to sit in the front row at school to see the blackboard. Incredible! Much later I found out I had glaucoma and now take drops three times a day to sustain an acceptable eye pressure.

One summer day ... I must have been six or seven ... Sammie and I went to town with Mom. While she was in the store, we each sat on a window of the car and banged as loudly as we could on the car top, having a grand old time. Suddenly the town policeman ambled over and asked what we were doing and mildly suggested that we get back inside the car. We, of course, did. I did not tell my parents about this but was semi-traumatized by the episode and refused to leave the farm for about six months. I constantly watched the lane to make sure no one (like the policeman) was coming for me to haul me away. I was convinced that I was going to the slammer if I showed my face in town. A fear of authority you say? Took me awhile to get over that. An episode for sure.

The Heat

Oh, the heat! We kids slept upstairs in two small five-foot high rooms with bunk beds that Dad built under two dormer windows in each room ... the key word being UNDER the dormer windows which funneled what breeze there was well above our heads. We received absolutely no breeze at all and sweltered on those hot summer nights. It was dreadful. I remember when Dad finally installed a whole house fan at the end of one upstairs room one summer, I thought I had reached heaven as it drew a fantastic breeze across my skin for the first time. To this day I still sleep with a fan slowly blowing air across me.

In the winter it was a different story entirely, as the only heat in the house came from the floor furnace downstairs and had to come up the very narrow winding stairs to our bedrooms. On freezing mornings, you would wake up with ice on your pillow (or later my mustache) from your breath having frozen, and hurry to take your clothes downstairs and stand on the beautiful, heavenly, floor furnace, pumping hot air on your legs. (You had to be careful when you came in with frozen feet in your rubber boots as often you would soon smell burning rubber if you stayed on too long.) It's one thing I miss in the modern house we now have ... that wonderful warming floor furnace.

Hunting

I was an amateur hunter back in my bloodthirsty youth. I say amateur because the most I would ever get was a few squirrels, rabbits, or ducks and a couple of geese flying over. But Jack and I would get up in the morning dark at about five, take a sandwich and a piece of cake, and go off in the freezing cold to Hal Lassiter's land about 45 minutes away. By the time we got there the car would finally be toasty, but we would then get out and trudge in our boots to our waiting place to hope the geese would come in to land in the fields of corn. Sometimes they did, often they didn't. Most times we ended up not getting any but calling it a successful hunt anyway because at the end we would lay back in the rising sun and warm up while eating the cake and sandwich we brought.

Other times we would go squirrel hunting or duck hunting after school or rabbit hunting on weekend mornings with Jack's dogs. (Jack one time accidentally shot his dog, thinking it was a rabbit. The shot bounced off his breast plate and the dog was fine, but Jack took some ribbing for that.)

Jack and I were hunting for food one time while our friend Hal, wealthier and worldlier, was hunting for sport. This came home to us one day when I carefully and silently snuck up on a flock of ducks in a pond on Hal's father's land. I blasted them with my single shot blunderbuss of a twelve gauge and got six of them. Hal was mortified that I shot them sitting on the pond rather than in the air, while Jack and I were oblivious to the sporting aspect of hunting and wondered what had gotten into Hal. We were hunting for food and sneaking up successfully on a flock of ducks was a huge accomplishment. Hal didn't think it was sporting, and when he went back to hunt the next weekend, he found a seventh duck that I had killed. Oh well.

Much later when Jack and I were adults and I called Hal's father (a wonderfully kind man) to ask permission to hunt his land once again, he refused to let me. Puzzled, it was only later that I guessed that Hal had told his father of my nefarious act and he was horrified as well. Of course, I am now ashamed of that act, and realize my transgression, but at the time I thought Hal was crazy.

We never really had a great deal of success hunting, but we had a lot of good times. One time we were hunting in a vast marsh up behind Bloxom and we came across about 20 or 30 dead geese just lying way out in the marsh, freshly dead, with no marks on them. We were puzzled and stunned, never having heard of such a kill off. We speculated that they had all eaten something poisonous, but we did not have the sense to bring one back to allow the authorities to figure out what went wrong (mainly because no one back then had the expertise to conduct a goose autopsy as far as we knew).

On the way back from that hunt, from way out on the marsh, Jack was leading us, looking for the opening in the woods where we had come out onto the marsh as we had another mile of woods to walk before getting to the car. As we passed the opening where I knew we should go in Jack was sure it was further along, so we continued walking the marsh until we got to a solid wall of trees. Only then did Jack realize we had passed the opening way back and had to reverse direction to get out as it was getting dark. We did of course, but it was one of the only times Jack had directional problems, and I suspected he was suffering from some confusion caused by a touch of hypothermia.

Self-Entertainment

Unlike today, kids back then were on their own to entertain themselves. This was particularly the case for us during the summer school vacation because both Mom and Dad worked. We had to think up games, or activities to keep us occupied, and our parents had no time to do "projects" with us or keep us entertained. So we played tag; took turns hiding and finding a worthless and empty perfume bottle all one summer as if it were gold; swimming (one hour after lunch to avoid cramps, of course, which we would count down to the second); pitching a ball up on the roof of the house and catching it; or throwing it over to Sam on the other side; taking the skiff out in the creek or sailing it around; or going in the woods to build shatter houses; or carve out our paths; or making "mud pies" with wet mud on cement in the sun.

I remember one summer when I was about 12 or 14 I bought, from a friend, a 12" x 12" 45 rpm record player for $5. It was the first record player we had ever owned. I had one record, "Greensleeves". I played that over and over all summer and that simple purchase and record led to my love of music. I moved first from "The Lettermen" (I was a hopeless romantic), then on to folk singers Joan Baez, Judy Collins, Leonard Cohen, Peter, Paul and Mary, Bob Dylan, John Denver, leading to The Moody Blues, Bob Marley, Nancy Griffiths, with some country music thrown in, then Pavarotti, now reverting to the classics of Sam Cooke and Louis Armstrong. Love music.

Another time Sammie and I got ring worm from a stray cat that we had adopted and had to wear some awful purple medicine on our sores. We got UV rays to try to get over it, which we finally did, staying home from school for a week or two. We looked awful. Just an episode.

Hurricanes

Every summer we feared hurricanes, barreling up the East Coast, and pushing water up the Chesapeake to flood the

Bottom of King Street in Onancock — 1962

Eastern Shore and bring havoc with their winds. And we had some big ones ... Donna, Carol, Hazel ... all would mean downed limbs and some damage to the house and barn. But flooding was the big fear. As each storm approached, we would have to make the decision whether to stay and weather it out on the farm or go to higher ground in town or to the house of relatives such as Jo and Kim Penland, my cousins.

The worst storm in terms of flooding was the Good Friday Storm in 1962, which was not even a hurricane, but a conglomeration of factors which caused the biggest flood of the last 100 years. The moon, the tide, and the wind were all aligned to give us the strongest nor'easter we had ever seen. The waters, which often would come up into the yard, usually had another two and a half vertical feet to go before lipping into the house at the top of the steps, which it had never done. The Eastern Shore, being almost completely flat, spread the water easily as it rose, reducing the danger.

In this storm, the winds were great, and pushed the tides higher and higher. Soon it surrounded the house and kept rising. Propane tanks were floating by in the field between the woods and the house. All manner of debris was swept away and turned up in the woods or in our yards. But when the water was just about to lip into the house, having flooded over the steps, it began receding. We were lucky, only losing the floor furnace, which rusted out a few months after the storm, being under the house and vulnerable to the flooding.

However, in low lying areas and towns like Chincoteague, the damage was great as boats were left high and dry and downtown areas were flooded. This has been the only time that our house has been at all threatened by flooding.

For us kids, each storm was an adventure, but not for Mom and Dad, for they knew the damage and cost of each storm and did not look forward to the consequences. One time, Dad, as a member of the Power Squadron, the local boating club, had to go out in the Bay during one hurricane to help save some stranded sailors, caught in the storm. We were very worried about him until he returned.

Sisters

Now a bit about the siblings.

Sam

Sister Sam and I had a somewhat competitive relationship. She was the last born, six years younger than Barbie, two years younger than I was as the only boy, the middle child. Sam had to make her mark by being the rebel as Barb and I had staked out the "goody-goody" roles in the family … and she did it with flair, breaking most of the rules. We fought a good deal as young kids, wrestling and arguing. I, being the supposed "gentleman", would not try too hard, but Sam, two years younger, fought for all she was worth. And truth be known, when we were both small, she could whip me a good bit of the time even when I tried. Sam was a fierce competitor.

She also would not be beyond stooping to a few low tricks. Like the times we had shucking contests, each taking a row of corn to shuck and toss into piles to be picked up later in baskets. We competed to see who could finish the 700 ft. rows faster. I could not figure out how she seemed to always be faster than me, until one day I began to realize that she was skipping every third cornstalk (at least that belief was what my ego required, being a helluva shucker myself).

Another time, we were fake dueling with dull table knives and suddenly Sam started howling, as if I had struck her jugular, just after mom had told us to be careful. I knew Sam wasn't hurt and wondered why she was yelling, until Mom came after me and gave me a short spanking for hurting Sam, after which I went into the living room to find Sam laughing on the couch. Ooh was I pissed.

But being a rule breaker, Sam had more fun than Barb and I put together. She had many friends and I learned later in life that many times when I had come home from college and gone to sleep after a date, Sam would have her friends over to gather and drink beer in the garage and party on. I don't know how many times she did this, but it was clearly more fun than sleeping. The "goody goody" was not invited. And when Wendy and I returned to live on the farm in 2008 everyone asked first about "Where's Sam, what's Sam doing now?", a testament to her popularity.

Sam was a trickster with a big heart. On one of the Christmases, she couldn't be home, so she sent "the 12 presents of Christmas" to a neighbor, who then put them in the mailbox, one each day, and Mom and Dad couldn't figure out where they were coming from until Sam called on Christmas morning. They said it was one of their best Christmases.

Sam had managed to snag, through hard work and being a good cook, a career as a chef on these 100-150 foot mega yachts, billing herself as the "Guiltfree Gourmet". She would travel with the weather out of Ft. Lauderdale often going to the Mediterranean, the Bahamas, or wherever the whims of the wealthy owners took them. After doing this for several years, broken up

Chef Sam, "The Guiltfree Gourmet"

by a year or two being a chef for a wealthy family in Idaho or Montana she had met on one of the yachts, her back began giving her trouble and she had to quit.

Being resourceful, she then published two huge cookbooks, with over 1,200 quick & easy, low fat recipes in each, that she had cooked on board the yachts. She sold them around the world at boat shows and online, selling them for about $50 apiece to women who said, "If he's buying a boat, I can at least buy a nice book." It worked. She became successful at it. Sam seemed to skirt the edge of all rules (and I joke with her that it's a wonder to me, the "good boy", that she stayed out of jail, but she did ... smart, our Sam).

Sammie and her long-time friend and husband Randy (must be a saint) got married awhile back and live in Ft. Lauderdale where Sam is nursing a chronic and fairly serious case of arthritis of the spine which restricts her mobility substantially. She runs a huge crew house (calls it her "castle") for the crews of the many large yachts that sail out of Ft. Lauderdale to the Caribbean and the Mediterranean. Quite successful.

Barb

Barbie and Doug Scott

Barbara Lane Miles was four years older and didn't hang around or play with Sammie and me as much as she would have liked. Being older, Barb was expected to help Mom around the house more than Sam and I were.

We were all outdoor types, but Barb learned all the female things, cooking, sewing, cleaning. She had her own large group of friends, particularly Jane Twyford, Amy Savage, and Marcia Dobson and was very popular, hitting her teenage years as very pretty, athletic and a cheerleader (as was Sam). Since Mom went to work early, Barb would make our breakfast and get us off to school.

Barb and Sam were both stars of their basketball teams and cheerleaders. That was all they had for girls back then - an unfair world. And basketball was quite different, as the girls could only go to half court as there were defensive and offensive teams, I assume so they would not wear themselves out running full court. The pace was so much slower than the game women play today. Hail to Title IX!

Barb was quite popular, being chosen Queen of the Athletic Ball one year and had many suitors as I recall. Barb graduated in 1960, before it was expected and the norm that intelligent girls went on to college. That expectation and perhaps the lack of family financial resources kept Barb from going to college, which I'm sure she must have resented, being quite bright and capable. Instead, Barb got married soon after high school to Doug Scott, her steady. She worked for the Army and eventually rose to become a GS 12, very

Barb

high up for a person without a college degree. She supervised a staff of 12 and was responsible for the budget of millions of defense department dollars. She did quite well.

Barbie and Doug were married for about 10 years and had two great kids, Chris and Lexa, now each with their own kids. Lexa works with State Farm and lives between Newport News and Richmond and has two kids, Austin and Breyden, and her fine husband Darrell. Chris works as a defense lawyer for the Federal Public Defender's office and is living in San Francisco with twins Georgia and Olivia and older sister Roxie, now at Wellesley. I couldn't ask for better nieces and grandnieces and grandnephews.

Barb was divorced from Doug after about 10 years and years later married an Army man, Mac, and did some sailing and traveling with him to several different Army postings around

Barbie and her family

the world before getting a divorce and striking out on her own. Barb now lives in a small town, Forks, in Washington State, where it rains A LOT, which Barb seems to love. Barb spends her time gardening and visiting and very much enjoying her large family, often taking summer trips with them to Nags Head, NC for vacations.

Barb is currently outfitting a mini-van to use in traveling around the country for an extended period of time, leaving in the fall of 2021 and renting out the two houses she owns in Forks. Quite the adventurer!

Parents

Mom

*Helen Mathias Miles
Mom*

Mom and Dad's relationship was interesting and had an effect on me which I did not realize fully until my mid-20s. Mom (born in 1919 and two years older than Dad) seemed sometimes to be a little disappointed in Dad. She had gone to Goldey-Beacom College for several years and had graduated, while Dad went into the Coast Guard in the late 1930s when he was 18 and served in the Pacific on the Hunter Liggett, which was a kind of troop landing ship.

Mom could be a bit judgmental about things. In the hospital, one hour after Dad died of heart disease in December 1996, after 30 days in intensive care, Mom told Barbie and me that Dad had had a fling in New Zealand during World War II in the Pacific. Apparently, Dad had confessed this to Mom when she found a picture of a woman in his wallet, and Mom, being Mom, may have held this over his head for their entire marriage. It seemed important to Mom to tell us about it, with some spite as I remember it, soon after his death.

While Mom doted on me, always wanting me to be the best

and praising me for my successes, Dad just plowed ahead, getting everything done. So, this was the situation … I worshiped Dad, Mom thought I was the greatest, and seemed to think that Dad was lacking in some way which left me in the position of having to not be too good, so I would not make Dad look bad, and yet not be too bad or lose Mom's love. To this day it has affected how I compete in life. Say in tennis, I invariably let my opponent get ahead at first and only then can I come back to win the contest. I fear losing the friendship of my opponent if I really did my best all out and trounced them, so I temper my game and just squeak by at the end. (Sam said basically the same thing, that in tennis she would call balls 'in' when it was very close to, if not actually being, 'out'.) I lay it all to my learning how to maneuver the relationship with Mom and Dad to get what I needed, the love of both.

While Mom probably knew the effect that she was having on me in keeping me at my best through conditional love, I am positive that Dad, being too busy to notice, was oblivious. Although quite successful by most standards, in many areas of my life, athletics, the White House, in other jobs, this dynamic seems to have limited me somewhat. I don't have much of a killer instinct, valuing relationships over results. Not an altogether terrible trait but limiting evolution-wise in this competitive world we have created or inherited.

Mom was an incredible worker. She held a full-time job at Pyrofax Gas after we all were old enough to go off to school. Later in the late '60s she got a job as an administrative assistant at NASA and she and Dad commuted an hour or so each way every day to Wallops Island. Mom kept the books around the house as she had a good bookkeeper's mind and was very meticulous.

Page from Mom's Ledger — Sheep Expenses 1953

Plus, she helped Dad around the farm, tending the chickens, milking our cow, and raising us. She was pretty practical and could be stern and not particularly affectionate, which I think was a little hard on us, particularly my sisters.

And an aside about our road, not our lane, but the mile long

Breezy Point Road leading to our lane. It started out as a dirt road, but one day Mom saw a rubber electric line across the road, the kind used to count cars that traveled over it. She organized the neighbors and she and they rode over that thing hundreds of times to show the highway department that we deserved to have the road macadamized. I can't imagine that they didn't figure out what happened as we only had six houses on the road at that time. But we got a new hard surface road soon after.

Mom was religious in a formal way though not too spiritual I suspect, going to church for the social and appearance aspects mainly. However, her numerous albums of sentimental clippings may belie that and show a sensitive side that she rarely showed us. Mom threw herself into community activities and did her part in the Cub Scouts, Boy Scouts, Girl Scouts and church bazaars, making six to eight pies or cakes to sell in each fair.

Every year, Mom organized parties for her church

A Five Miles Farm Lawn Party

congregation on our lawn which were a big hit as we had a beautiful creek view. In fact, we were known for our lawn parties and regularly during the summer would have all the relatives and friends over for elaborate parties on the lawn, under the shade trees. Wendy and I to this day enjoy giving such lawn parties, though certainly not as elaborate or as frequent as then, as we socialize with 10 to 12 friends usually, back and forth to their houses for dinners and such. Mom and Dad rarely went to dinner at their friend's or relative's houses, and almost never went out to eat at a restaurant, and when they did it was a special treat. It just wasn't done in that day as it is today.

Mom also had a good heart, taking food to all the older adult shut-ins around Cashville (the name of our nearest town, consisting of only a crossroads and three churches). At times she seemed to want to be seen as a "good person" by others more than she wanted to be seen as a good mother by us.

One such older neighbor, about four miles away, was Will Burke and his wife Etta. Mom always took them food and for about ten years after Etta died, Mom did everything for Will, cleaned his house, fed him his meals, took care of his goats, etc. He relied upon her greatly and when he died, he left Mom and Dad his small house and farm, worth about $60,000 at the time. He had no relatives who cared for him. I was a little wary of this as Mom helped Will make out his will, but she and Will got a lawyer to draft and witness the deal and OK it. She recognized the appearance of things, but Will very much wanted to reward her for all she had done over the years, so I guess it was all right as he clearly documented his intent. It had waterfront but was swampy and no one could build on it. Later, they sold it for $60,000 to a Mr. Slayton, brother of the astronaut, Deke Slayton.

Dad used part of that money to buy his 37' Irwin sailboat, the Cormorant, which they sailed for years.

Mom was quite class conscious and felt shy and out of place with folks she thought were above her station. But she so wanted us as children to fit in and did everything she could to do the normal things that parents do for their kids ... parties, overnights, etc. I remember her being terribly embarrassed because I was the pitcher in a little league game and repeatedly balked as my foot slipped off the rubber on the pitcher's mound as I threw the ball. The umpire and coaches came out to check why and found it was because my tennis shoes did not have any tread on the soles, being old as the hills. Holes in them too, as Mom put linoleum inserts in them to keep the water out. Mom was mortified! Never got over it I don't think. Mom was thrifty to the extreme to say the least. Probably had to be.

Mom followed our progress in school and me in college, keeping numerous lengthy and detailed scrapbooks of all our

The Cormorant — *Dad's 37' Irwin sailboat*

Mom aboard the Cormorant

stages, events and honors… with pictures, newspaper clippings, etc. Mom, as did her mother Big Momma, also kept many large scrapbooks of poetry, letters, and inspirational sayings, both of hers and others. Hallmark card types of poetry and sayings - inspiring, tearjerkers, sentimental, nostalgic. It's where she seemed to express her tenderness and heart, rather than to us, the children, to whom she showed her practical, less sentimental side.

Mom also sold Hammond organs for a time and loved playing them, these big bulky piano-like instruments, which she sold aggressively around the Shore. She loved music and particularly poetry, and wrote many poems about us kids, Dad, and others. She wrote well and often. At age 80 she edited and published a book, "Consider the Sparrow", that my grandmother, Big Momma Mathias, had written about her life from 1893, born in NY State, through 1921 when they moved to the Eastern Shore, and on to the 1960s. She died in Florida in 1976. Mom sold that book all around the county. Then she started on her own book, *The Sparrow Flies South*, about her own life and ours from her birth in New York State in 1919 through the 1970s. She finished it, and marketed that too, selling about 500 copies of each.

In the early '80s after Dad had retired (in 1972) and Mom had retired from NASA also (in 1979 I think) and all the kids were out of the house, they took three winter trips. They sailed down the Intracoastal Waterway to Florida, spending the winter on the sailboat, coming back in the spring. Just sailing from port to port, having friends join them from time to time. Among the happiest times of their lives Mom would say.

In 1999, after Dad died in '96, we threw a large surprise party for Mom's 80th birthday. All her friends were there, and each brought something to eat on a beautiful July day. It was a success. I wrote a poem which captures Mom from my perspective.

To Honor Mom on Your 80th Birthday
From Your Children

You came out of the North as a precocious young girl,
so eager to please, to take on the world.
You were the youngest of three, Alice and Robert led the way,
to the whole clan you see gathered round you today.
You landed in Greenbush with Bessie and Al
and survived the depression, no one knows quite how.

Your childhood was happy on Virginia's Eastern Shore
and you grew up well, above the 5 and Dime store.
A worker you were an easy child to raise,

helping here and there to earn your Dad's praise.

As you grew to maturity you met a boy named Abie,
A quite handsome lad though a bit wild and crazy.
And thus it was that he won your fair heart,
though it took four years through some fits and some starts.

So you became his bride and a hard working wife
and perhaps as important, a good companion for life.
But then the war came and Abe went to his duty,
And you stayed and prayed and knitted little booties.

Yes, Barbie came first, then Kim and Sammie made three
and with Abie now home you had your whole family.
We lived at Kerr Street till Dad used all his charm
to win the city girl over to our own Five Miles Farm.

And life on the farm proved a wonderful way
to raise kids and live close to nature each day.
With sheep and then cows and corn and rye grass,
we had all we ever could want or could ask.

With the kids all in school you went back to work
With energy to burn you weren't one to shirk.
With sailing on weekends o'er to Weir Point and back
a good garden and fine family your life did not lack.

And when the kids were all gone to their lives far away,
you never stopped helping in just the right way

With support and love just a word here and there
you let us all know just how much you did care.

And when one day Abe said, "Come, we're sailing away
to the islands, the sun, it's our time to play!
You jumped right on board with canned goods and all,
you became a first mate ready at the skipper's call.

Yes, you've lived a full life Helen Mathias Miles,
Full of work and some worries but faced all with your smiles.
Whether putting up vegetables or canning the corn,
or ironing, or sewing, whatever was torn.

You never complained about the work in our days
just did it and waited for a small word of praise.
Though a Northerner you were, now you'd never know,
for your southern fried chicken ranks the best in the show.

A whirling dervish who won't sit or idle be,
we all want to know where you get your energy.
Never one for fashion you paid it no heed,
and through sacrifice of your wants you met all of your needs.

Yes, thrifty you were and are so today
but when it comes to yourself secondhand is the way
But as sparing as you are in tending your own needs,
When others are in pain their call you do heed.

Your generosity is well known among friends and neighbors,
In giving to others, you spare no labors.

Taking meals to the elderly, building houses for the homeless,
your churchwork, your caring, your charity is boundless.

And as we celebrate this day we want you to know,
how much we love you in ways too numerous to show.
For your life full of giving, for your life we have shared,
for the treasure of memories, for how much you have cared.

Though your Abie has gone now, watching from above,
it has certainly not stopped you from spreading your love.
So what lies in store for one with such zest,
and always insists on giving others her best.

Of course, there is no real way of knowing,
surely a life full of caring, learning, and growing.
So, we gather today your life to retell,
and we give love and thanks that here with us you dwell.

Love,
Barbie, Kim, and Sam - July 3, 1999

Dad

Dad's lineage on the Eastern Shore goes back to a Roger Miles, who sailed over from England in 1657, possibly as an indentured servant (a common practice at the time to secure money for passage). This meant that he had to split his farm proceeds and labor with another for a period (usually seven years) to pay back his portage to the States. We know this because a renowned genealogist MK Moody Miles, who lives and works on the Shore (look up "The Miles Files" on Google) did a complete 300-page genealogy workup for me, my family tree and all ancestors, for free as a surprise favor. I had recruited him for the Heritage Committee for the new library and we had become friends. This genealogical workup shows information about our ancestors through land records, court proceedings, and other historical records. MK is a nationally and internationally recognized expert on Eastern Shore genealogy.

Dad was a rather amazing man. He was taciturn, not saying much, like a lot of men of his generation (born in 1921). But he was a thinker with a sensitive streak. He held down a fulltime job at NASA, at first as a carpenter and then rising to the job of Chief of Logistics for the NASA operation at Wallops Island, which really meant making sure that the building, grounds, and launch pads were maintained and kept in good shape with a team of electricians, carpenters, plumbers, etc. That sounds like a big job now, but it was a much smaller operation at Wallops back in the '60s.

Dad's first boat, Helene

Dad's second boat, Long Wind

But Dad also kept the ten acres of cleared land we had in production in one way or another through the seasons. And we all worked hard on that land. I remember one day I stayed home from school to disc the fields in preparation for planting corn. I accidently, through inattention, allowed the tractor to slip into a ditch which laid it over at an acute angle. Being afraid to try to drive it out, I left it there, almost on its side. Now this happened one month after a close neighbor had been killed when his tractor turned over and fell on him, so I could imagine what Dad was feeling when he came home, drove up the lane, and saw the tractor lying almost on its side in the ditch. But he said nothing when he found me safe, just drove the thing upright and out of the ditch and back to the barn.

Dad also built five or six boats in his adult life ranging from two 23 and 25 foot sailboats to an 18 foot outboard and two small skiffs and a sailing dingy. The 25-footer was a model skipjack, whose mast he picked out very carefully from the many pine trees in the woods, dragged it out, and skinned it and outfitted it with tackle.

The family would take trips to the mountains of Virginia, West Virginia, and North Carolina. We would look forward to those trips. I think Dad was the instigator of these as he loved to ride, often taking Sunday afternoon rides with Mom all over the

Shore, particularly after they retired.

But Dad also had hobbies, usually one at a time, like raising homing and specialty pigeons, such as tumblers. We would take the "homers" 30 or 40 miles away and release them and wait for them to return, which they invariably did, sometimes it seemed before we got back home. The tumblers would fly high in the air and seemingly crumble and drop and catch themselves and fly again just before they hit the ground.

And for a while Dad trapped muskrats, setting out maybe a dozen traps around the marsh. A lot of people did this in the 1950s, selling them for the furs. It didn't last long as there were not too many on our creek. Dad also tried to raise goats, laboriously fencing in 23 of our 25 acres of woods land to keep them in. His objective was to have them clear out all the low underbrush, leaving a park-like setting. It did little good as they all died, one by one, from eating leaves from cherry trees, which were poisonous to them.

We had peacocks for a time, which were beautiful but noisy and messy. I loved the strutting peacocks and their gorgeous feathers. And at first, we had chickens and our job was to find the eggs which they would lay all around the farm, mostly in the hayloft which made finding them rather easy. One time older sister Barbie tried to hatch an egg by sitting on it for a full day, to no avail.

All the critters—sheep, cattle, goats, peacocks, pigeons—Dad took care of with our modest help, building pens, barns, hutches, and fences for them and feeding them ... all this in his spare time. He also aspired to be an artist, and sketched and painted with oils and watercolors, taking classes from Willie Crocket. He carved ducks, not very well, but he tried, and succeeded in carving a variety of them, the best being a pintail. He then painted them.

I admired Dad and wanted his praise, working alongside of him. I watched how he did things and his persistence - like when the tractor would get stuck, completely, up to the axles in the mud in the woods and I said to myself that there was no way we were going to get it out. But Dad always persevered and we miraculously, in my mind, dug it out and we went on about our business, raking shats, cutting and hauling hay, or gardening.

Oh, Dad also raised a full 4,000 square foot garden each summer, and shared the produce with all the neighbors, who generally recognized Dad as the best gardener around the area. Mom and Dad would put up jar after jar of peas, corn, beans, beets, and any specialty crops that Dad would want to try that summer (he was a tinkerer, always trying something new it seemed). I have many mental pictures of both of them shelling

Dad's best picture — The Osprey

peas, husking corn, picking pole beans, or pulling beets, and then preserving or freezing all for later use. And Mom would keep meticulous records of how many jars of each they would can or freeze.

Dad also modeled for our famous artist neighbor, Charlie Dye, as we all did, for $5 an hour which was a princely sum back then for a kid. Charlie was a painter of magazine covers in the style of Norman Rockwell, (whom he occasionally substituted for I understand). He later became a famous western artist whose works now sell in excess of $100,000. We would pose for Charlie in child poses for about an hour and Dad did also, and we were all on the covers of several magazines. Charlie specialized in sporting magazines like *Outdoor Life and Sports Afield*. I have a magazine that Dad posed for, an *Outdoor Life* issue with Dad on the cover, resting, exhausted, against a log with a smile on his

Dad planning his garden

Dad on the cover of Charlie's Outdoor Life
(Image used with permission)

face and shouldering a large buck deer. It was called the "Happy Hunter". I also have the pictures of Dad posing for the picture that Charlie used.

Charlie also had a sailboat and loved to sail. One of my fondest memories was most Sunday afternoons in the summer we would sail out to Weir (pronounced Wire then) Point, and everyone would bring picnics and we would swim with the other kids from nearby towns, as many families would gather there in powerboats and sailboats. Dad would race with Charlie and Doc Conboy, our veterinarian, who also had a sailboat. The Weir Point Sundays continued until the country club was built and many of the wealthier folks joined and spent Sundays there instead.

Later we sailed and raced against Judge Northam, a neighbor and the father of our current Governor, Ralph, who I think Dad taught to swim. Judge, his interesting wife Nancy, and his kids Ralph and Tom, a local lawyer, were our closest friends on Breezy Point Road.

Dad was a truly amazing man, doing all this while maintaining a fulltime job. Back in 1972, at the age of 52 and having achieved his 30 years in the civil service, Dad retired from NASA, disliking intensely the job of managing men who used to be his equals and pals, before he took his supervisory job. I think he felt that, as a supervisor, he should call the men on some of their slack off habits which Dad knew about from his days as their peer. He could not resolve this issue of how to handle his friends as a supervisor, and he lost one or two friends because of it. I think his final annual salary in '72 was all of $18,000 and change after 30 years with the Civil Service, including his military service. Of course, this was 50 years ago when $18,000 was a decent salary on the Shore.

Sailing

In addition to building large and small boats, Dad taught all of us kids how to sail by the age of six to eight and we loved it. It became a big part of our lives at different stages, as all of us either owned sailboats or sailed on them for extended periods of time in our lives. Dad was a great sailor, having sailed from childhood. I once saw him "sail" his 25' skipjack away from the dock, on a completely, dead calm evening, under bare poles (without any sails) through our narrow Parker's Creek channel, and over to our neighbor Charlie's dock. I was astounded! How did he do it? Dad had sensed that there was sufficient gentle breeze above the surface of the absolutely calm water to allow him to maneuver the boat using just the windage of the boat structure, mast and boom. I wish I had a video of that: Dad "ghosting" along slowly through a mirror-like creek.

Dad had a good friend later in life named Jerry Brown, who had a sailboat, but was too old to sail. Dad sailed it for him and took many, many trips with Jerry across the Bay to Tides Inn, Irvington, and Deltaville and up the bay to Crisfield, among other places. Jerry gave his boat, an Irwin 27, called the *Sin*

Nombre (no name), to Dad, with the provision that Dad would continue to take him sailing with him. Later they sailed on Dad's *Cormorant* (Dad's favorite bird). They had some fine times together.

Dad was one of the founders of the Shore Little League in 1958. It was just an informal group of fathers who got together to plan and organize four little league teams, build the fields and fences, recruit the coaches, hold tryouts, arrange schedules, and hire umpires. I was on the Fireman's Team with Little Ronnie Killmon as our coach. We won the championship that year, the only year I was eligible, as I was 12. I played as a utility guy, playing about half of the positions as needed, though my favorite was shortstop. While I was the fastest player, I was not the best, as Bobby Taylor and Jack Phillips were the stars in my eyes.

As I mentioned, Dad served in the war and did a tour or two in the Pacific with the Coast Guard. He drove the LSTs (or LCTs)

Me, sailing the bay minus 50 years and 50 pounds

the landing crafts with the drop-down bow, allowing the troops to wade ashore. Although he was at the battle of Guadalcanal, he never talked about the war except one time he said he was stranded ashore on a beachhead when he tried to unload his men too close and ran aground and couldn't get off. He said, without a weapon, he just found the deepest hole and waited until the shooting stopped before coming out.

Around 2015, I received a call from a friend saying that she had seen a post on Facebook from someone who had bought a bureau and trunk set that we had put up for auction back in 2008, when we moved into the house from New Hampshire. In a secret compartment this person had found about 70 letters from someone named Abie to a woman named Helen. She asked on Facebook if anyone knew anyone with those names. My friend,

The Miles Family

knowing me and my parents, called me and I have the letters. These were love letters from my Dad to my Mom before they were married in 1941, when he was stationed up and down the East Coast with the Coast Guard, and just before he went to the Pacific. They were the letters from an enamored 18-year-old to his future bride and although expectedly juvenile, were revealing of the relationship and Dad's love of Mom.

Yes, Dad in his own way was a wonderful man. I looked up to him a lot, and sought, and knew I received, his approval.

So that completes the picture of the Miles family and our origins, not too unusual for the times, but each with our own quirks.

The Early 1960s

Christmases

Christmas was always a magical time for us. Mom and Dad would hide the presents until Christmas Eve and Sam would take it upon herself to find where they hid them and usually did, not telling the rest of us. (I would not want to know what I was getting, wanting to sustain the anticipation. This delaying of gratification was a trait throughout my life, as I always wanted to do the hardest task first, eat desert last, etc. I recognized that I was different in this respect from many.) We would all, when young, get up early, and the first one up would rouse the family and we would immediately start opening presents. Later, of course, when we were in our teens we would pretend to be above the anticipation and have breakfast first, and then open the presents.

Mom, of course, bought most of the presents as Dad was too busy and didn't have the ideas or know where to buy things. But he would preside and get a kick out of all the festivities of opening the presents. My favorite Christmas was when I was twelve and wanted a 22 rifle of my own, as well as a Boy Scout uniform as I had just joined the Scouts. Mom said I could not have both as they were too expensive. BUT on Christmas morning, I opened both! Both used and not new, of course, but still they were mine.

Later, after I had left home, and returned for Christmases, I started being the Santa, buying all sorts of small presents for everyone, so we still had tons of presents to open, even though they were not worth much. I enjoyed this very much as many were anonymous gifts that could have come from anyone in the family. Yes, Christmases were special to us, and to me.

School

Generally, I liked school, as it was our main social life. At the end of the summer, I looked forward to going back to school with both anticipation and trepidation, for there was always something to have to get used to, particularly bullies who picked on small kids (like me who was quite skinny back then). But since I did very well at school, always leading the class, and once getting 56 A's and no Bs on my monthly report cards in seven classes over eight grading periods. Proud of that. As I recall, in one seventh grade class, the teacher often sent me out of the classroom with another student who was having serious trouble reading, to sit with him and teach him to read for an hour each day. Wasn't too successful at that.

My first grade class at school

My senior class

Every year we had reading tests given by the Weekly Reader and I always was reading at a level way above my grade level. Once in the fourth grade, I was reading as an eleventh grader. I was pretty straight and well-behaved EXCEPT when there was a substitute, who for some reason, seemed to be my excuse to let loose and be terrible. On one occasion leaving one of them in tears by my behavior. I now feel quite bad about that.

The Tooth

Kim

METHOD OF GRADING

A—Outstanding
B—Above Average
C—Average
D—Below Average
E—Conditional
F—Unsatisfactory

Six Weeks	1	2	3	Av.	4	5	6	Av.	Final Av.
Reading	a	a	a	a	a	a	a	a	a
Language	a	a	a	a	a	a	a	a	a
Spelling	a	a	a	a	a	a	a	a	a
Writing	a	a	a	a	a	a	a	a	a
Arithmetic	a	a	a	a	a	a	a	a	a
Social Studies	a	a	a	a	a	a	a	a	a
Science	a	a	a	a	a	a	a	a	a
Art	a	a	a	a	a	a	a	a	a
Music	a	a	a	a	a	a	a	a	a
Health & Physical Education	a	a	a	a	a	a	a	a	a
Personal Conduct	a	a	a	a	a	a	a	a	a

Personal Conduct is meant to give some indication of the pupil's development in following areas of personal and social living.

1. **Social Habits**—Respects rights and property of others; takes care of personal belongings; follows rules and directions; practices good manners and habits of good sportsmanship; accepts responsibilities.
2. **Work Habits**—Works independently; is attentive; uses time and materials wisely; completes work and assignments; is cooperative.

LEVELS OF READING (Check)

Six Weeks	1	2	3	4	5	6
Reading Readiness						
Pre-Primer						
Primer						
Basic Reader	✓	✓	✓	✓	✓	✓
Supplementary Material	✓	✓	✓	✓	✓	✓
Special Material						

Seventh Grade Report Card

One time in the second grade I went sliding down the hall with several other guys on the grit they put down to clean the halls. A heavy upper-class girl ran out of a door and collided with me, coming down on my head and chipping my front tooth in half. I would keep that half tooth in my mouth uncapped until I was 18. The story I was given then was it had to be fully grown before I could get it capped … But I suspect the real story was that it was too expensive to get it fixed. Anyway, I took quite a bit of ribbing for that throughout my school days.

One day at school in 1962 I heard that Big Daddy had bought me a car. I was so excited to get home to see this new car. I got home. It was not new. It was a nine-year old '53 chevy that ran fine but was no sight to see. I just hope my disappointment did not show too much as it was a very, very, nice gesture. And it served me well during my high school years.

The 1953 Chevy

Outside of the idyllic life on the farm, school took center stage. I was a loner, I guess. A straight arrow for sure, I didn't run with the gangs (at that time just a bunch of guys who hung around together... not like gangs today). Because I was smart and a pretty good athlete (in some folks' minds), people looked at me as different, a bit of a loner. I also didn't participate in the beer parties and weekend gatherings as many did. Thus, I felt like an outsider much of the time, never learning the small talk, kidding, and male relationships that others of my friends did. There was a reason, of course … I HAD A STEADY GIRLFRIEND! The main reason for my being an outsider though was Robin. More about this lady later.

Athletics

I happened to do very well as an athlete, playing all four sports and being pretty good in all, particularly football and track, where I received multiple honors and was the state 100-yard dash champion my Junior and Senior years. Some old-timers have said that I was the best all-around athlete to ever come off the Shore. But I had known of another athlete, Little Ronnie Killmon, about five years ahead of me, and thought he was the best athlete ever. (I suspect that's the case with most folks…you remember an older person as your idol and feel that no others can compare.)

An example of this might be Bill Sterling, a little younger, long time local newspaper editor, celebrated sportswriter, and athlete in his own right, who wrote a book called *Still Browsing*. In it he compiled the top newspaper stories and columns he had written in his career. He was kind enough to include a full-page, and very flattering, article he had published upon my return to the Shore.

In the article, he concluded: "Younger generations and those who have moved to the Shore in the past 30 or so years may not realize it when they see someone who looks much like a college professor, but there was a time when Kim Miles was the fastest and one of the best athletes ever to compete on the Eastern Shore. But, more importantly, the term 'student-athlete' never fit anyone better than Kim Miles."

This was very kind, and flattering, as I had gained about 40 lbs. from my 160 lb. playing weight. (And the beauty was, I only had to pay him $500 to do it! Joke here, as Bill, being a man of integrity, refused all my attempted bribes ... still joking.) Bill and I became good friends, and we play golf often, where I have yet to equal or beat him in a round. So much for the "best athlete" part. Golf's a humbling sport.

As an athlete, I was just doing my best and enjoyed the strategic thinking that went into being the quarterback, or shortstop, or the captain of the basketball team. I didn't see myself in that role as "best athlete" as I have also learned of another athlete, Larry Burton, graduating after me from a nearby school, Mary Nottingham Smith, who better deserves the accolade "Best Athlete from the Shore", as he went on to the Olympics and played in the NFL. A fine man.

I never really focused on being the star, as I was taught from an early age that to toot one's horn was unseemly and wrong. Humility was the order of the day back then. You just didn't brag or boast. (Of course, you would never guess it from reading this puff piece of a memoir.) Therefore, I also tried to be the best at being humble (heh, heh). But my mother wasn't so hesitant to brag on my behalf.

Winning my first 100 yard dash

I remember when the football coach Thomas Ray Parks came by the house on a hot summer day before I started my 9th grade school year. I was on a tractor-drawn wagon in the garden behind the barn, knee deep in manure that I was spreading from that wagon, the same manure that I had just pried out of the cattle stall. I was sweating, with just my cutoff jeans on. He wanted to make sure that I was coming out for the football team that year. I assured him I was.

I had two good coaches back then - one Freshman and Sophomore year (Thomas Ray Parks) and one Junior and Senior year (Trent Serini). Both were good but used different training strategies. Coach Serini got us in better shape and was a great defensive coach having played college ball for Oklahoma State. He was also more professional and more of a disciplinarian,

Footbacll action against Central
(Image used with permission)

while Coach Parks was more laid back and focused more on offense. They had traded schools in our junior year, Serini to Onancock, and Parks to Central, which angered Coach Parks because he had seen the talent on our upcoming Onancock team and didn't want to leave Onancock. (The rumor was that Serini at Central had benched a couple of star Central players for missing practice which had angered some parents who took their case to the Superintendent to get him shifted to Onancock. Football was king back then and parents had power. Don't know how true that story is, but it has the ring of truth given the times.)

I do remember one game my senior year when I was getting hit way after the whistle, when the play was dead. After this happened three of four times as I lay on the ground having been tackled illegally two or three seconds after the play was whistled dead, I dug my heel into the player's back and asked him "Why are you doing this?" Scared of my anger, he said "Coach told me to tackle you every play even after the whistle blew." I immediately ran over to the bench in front of all the stands and in a rage asked Coach Parks, "Why are you having your players hit me after the whistle"?! He didn't respond but I'm sure was embarrassed by it and should have been.

An Honor
(Image used with permission)

One night we were playing our main rival, Central High School, for the Championship. A win would be considered a small miracle, since the Central line outweighed ours by an average of 30 pounds per person and they had an enormous fullback who outweighed ours by 80 lbs. We had our line practice all week against some heavy alumni who tried to train our small boys in how to handle big opponents. It seemed to work as we won 20-7. I think I scored a touchdown and threw to Jack for another (so much for humility) and handed off to Bobby Taylor for a third. And the line, led by Hal Lassiter, George Parker, Chester Jackson, Johnny Kellam, Bill Valentine, and Tommy Duncan, did a great job. That night I improvised a play that worked like a charm several times in fooling the defense totally and allowed us to score. Very proud of that.

I also remember one day after we lost our only game of the season, I overheard the Coach say to the other players, "Well, Kim just didn't have a good night last night". I felt that too much stress had been put on me as I had scored two touchdowns that night... just not enough to win as we lost by one touchdown. I was lucky to play at all, having had the flu and was home for three days in the week prior to the game.

Sports was a big part of my high school life. I went on to win all sorts of honors, had my picture in the paper quite a bit and had a lot of pressure put on me. We won just about every championship my junior and senior year. I was the captain of our basketball team (better at defense than offense), state champion in track, a shortstop on the baseball team, and QB on our football team, where we often had 2,000-3,000 people show up for a Friday night game.

However, I very often got more credit that I deserved. For

example, the picture below was in the paper with the title "MILES STOPS PRINCE!" As anyone can see, about the only way this 140 lb. kid was going to stop that behemoth of a fullback was if he tripped over my face mask while going over me, which I think he did.

I remember one prank that Jack Phillips, my best friend and the captain of our football team, and I pulled one Friday to motivate our team. We were playing our main rival, Central High School, for the championship that night. The previous night Jack and I had created a large poster, listing quotes and slogans derogatory to many of our team members, and signed it as coming from several of Central's key team members.

Friday morning early before anyone got to the school, we propped it against the front door of our school where everyone could see it. We waited across the street to see what the reaction would be. As expected, our team members, as they arrived, were incensed at some of the things said about them by our rival. "Joe, yo mama wears army boots!" "Kim, you're too slow to get out of your own way!" "Hal, whoever told you that you could play football? They lied." Pretty juvenile, but we loved it.

Well, our Principal, Mr. Hoppes, was very angry and

The Caption Was "Miles Stops Prince!"
Oh really?
(Image used with permission)

called the Principal of Central to complain. Their principal asked the Central team members about it, and they denied doing it, so Mr. Hoppes came back to us for an explanation, and we had to confess. Mr. Hoppes had to apologize to the other Principal. But the deed was done and to his credit, Mr. Hoppes did not tell anyone, even the other Principal, about it until the next day. So, our team went into the game with extra motivations to win … and we did. Only after did we spill the beans.

There was only one indoor basketball court on the middle Shore, and we had to share it with other teams so only practiced there one day a week. But I practiced at home with a hoop on the barn. Unfortunately, one side of my "barnyard court" was fenced in by the cattle fence so I could not shoot from that side, and I had to climb over the fence when the ball would bounce over it many times a day. Being in a barnyard, the ball also became covered with chicken and peacock crap as I practiced, so it wasn't the easiest ball to shoot. But I would spend hours shooting baskets. One memorable time hitting ten three-point shots in a row while practicing.

The Break

Swish… I was at the barn shooting baskets in the rickety hoop on the side. It was getting dark. It was about March, the end of basketball season, and the air was chilly, but I was sweating from the practice. The ball had a good bit of chicken and cow crap on it and my hands were dark with stain. Bumpty bump … a miss … and again the ball bounded over the fence which prevented much right-side shooting practice but gave me a lot of exercise retrieving it.

Suddenly, as expected, a call from Mom, "Kim, dinner's

ready!" I trudge to the house and enter a kitchen filled with the smell of frying chicken and baking rolls. Immediately my glasses fog completely from the steam. After washing my hands and clearing my glasses, I noticed Dad sitting at the table reading something. I quickly set the table as usual and asked Dad what he was reading.

"You got a break," he said. And explained that I had been admitted to a small college in New England. "And they're giving you a pretty big scholarship." A wealthy Eastern Shoreman, Lucius Kellam, had gone to Trinity College and graduated in 1935. He took an interest in me and suggested that I apply to his college, which I did. I was stunned, for the college was pretty selective and a small-town kid didn't seem to have much chance against the guys applying from the elite prep schools. And I had not even applied seriously. I had reconciled myself, like many of my friends, to going to a Virginia school - UVA or William and Mary, following the regular path of graduation, marriage, returning to the town and living an expected life.

But now things were different. The promise of a totally new environment, new kinds of people, away from home, on my own! Away from the expectations of others, and the straight jacket of normalcy I often placed, and felt placed, on my shoulders. For a young boy who had just turned 18, it was exciting ... but very scary.

"You've got a decision to make," Dad said, as Mom began putting the dinner on the table. "It's a long way from home. Your mother and I won't be able to help you much."

"But," Ma said, "It's a much better school, hon. And think of the opportunities it will give him with this good break."

I sat there and ate dinner. I knew it would be hard for them, and me, to leave the farm and go north, when all my friends were staying near in Virginia. Trinity was the far better school, since UVA did not have the fine academic reputation in the '60s that it does today. I also could have almost a free ride at a less expensive Virginia school, but the northeast school, Trinity College, would only pay for about 2/3rds of my tuition and board and was much more expensive. That night, after the game, I didn't sleep much thinking of the pros and cons of this new chance.

The next morning, a Saturday, Dad and I raked shats, started preparing the garden, and fed the sheep, just beginning to bear young. I knew I would miss these times working with him on weekends, something I could do more often if I went to school closer to home. We didn't talk about much of anything that sunny morning. Not unusual. That was Dad.

When Mom called us in to lunch, and we were seated at the table, I looked up and said, "I've decided, I'm going to go north to that school."

And Dad said, "OK, boy, but what made you choose that?"

"Well," I said, "It's just that … I gotta break."

He may have understood my meaning … needing to break away from my previous life, away from expectations, and toward newness and opportunities, but I didn't tell him that.

The Trip to Trinity

Although I was accepted, I still had a firm decision to make as to whether to go to UVA, William and Mary or Trinity. Thus, I wanted to see the Trinity campus. So, Dad and I planned a trip to see the school. Lucius Kellam, understanding my parent's situation, gave us $100 to make the trip, as he wanted me to choose his alma mater, where he had excelled.

In the late winter of 1964, we took a bus from T's Corner,

20 miles north of Onancock, to NYC one afternoon and Dad slept most of the time, while I sat wide-eyed contemplating my future. I remember we burst out of the Lincoln Tunnel at night with the bright lights of the NYC skyscrapers right in front of us. WOW! Dad woke up with a start and I saw fear in his eyes, as momentarily he forgot where he was. We took a cab to a hotel and the driver looked at Dad with a semi-angry face as Dad did not give him what he thought was a sufficient tip. Dad, feeling a little cheap then made a point of heavily over-tipping the bellman who carried our bags up to our room. I came to see Dad as very human on this trip, a fish out of water in the big city, and I sensed that, in many ways from now on, I would be the one leading him rather than him leading me. A break indeed.

The next day we took the train to Hartford and a cab to the campus to have our tour and my interview with the admissions staff. It seemed to go well. (I later learned from my records that the interviewer had termed me "a real delight", I suppose due to my naïve excitement.) We left that day for the trip back home. I had made up my mind to go north, to get away to something new, attend a smaller, better college if I received the promised financial aid, as it was an expensive school.

I know now that I had a wonderfully successful experience at Trinity. Whether I would have had an equally satisfying experience at a Virginia school I don't know, but it would have been very different, and I'd never give up the Trinity experience or friends for anything.

The Trinity Experience

All that summer I spent anticipating leaving in the fall for Trinity College. The College sent a booklet with the names, hometowns, and pictures of all my soon-to-be freshman classmates. I memorized every last face, name and hometown in the book ... all 260 of them. Not much to do on the farm on hot summer days.

They also sent a suggested wardrobe for all incoming students, two suits - a summer and a winter one; good shirts and pants and everyday ones; hats, ties, three kinds of shoes, overcoats and jackets, the works. Mom dutifully began aggregating all these things, few of which I had, from thrift shops, from friends and neighbors, hand me downs, or anywhere she could fulfill the list. She finally had it done and was quite proud of her job.

After a summer preparing for the new college experience, my parents packed me up and we drove to Hartford. We settled me into a new dorm, a post-WWII built brick building with little personality and small rooms, perhaps the least sought-after housing on campus. My parents left and I unpacked and looked around for something to do, picking up a football game on the Quad. After leaving, my parents got as far as Rhode Island, but turned around, worrying that I would be homesick already. They got back to campus and saw me playing football with a bunch of guys and didn't bother to check in, just went on their way, satisfied that I was going to adjust OK.

The wardrobe that Mom had scrounged and packed so carefully soon went by the wayside. As neither she nor I guessed, no one at college ever used almost any of the clothes on that list. This was the '60s. At an all-men's college. Most students just wore jeans or khakis, sometimes clean, sometimes not, and most wore the fashionable shoes at the time ... old loafers taped with duct tape as if they had holes in them. Suits were never worn. I can't remember what I did with those clothes, probably gave some away and brought some back home on a vacation. I felt so bad for Mom who had worked so hard to match "THE LIST".

The first night on campus, the upperclassmen organized a demonstration and march on the Capitol, which we as freshmen, gladly participated in, as a lark. We all marched downtown, did nothing and marched back, stopping by the Washington Diner on the way back. That diner, Phil's, and the Silver Dollar were favorite restaurant/bar hangouts for students. The march was to protest new regulations about drinking on campus as I remember. Quite exciting, but it was but a harbinger of things to come as it foreshadowed a politically active four years at Trinity from '64 to '68. (Clearly, we were not in Kansas ... or Onancock, anymore!)

My roommate was the son of the US Ambassador to France in Paris and from a distinctly different wealth class (he had shoehorns for his SOCKS no less!). I suspect the admissions folks put him in with me so he could educate the country bumpkin in the ways of a more sophisticated urban life. We got along well but did not become good friends as he was very formal and quiet, and previously had had a butler and a maid to do his wash (I showed him how).

I dove into my studies and, of course, made friends quickly as I had memorized every face and name in my class, startling many when I would say "Hello, Fred, how's Winnetka?" to a complete stranger, walking along the Long Walk, a fixture at Trinity.

I also began to realize just how much of a fish out of water I was. I kept hearing about some "great quarterback from Texas" who had been recruited and enrolled, and I wondered if I would be able to make the freshman football team with that competition. Until someone told me that it was me that they were talking about.

Actually, nothing could be further from the truth about the recruitment, as little was made of my athletic ability by Trinity in "recruiting" me (recruitment consisting of a letter listing my acceptance and scholarship). I did make the freshman team but, in an early practice, separated my shoulder and was taken to the hospital for x-rays. After waiting awhile, the assistant coach must have gotten tired of waiting for me and left the hospital, while I got my x-rays and was strapped up. When ready to leave,

A pre-season game in the Yale Bowl
(Image used with permission)

Clipping from The Harford Courant
(Image used with permission)

I noticed no one was around to take me back to campus. So, I had to walk, and for the first time, began to have the realization that I was truly on my own from now on and would be considered to be an adult, able and expected to care for myself. I spent the season on the bench with the injury but still attended every practice and made the Dean's List as well. Hot damn!

One thing I was surprised about was that, for many of my classmates attending Trinity was a disappointment, for it was not their first choice for a college, not having gotten into an Ivy league school. There were a lot of Harvard and Yale rejects there. This may sound naïve (which I was the very definition of), but I did not even know about the Ivy League schools, like Harvard, Yale and Princeton, when I was applying to colleges. The guidance counselor never told me, probably assuming that a small-town kid from a school of 500 kids in grades one through twelve would never have a chance.

My second year at Trinity, I did play on the varsity team and on the opening play of our first home game took the kickoff and ran it back for a 100-yard touchdown, still a Trinity record. This would not be so eventful except that it caught the attention of the school Public Relations head, Robert Herron, who had a national reputation in the sports world. He would go on to herald me as much more than I was, as a student athlete, resulting in numerous regional and national scholar athlete awards and experiences. This is speculation, but it is hard to see how I would have gotten the national honors and attention I did without someone being alerted to my existence and promoting me nationally.

I became involved in campus leadership positions, on the Freshman Executive Council and subsequently in the Student Senate of which I was later voted President, after a competitive campaign from two very capable student opponents.

In my junior and senior years, I became the leader of two big undertakings that took up considerable time but were particularly important, both to the college, and to my development. In my junior year I started a research study involving a campus wide survey of students' social habits and

A Busy Man
(Image used with permission)

attitudes called "The Social Evaluation". It involved organizing and carrying out extensive questionnaire surveys of almost 90% of the students. The results made a strong case for the college providing better social opportunities for the many students not invited to join fraternities. It led to the College building a place for independents to meet and socialize outside of fraternities. I was enormously proud of that.

In my senior year I conceived, organized, and led a much more ambitious Course Evaluation, where, following registration, each student sat down and evaluated faculty courses and the teachers they had taken in previous years on about 40 criteria. About 95% of the students completed the evaluation as part of the registration process, rating the courses and teachers. It made quite a stir as some professors and their classes were panned on a ten-point scale for each criterion, while others were rated deservedly highly. It was the first College-wide course evaluation in the nation, and I was damned proud of it.

The Wreck and the Draft

At that point, the military draft for Vietnam was in play and all of us were called up to get registered for the draft, not to necessarily go into the service (I had a college deferment) but to register and get a physical. I remember, I think in my sophomore or possibly the start of my junior year, that I went home for my registration and a medical checkup with all the other boys in my town. It just so happened that the Saturday night before the check-up on Monday, my friend Hal Lassiter, whose parents were out of town, threw a party at his house. At that point in my life, I had never had any hard liquor and not very much beer. But I did try hard liquor at this party, drinking it like beer, and the last thing I remember was playing Twister with others on the floor of his living room.

The next thing I remember was the police officer in town, who happened to be the sponsor or some such role with our MYF (Methodist Youth Fellowship) group, asking me if I was OK, as smoke rose from my parent's new car which I had totaled into a telephone pole across from Williams Funeral Home. I then remember being on a stretcher in the hospital emergency room 15 miles away and the doctor stitching up my tongue which was badly lacerated. It was a Saturday night and there were several other patients there awaiting care, wailing and yelling, most drunk like me.

Clearly I had had much too much to drink at Hal's party, but I insisted I drive home. Hal, recognizing this, had taken my date in his car and followed me as I, very slowly, weaved my way across the Mt. Prospect bridge, and down Market Street before slowly plowing into the pole. (I have always accused Hal, kiddingly, of really trying to snake my date, Barbara, that night).

I was finally released from the hospital into my parent's care and went home to sleep it off all day Sunday. I was mortified since I had been the president of my MYF, a model "good boy", who was supposedly making it big in a good northern school, now having gotten drunk and wrecked his parent's car. What a lesson!

On Monday, I got on a bus with many of my classmates and went for my medical checkup for the draft. I remember we were lined up, half naked, and the doctor went down the line asking us to open our mouths while he checked for god knows what in our mouths. Since my tongue was about three sizes too big, with visible stitches across it, I knew he would ask me about it. But

NO, he looked in my mouth for a few seconds like everyone else and passed on to the next person.

At that time in 1965, I think they were taking anyone who could walk into the army to go to Vietnam. At one point they had 500,000 of us over there. Since I had a temporary educational deferment, I was not too worried about being drafted until I graduated, but the fact that I had passed the physical and was in line to be drafted worried me.

I returned to school and continued the endless debate about the war. All my roommates, being against the war, talked about what they would do when our educational deferment came to an end when we graduated. I made it a point to learn a good bit about the origins of the war, our rationale for being there, and had given a lot of thought to how I felt about it, concluding that we were on the wrong path and that we should not be there.

We had endless talks about conscientious objector status, fleeing to Canada, enlisting or waiting to be drafted and then working from within against the war, refusing and going to jail, the whole gamut of options. Others talked about getting medical deferments for flat feet or other ailments. My Vietnam dilemma, which was very real to me, was solved by serendipity … I contracted sarcoidosis.

Boeck's Sarcoidosis

It was around the spring of my junior year that I developed a bad cough or bronchitis. Going to the doctor he noticed that my lymph nodes were quite swollen and checked me into the hospital for tests. At first, they couldn't find any particular cause. However, one test … the Kviem test, where a small incision and injection was made on my arm, came back positive when it did not heal properly, evidently the indicator that I had Boeck's Sarcoidosis. I remember the doctor (who just happened to be the world's foremost authority on Boeck's Sarcoidosis based in Hartford Hospital) saying "Well I have good news and bad news. The bad news is that you have sarcoidosis. The good news is that you won't be drafted for Vietnam." Evidently the Army didn't like the idea of having to care or pay for the care of someone with sarcoidosis, a serious and potentially debilitating or fatal disease.

Little was known about this disease at the time except that it was an immune system disease which was seen mainly in Scandinavian, Black, female, and southern populations, and suspected to be associated with pine trees for some reason. And since I spent a good bit of my after-school time sitting on pine needles in wait for squirrels to begin moving at dusk, it made some sense. It manifested itself by swollen lymph nodes in key organs, which over time damaged the organs. My sarcoidosis was lodged, as is often the case, in the lymph nodes around my lungs which I was told caused my lung capacity to be diminished by about 20%. It was a rare disease which was not curable but could be treated with steroids to keep it in check. However, in about 40% of those who get it, it goes away naturally, and pops up later in life in about 60% of those in whom it disappeared (I may have the percentages wrong, and I'm sure that they know much more about it now, 50 years later.)

Since taking steroids was not an option that was desirable, they chose to watch my case and see if it went away naturally. And indeed, it did, as they tested me six months later and it was gone, or at least dormant in my body, hopefully not to reemerge. All this to say that this solved my Vietnam dilemma which was very real to me. But I am always watching for it to return, and they say my immune system is affected somewhat. And a later cardiac MRI found some damage to my heart caused by the sarcoidosis.

The Florida-Bahamas Lark

A brief adventure one spring break. Tom Nary, in our senior year I think, was playing with the baseball team and making a trip to Florida with the team to play down there. I was down there visiting with my parents also and decided to drive Tom back to Trinity. At the end of his spring training, we were starting to head back when we saw a billboard advertising $29 round trip flights over to the Bahamas. We knew Tom's girlfriend was over there with some of her friends, so we counted our pennies and decided to go, meeting up with her friends and sleeping on the floor for a night or two before heading back. The one memory I had was Tom and I going to a casino in Nassau, and as we entered, seeing Sidney Poitier being driven up in a huge black limousine. He got out, went up to the doorman, who was quite impressed, and gave him a hundred-dollar bill as a tip. We were impressed as well.

However, when we returned to the mainland, we were in Fort Lauderdale, a thousand miles from my Virginia home and had little moola. We spent frugally on the two day drive home, and had just about made it to Virginia … about 50 miles short when we were afraid we were going to run out of gas, with ten cents in our pocket. We tried every ploy to get a gas station's operator to give, or loan or trade, us some gas but to no avail. We limped home to the empty farm (parents were still in Florida) on a wing and a prayer. We were forced to try to find any money in the house - change in the chairs and sofa, behind the desk, anywhere, only to come up with just a few dollars, not enough to make it back to Trinity. Finally, I think I was forced to borrow money from a neighbor to make the trip back, which we did, learning not to leave home without a decent supply of dough.

The spring of 1963 was memorable to say the least. There was an election going on as Lyndon Johnson had announced that he would not run again for president. Hubert Humphrey was the Democratic establishment candidate, while Gene McCarthy was the outsider, firmly against the war. He had the support of most active students (most were not active) on campus and many worked for his campaign. I did not, having many other things to do, another minor regret I had. Around that time Martin Luther King was assassinated, resulting in demonstrations at the College, and later Robert Kennedy was killed, a truly sad spring.

And speaking of regrets, many in our Theta Xi fraternity became involved in the theater on campus and had roles in several excellent plays. I remember "Marat Sade" and "The Fantasticks" as being particularly influential in their lives while they were practicing, and I felt that I had missed an opportunity. I really was too shy to put myself out there, and too busy with the Course and Social Evaluations to put the time in, but I was sorry for that, as it seemed so much fun and the central conversation theme for a while.

The Sit-In and Takeover

During the spring of 1968, my senior year, there occurred an event which made an important impression on me and shaped my thinking and much of my life after college. At that time, the activists within the student body and the Black student's organization, were concerned about the small number of Black students enrolled on campus. As President of the Trinity Senate, I had been discussing with the administration ways of increasing recruitment of minority students, to little effect. One spring day after my tenure as President ended, I saw a group of about a dozen Black students who formed the Black student association on campus, striding towards the administration building. I asked them what they were doing, and they said that they, along with some members of Students for a Democratic Society (SDS, the "radicals" on campus), were going to sit in at the Trustees' meeting going on at the time to protest the lack of minority students on campus. I decided to join them, as nothing I had been able to do had had any effect.

We entered the building, and soon many other students joined us, sitting outside the room where the Trustees were meeting. Demands were made and passed through the door for the Trustees to develop plans to increase recruitment of minority students. This was met with consternation by the Trustees who demanded that the students (who ultimately numbered 168) leave the building. At that point, the students decided not to let the Trustees out of the room until their demands were met in some form. So we sat. I did not agree with keeping them in the room as there were older men in the room and I felt that we could make our point by continuing our sit-in without confining the Trustees. However, I was not leading the sit-in, as the Black students and the SDS leaders were. But I stayed to see how things would play out.

Ultimately, after about five hours, we allowed the President and the Trustees to leave the room. I, being near the head of the line of students next to the door, got ferocious looks from several of the Trustees who recognized me from my days as

Clippings from the sit-in
(Image used with permission)

Senate President, or as an athlete. We continued to take over the administration building for the next two nights and three days, not allowing anyone in but students.

On the third day the Trustees gave us an ultimatum: either leave or the police would be brought in to remove us and we would be arrested. We divided into two groups, those who would stay and be arrested and those who felt we had done enough to make our point and could leave. I was in the latter group which had about 2/3rds to 3/4ths of the students. Joe McKeigue, my idealistic and committed roommate, was in the former group. Finally, before the police would be brought in (an act to be avoided since the College felt strongly that they were acting in locus parentis, in place of the parents, and thus did not want the police involved in settling College problems or disputes) the Trustees agreed to develop ways to recruit more minority students.

Then came the punishment phase. We didn't know whether we would be kicked out of the school or what, as it was less than a month or so until graduation. The Trustees decided to place on our records that we had incurred "administrative discipline" or some such wording and did not seem to follow through with their promised actions to recruit additional minority students. The students were incensed, and there were some threats among some of the more activist students about burning down some college buildings or writing to all the incoming freshmen telling them not to come to the college. (I remember there was considerable discussion of Saul Alinsky's brand of aggressive social activism and community organization in Chicago, where his philosophy was "Get 'em by the balls and their hearts and minds will follow".)

I received what can only be called hate mail from two of the Trustees saying, "How could I have done this when the College had done so much for me" (a stance my parents took as well as they were terribly upset and confused by my clearly unexpected action. We did not speak for several months after that until George Higgins, a psychology professor and my college faculty mentor, sent them a letter explaining the situation). And I convinced them that I was doing it for the College and because it was the right thing to do. Dean Vogel called me in and in a rage, gave me holy hell for "leading the demonstration" which I told him I did not do but felt I had to participate. A despicable man in my view, but my view was highly colored at the time, and he had his job to do.

At that point things were getting out of hand, and I called a student body meeting (I don't know on what authority I did this as I was not the Senate President at the time) to discuss the issues. I persuaded a Trustee, Chuck Kingston, who I had befriended and who was reasonably sympatico to our cause, to attend the meeting and state what the Trustees were willing to do. It seemed everyone showed up in Krieble Auditorium that night. All sides had their say and the issue was diffused when the Trustees agreed to a plan to increase minority recruitment and enrollment at the college.

However, at that point the faculty, some of whom were sympathetic to our cause, were outraged that the Trustees would take on student disciplinary actions, which the faculty felt was their authority alone. They rebelled and were at odds with the Trustees on the issue, threatening their own action. Finally, a student-faculty committee was set up by the faculty to interview all 168 student protesters and decide on the appropriate punishment. I think Dan Goldberg, a roommate, was on that committee. This was accomplished and the punishment included 30 days of community service and the notation on our record of the disciplinary action.

Many years later, the Trustees decided that the notation on each record would be expunged if the student sent in a request to do so. I wrote a letter to Dean Smith (lotta Deans back then) stating in effect that I had expected to be punished and that the cause was worth it and to please leave the notation on my record. I said it was up to the Trustees to determine if the punishment was justified, not the transgressor. Thus, it was up to them to expunge the punishment from the record if they wished. He asked if he could read the rather personal and heartfelt letter to the Trustees, and I agreed. Later, after multiple jobs at the Executive Office of the President, the Ford Foundation, the Justice Department, and others, I do not think this "Administrative Discipline" notation had any effect on my career. I was never asked about it and, as far as I know, it stands on my record to this day, one of only two that remain I am told.

Fraternity Impact

I joined a fraternity in my sophomore year, having gotten four bids from every fraternity on the street, probably because of my athletic reputation (you get one to four bids depending upon how much the fraternity wants you to join their club). I certainly didn't know many people in most of the fraternities. I chose Theta Xi. Joining Theta Xi was a significant step in my college life, and later life. I joined many of a group of my friends, who have remained close friends to the present day, gathering each year for a long weekend to share our lives with each other.

During the COVID pandemic, which is ongoing as I write this, we have a weekly Zoom call, discussing events going on in our lives and in politics, this during Trump's last year as President and Biden's first.

The fraternity experience was also important as it gave me access to some of the cleverest and funniest people I have ever encountered. No one lived at the fraternity, but we gathered each night to eat dinner. To this day the after-dinner banter was the most sophisticatedly humorous I have ever experienced. I laughed like I had never laughed in my life, before or since.

The Pranks

And there had to be pranks. One of the best was when I remained in school one spring vacation and a fellow schoolmate, Bob King, had a contraption which you used to hoist a tire with a net to hang it on top of the flagpole. Although seen by a campus guard who looked the other way, we accomplished the feat one night and when the students returned, they saw a mysterious tire atop the flagpole with no good explanation of how it got there. Explanations ranged from a passing airplane losing a tire, to someone tossing it

TIRED – The campus flagpole was capped with a rubber tire late Friday night by some unknown pranksters. The tire remained aloft all weekend, while officials tried to think of a way to get it down.

Did it drop from a plane?
(Image used with permission)

Theta Xi Fraternity Brothers
(Image taken by the author)

from the nearby chapel. None fit and the fire department came eventually with a 100 ft. ladder to take it down, unfortunately at some expense to the college.

Another time my friend George Fosque and I planned to hang a surprise 15 foot "End the War" scrolling poster at the Connecticut Democratic Convention where Hubert Humphrey, then backing the Vietnam War, was being nominated and elected as the state's Democratic choice for President. (I knew of George before going to college as his parents were living in Onancock, and I had heard George was going to Trinity, so looked him up when I arrived and became fast friends.) For this prank, George and I posed as press corps, got into the high up press box and set up the poster to unscroll at the proper time. Later just before Humphrey spoke, we snuck back into the press box, using a back door we had taped open for that purpose. We lit a cigarette on a saucer which, as it burned through a string holding the poster tight, would allow the long poster to drop. Alas, when we went back later to see what had happened, we were told by a guard that just before Humphrey spoke, John Bailey, the Convention Chairman, had seen and questioned the rolled-up poster, poised to drop, asked what it was about, and after reading it, of course had had it taken down. Ah, the best laid plans …

In another instance, I assumed my adopted role of Casper, the ghost, a role someone took on to play tricks each year on the Medusa, the honorary student disciplinary group of seven students. In this role, one night I figured out how to steal, from a showering classmate, David Chanin, the keys to the Medusa room where the Medusa met on campus and kept their robes. I stole their robes, then called all the hotels in Hartford to find out where they were having their annual secret meeting. I went in and hung the missing robes on their chairs with the sign that "Casper had struck again"! Pretty cool I thought. Definitely juvenile, but cool.

The Rhodes Scholarship Experience

Throughout my academic career, even in high school, I had heard about the Rhodes Scholarship … an award given to 32 scholar athletes throughout the country, four in each of eight districts, six or seven states in each district, I think. This earned the student a scholarship to do graduate work at Oxford and was a highly prestigious honor. In college I thought I had a shot at it even though no one had ever applied, much less won, a Rhodes from Trinity (since then, I found out there was another Rhodes applicant who made it to the finals 40 years later, in 2008, before she lost out).

I found out how to apply and started to process an application on my own. I did not have a faculty adviser to help me, but I did have to get letters of references from my coach, Dean Heath, and other faculty and friends which I had them mail directly to the Rhodes Committee without me seeing what they would say. I thought this is what the Committee expected. This turned out to not be too smart as Dean Roy Heath gave me a not too flattering comment on his recommendation. (In my Freshman year in the first weeks on campus, Dean Heath had invited groups of 8-10 freshmen to his house for dinner over the course of a month or so. I was invited to one and had not heard of these dinners so thought it was just a formality and did not go. I don't think he ever forgave me for that). His negative comment was noted by one Rhodes judge in the finals with a question in the margin of my application, which they returned to me.

After submitting all the necessary paperwork, I waited until I learned in the fall of 1967 that I had surprisingly been selected to compete in my state, Virginia, with about 12 others, out of a hundred or so applicants, to see if I would be one of two selected to represent Virginia in the Rhodes Southern District finals in Atlanta (or maybe it was Birmingham, Alabama, I really don't remember). They flew me to Richmond where I took a car to UVA to meet with the Rhodes Selection Committee. This was done at a "smoker" which turned out to be all of us mingling in a room for two hours in our ties and blue glazers, sipping sherry and talking with members of the Committee. I was thoroughly intimidated and don't remember talking to anyone in particular.

The next day we were lined up and, without any interviews, I was one of the two selected from the 12 as Virginia's Rhodes

Scholarship representatives to be sent to the finals. I excitedly sent word back to Trinity, expecting folks to be a little excited, but they did not seem to be, perhaps because they did not think I had much chance in the finals or few knew I had even applied.

They flew us immediately, as I recall, to Atlanta, for the finals. This was serious business. I was sitting on the plane with the other winning candidate selected to represent Virginia, a cadet from the Naval Academy, Dennis Blair, all decked out in his spiffy military uniform. (I later learned that the military academies competed with each other in the number of Rhodes Scholars they produced. They spent considerable time, faculty, and expense preparing their Rhodes candidates for six months, knowing the Selection Committee members, honing letters of recommendation, writing essays, etc.) I tried to make

*Two State and One National Rhodes Scholarship Winners
(Image used with permission)*

conversation with Dennis on the plane, but he was distinctly quiet and standoffish, to the point of being rude, I guess seeing me as competition, and not to be befriended.

After another smoker the night before the competition, each of the candidates (14 or 16 this time) was scheduled for a long interview the next day with about 12 former Rhodes Scholars.

The time for my interview arrived. The candidate would sit in the middle of a room with the interviewers lined up on each side sitting against a wall, asking questions. I don't remember all the questions but several stuck in my mind. I was asked about my supposed expertise in conducting multivariate data analysis. I had no idea what they meant and said so. They asked me hadn't I reviewed the references submitted for me by the faculty and others. I said that I did not know I was supposed to and indeed thought I was not, since the recommendations should be made without the applicant seeing them to insure honesty (so-o-o naïve). And I asked, did one reference suggest that I was accomplished in multivariate analysis? They said yes, and then it hit me, they were talking about Chi Square analyses, which I had become quite expert in during one summer working with the college professor, George Higgins. I admitted my confusion and laughed about it.

One questioner was particularly hostile to me. It was one of McNamara's whiz kids, Alan Enthoven, who was a former Rhodes Scholar and, I later learned, the leader of Robert McNamara's "best and brightest" in the White House, advising Johnson on the war. He asked several questions about the Vietnam war, one of which was what I thought about the use of napalm. I said I thought it was a particularly gruesome weapon, whereupon he said, "Can't any weapon used in war be a gruesome weapon?", where upon I sort of gritted my teeth and said "I see your point" not wanting to appear too argumentative, whereupon he laughed and said "I didn't think I was making a point", getting a laugh from the interviewers. I should have made a more thoughtful response about it being a particularly indiscriminate weapon, often taking civilian lives along with the enemy. Shoulda, coulda, woulda.

In any event, all interviews were concluded, and the questioners deliberated for about two hours while we mingled outside. They then came out and lined us up. We were congratulated on making it to the Finals as our State's winners, and then began to read out the winning four names. I was not among the first three, so my chances were looking pretty dim. They read the fourth name, not mine, and again said what fine young men we were to have made it this far.

At that point it was over, and I started to turn to leave. Immediately four of the interviewer judges came rushing over to me expressing condolences at my losing. They asked me if I wanted to go to Oxford next year anyway, just not as a Rhodes Scholar. They would help make it happen. I quickly (too quickly, in retrospect) said no, that I had planned to attend the Woodrow Wilson School at Princeton if I had not won the Rhodes. I was a little heartened by the fact that none of my other competitors who lost had any judges come up to them afterwards, suggesting to me that there was some controversy among the judges as to whether I or another should be one of the four picked. But I lost.

As it turned out, the other candidate from Virginia, the Naval Academy graduate who flew down with me and had been so rudely taciturn, won. They rarely chose two from the same state and he was certainly accomplished and was probably far more practiced and smoother in his interview I'm sure, so he probably deserved it. Blair was a high-ranking cadet in his class and went on to become the Commander of the Pacific Fleet, won many honors, and subsequently served a short-lived career as the Director of National Intelligence under President Obama.

He was fired by Obama for what some thought was not being able to successfully coordinate the many agencies in the intelligence community (a difficult task at best). He had been involved in some controversies involving disobeying orders and not following Obama's directives (Wikipedia).

I much later learned that Bill Clinton had won the Rhodes that same day in an adjacent district. I also learned that in the same class of 32 Rhodes winners who were picked on that same day were Robert Reich, the future Labor Secretary, and Hank Paulson, the future Treasury Secretary who helped immensely when the economy tanked at the end of George Bush's presidency from over-leveraged consolidated mortgage instruments. Several other famous persons were among the 32 winners that day, but I never heard from the other two winners in my region, one of whom I deemed to be of southern gentility and undistinguished character but with a long name ending in Beauregard, or something similar.

Somewhat disappointed, but not terribly, as I had figured I was a long shot, I limped back home to Trinity. Few on campus were the wiser that I had even competed for the Rhodes much less made it to the finals and perhaps almost won (in my humble opinion).

A Night to Remember

Some short time after the Rhodes experience, it all started

innocently enough. In the fall of 1967, I had been nominated, and awarded, one of 12 National Scholar Athlete Awards by the National Football Foundation and Hall of Fame, a group of prominent citizens, sports enthusiasts, and businessmen who had set up a Foundation and Hall of Fame for accomplished Scholar Athlete football players. I played quarterback for Trinity, and while a fine athlete, had no business winning this award for my athletic skills. It must have been the work of our college's public relations director, Robert Herron, who had taken a liking to me from my freshman year on. He was nationally known and must have nominated me, and I think must have pressed the Committee to award the honor to me based principally on my leadership role in the College, and my academic record. I suspect due to his work, I also later won one of 32 national NCAA Scholar Athlete Awards, which is another story.

In any event, every year the National Football Foundation held a very swanky 1,000-person dinner at the Waldorf Astoria in NYC in early December, inviting all the notables in the sports world to honor the 12 awardees, plus a few political and business types. So, the captain of our team, Larry Roberts, and I took the train to NYC. We went up to our room and struggled to figure out the tuxedos they rented for us to wear as it was a very fancy affair. Then Larry took his seat in the audience somewhere and I met the rest of the awardees upstairs for pictures and the TV cameras and interviews, and later went on stage for the event. Clearly this was a bigger deal than I had been led to believe.

We were aligned in chairs across the front of the stage each next to a sports notable sitting with us in a line. I happened to be sitting next to an old codger named "Greasy" Neal whom I did not know from Adam. But everyone else seemed to. As the klieg

The NCAA Scholar Athlete Award Presentation
(Image used with permission)

lights shot through the air around this massive Waldorf ballroom with tiers of seating up in the balconies, like at the Academy Awards (as a small-town farm boy I was most impressed, not knowing what to expect when I came to this event).

Before the start of, and throughout the dinner event, famous sports stars would come up to Greasy Neal to shake his hand. Mickey Mantle, Yogi Berra, Joe DiMaggio, Johnny Unitas, Y.A Title, Frank Gifford ... seemed like everybody wanted to say hello to Greasy. And Greasy, being the gentleman he was, introduced me to each of them as they came up to the front of the stage. I, of course, was eating it up.

After a while, Ed Sullivan, the host of the evening, started the show, by announcing the famous guests, and then individually announced the 12 Scholar Athlete winners. We each stood up as our names and accomplishments were announced, and I gave the thank you speech (very short) at the end (more work by the PR guy I suspect, to give me that honor). After the evening had a few more awards (Leverette Saltonstall got Man of the Year or something like that and Richard Nixon was honored in absentia), it became clear that Ed Sullivan was more than a little tipsy at the podium. At that point, he lost his place and began to slur his words, and to announce, once again, each of the 12 awardees names. We each began to stand up again in turn as he slurred out our names to the hushed silence of the huge crowd. I was only hoping that I did not have to stand up at the end and again give my thanks on behalf of the awardees. At about the sixth awardee, someone came up to the podium out of the wings, and gently escorted Ed off the stage and the ceremonies were concluded by another person.

Right after the ceremonies, we were escorted off stage to a room where pictures were taken and the TV cameras recorded us again, stating our names and colleges. I then got on the elevator with a famous sportscaster of the time (who shall remain nameless to protect the guilty) who was almost falling down drunk (seemed drinking was the thing to do at this event), then I was taken to another room upstairs where we were given our silver bowls with more pictures and citations and sent on our way.

At about 11 p.m. I came down and found Larry in the bar drinking with a couple of businessmen from Georgia. He called me over and introduced me as "Kim King" who was a well-known All-American quarterback from the Univ. of Georgia (I think). Astonished, and a little embarrassed and fearful that they knew what this guy looked like, I played along. They bought us drinks and ended up asking us if we wanted summer jobs in their business, Larry bullshitting and scarfing drinks all along the way. We told them we'd think about it, took their cards and ambled out into the Waldorf lobby.

Just then, around 12:30 or 1:00 a.m., we saw Bobby Kennedy walking past. This was about five months before he announced for the presidency and six months before he was assassinated. We, still in our tuxedos and feeling important, looked at each other and said, "Let's follow him." And did for about three blocks until he stopped and bought a Sunday morning *New York Times*. At that point we looked at each other and wondered what in the hell we were doing and why we hadn't been arrested already for stalking Bobby Kennedy!

We returned to the Waldorf and asked a taxi driver where the happening places in Times Square were. At that time topless bars were just coming into the fore, and we ended up being dropped off at some bar called something like the Kit Kat Club, supposedly hot at the time. Indeed, it was a topless bar with the ladies on a dance strip behind the bar. We took our seats at the bar and had drinks, taking in the sights. After a while I needed to take a leak and left Larry at the bar. When I came back, Larry, obviously well-fueled and taken with a particular lady dancing behind the bar, had one knee on the stool, the other up on the bar, reaching for the dancers. It was a race between me and the bouncer to get to Larry, which was a tie, whereupon we were not so gracefully escorted out.

Out on the street, we found another cab, asked the same question and the driver suggested that the best place to be at 1:30 a.m. was the Copacabana. Dropped off there, Larry went up to the ticket guy and introduced me as Gary Beban, the Heisman Trophy winner that year, and also one of the 12 Scholar Athlete Awardees in town. The guy knew about the Waldorf honorees and was impressed with Gary Beban, but obviously did not know what he looked like. He escorted us in and to a table right down front whereupon he again introduced us to the other folks at the table. The only one of which I remember (things were getting fuzzy by then) was the comedian Buddy Hackett, he with the lazy eye. They bought us more drinks and we talked a little and watched the show for a while, until we both excused ourselves to hit the head.

While in the men's room, Larry once again began talking to me (Gary Beban) with another gentleman between us at the urinals. The fellow looked at Larry, then slowly looked at me and said, "I know Gary Beban, and you're not Gary Beban," whereupon, Larry and I figured the jig was up and slunk out of the Copa.

Since it was about 2:30 or 3:00 a.m. by that time, we thought we'd walk back to the Waldorf Astoria, not giving much thought to the safety of two guys in tuxedos on the streets of NYC at that hour. As we walked along under one of the canopies that extend to the street from some bar, I heard a "THWAP!". Larry had reached up and swatted at the hanging edge of the canopy as he passed under. Unfortunately, he also hit the aluminum brace supporting the canopy, bending it into a nice, but gentle, "V". We walked a few steps and then about five or six fellows poured out of the bar and came toward us. I started to explain and looked to my left to see Larry running full speed away. Turning back, I saw they were (for some reason) coming toward me. I smiled a little and started back pedaling and explaining about the mistake. Seeing one of the guys had a broom handle, I turned and started loping away, knowing that as a pretty fast 100-yard man, I could outrun these guys easily. At that point I heard "BLAM", a gunshot! Not caring whether they were firing a warning shot or not, I kicked it into high gear and Larry and I did not stop until we got back to the Waldorf.

Back at the Waldorf at around 4 a.m., I had two messages:

one from my parents who had heard, from a neighbor, about me being introduced on Walter Cronkite's CBS national news (again I suspect the work of the Trinity PR guy, Robert Herron. Must have been a pretty slow news night on CBS News). It was a surprise to them as I had not told them I had even won the award, much less was going to NYC to get it.

The second call was from Pari Caldwell, TWA's Stewardess of the Year in '65 or '66 (her off hand boast to me, unproven) whom I had met the year before at the Harvard Business School Internship program during a summer in Cambridge, MA. I think she was just roaming around the campus looking for some eligible Harvard Business School person to engage. She had seen me on TV that night also and said she was catching a late-night flight to NYC from Chicago and would see me around five a.m. for breakfast. Since it was already about four, I tried to catch some sleep before Pari knocked on my door around 5:30, when, to avoid waking Larry, we went out to a nearby diner and had breakfast as the sun came up in Manhattan.

So that was my night to remember … Greasy Neal, Ed Sullivan, Robert Kennedy, National TV, Walter Cronkite, the Topless Bar, the Copacabana, getting shot at, and Pari for breakfast.

A second honor, the NCAA Scholar Athlete Award, was awarded, again in NY over a weekend, not long after. This was given to 32 Scholar Athletes from colleges around the country. However, this weekend was nowhere near as exciting, although we were feted at the 21 Club and the Biltmore with our picture on the front page of the *New York Times*. My selection for the award and choice to give the thank you speech, again was probably the work of the college PR Director. I ended my Trinity College years being selected for Phi Beta Kappa… (and they never found out about the altercations of my transcript! Hey, we weren't in the Administration building for two nights for nuthin'! Okay, kiddin' again.)

Post College Experiences - The Early 1970s

The European Motorcycle Tour

After graduation from Trinity in the summer of '68, three friends and I decided to go on a tour of Europe on motorcycles. In July we landed in Lisbon and George Fosque and Stu Edelman separated from Tom Nary and me, George to Paris to later pick up his motorcycle in London and Stu and his wife Leslie did it up right by renting a car and touring by auto separate from us. Tom and I were to make our way by train to London from Madrid via Paris where Tom and George would pick up their bikes, both brand new shiny BSAs and Triumphs.

I had no bike, but in Madrid, Tom and I were walking past a garage where a for sale sign was on a small motorcycle being worked on by a group of mechanics. The cautionary words here were "being worked on" which I ignored and bought the bike for $250, a Bultaco off road two-cylinder racing bike, not the bike you toured Europe with, but little did I know.

Abandoning the idea of taking the train, Tom and I set off with Tom driving, since he had experience driving and I had none. This small bike was not built for two people. It was a hot two-cylinder racing bike, which meant adding oil to the gas, which we did of course, but little did we know, it burned out spark plugs regularly. I learned quickly though, as every 400 miles it stopped running, and finally one mechanic told me that it ran hot and burned spark plugs, and from then on I took a supply of spark plugs with me, changing them every so often.

We packed all our stuff on the bike, and after an embarrassing start when Tom slammed the accelerator on sand in front of a group of bar onlookers, putting us down, we collected our scattered backpacks, got up, and this time slowly took off. Our first stop was in Pamplona for the running of the bulls. There we met an old girlfriend of Tom's traveling with her friends. After watching the running of the bulls, not running with them (we watched from the stands, not wishing to ruin our trip), the girls offered to put us up in their hotel "on the other side of the hills a few miles".

The 250 Bultaco Off Road Racing Bike

Around 11 at night we left Pamplona on our bikes and started over the "hills" to a small town where they stayed. Well, we went up and up ... and UP ... by way of multiple switchbacks, finally making it to the top after an hour where we read the sign - "You are now at the highest point in the Pyrenees". So much for the "hills". Then we started down and the buses came, finally catching up to us, and taking revelers across from Pamplona. Unfortunately, the buses took the sharp switchbacks by scraping the inside to avoid going over the cliff. Also, unfortunately, the only place for us to stop that was halfway level to let the buses pass, was on the inside of the switchbacks, causing some anxiety-producing moments.

We made it to Elizondo, a beautiful little town on the other side of the Pyrenees, around one a.m. Found the hotel and entered. Only to find that the proprietor, who did not appreciate us waking him up, would not let the girls know we were there, protecting their virginity I assume, from a couple of scraggly appearing bikers. He told us of an inn, where we were escorted to a room on the third floor with wonderful feather beds and had the best night's sleep of the trip. We met up with Tom's friend and her friends the next day for a day trip and picnic among the glorious mountains of Spain.

The next day we left for Paree, only to be stopped at the border, as we had neglected to obtain, because we did not know about it, some form needed to cross the border from Spain to France (this being well before the European Union was established). Not knowing where to get it or how, we promptly went to the nearest large town, and found an IBM office. We explained our predicament and asked to see their forms. We found the most official and complex one, in English, stamped it with several official looking ink stamps the office had, and headed back to the border.

This time the Spanish officials looked at the form and our passports and waived us through. A hundred yards on, the French officials were a little trickier. The official looked at the form and asked us in French what it was. We pleaded ignorance of the language and what he was asking, looked puzzled and surprised to be stopped. After a few Bud Abbott and Lou Costello minutes of "Who's on First", he got frustrated and waived us through. We roared away, glad to have escaped the slammer. Post 911 I suspect inspections have gotten much tighter, although there are few if any border checks between EU countries now.

We finally got to Paris, and then were on to London, and at Tom's frustrated urging I learned to handle the bike. I almost killed myself on the first day when touring the English countryside, George, in the lead, took a quick turn right between two small hills and down a hill to the left. Following closely behind, I tried to take the turn but hit the further curb, and as my hand accidentally gunned the gas when hitting the curb, I shot up the hill, narrowly missing two trees by an inch or two on each side, and went airborne on the other side, coming down near George who had turned left and waited for us down on the other side of the hill. Whereupon George, seeing me fly between the two trees and sail over the hill, said "Hey Miles, not bad for your first day!" That was only the first of three near-death experience I had on that trip on the bike.

That was the first few days of a whirlwind trip across Europe, hitting about six to eight countries, including Wales, where we looked up a branch of my Mathias relatives on a sheep farm.

My two-cycle engine blew in Switzerland from coasting down the mountains for miles without giving the engine gas, which it needed for the oil. Luckily, I found a wonderful Swiss family whose son was a mechanic and fixed it in about a week for a pittance. George kindly stayed with me several days before leaving for Italy and France on his bike.

After the motor was fixed in about six days, I took off and found myself on the shores of Nice where I parked my bike on the shore along a boulevard lined with beachgoers and went in search of a spark plug. At a drugstore, I met a couple of friendly guys who told me in halting English and using my little French, about a camp where I could spend the night in their huge tent. They led me there and I took out my bedroll and got in the tent they assigned me and slept.

The next morning, I went back to town to fix my bike only to find it as the only vehicle on the entire seaside boulevard along the Shore, parked alone. Evidently, I arrived just before the start of a huge holiday parade and all cars had been removed. I had missed the street sign that told of this. I immediately changed the plug, jumped on the bike and tore out of there. When I was racing by a porch heading out of Nice, George, who, unbeknownst to me, had stayed overnight in Nice, saw me, hopped on his bike and caught up with me, and we agreed to meet in Lyon for the trip back to Paris.

In Paris we stayed at a hostel on the left bank, "Hotel St. Andre Des Arts" which turned out to be two blocks away from the student riots of '68, which were underway at the time. At the same time, the Chicago 7 trial and hundreds of anti-war demonstrators were protesting the Democratic convention in Chicago with Mayor Daley at the helm. Exciting times.

Off to gorgeous, canal-filled Amsterdam. We toured the city that day and were intrigued by the women displaying their wares in the windows of the red-light district (prostitution being legal in Amsterdam). Staying at a YMCA in Amsterdam that night, I got up the next morning to find that my bike starter pedal was missing, rendering the bike useless. Told of my mechanical problem that night, the woman proprietor of our hostel said, "not a problem" and proceeded to take down the info about my bike and what was needed. The next morning a motorcyclist courier growled up while we were having breakfast, with the exact part I needed. She had ordered it from Madrid (it was a Spanish bike) and it had been sent overnight, reminding us of just how small Europe is. Overnight shipping was unknown back in '68 in the States.

During this European trip we stayed in tents, hostels, cheap inns, barns, under trees, wherever, to conserve money. The trip was awesome. I reveled in the antiquity, the ruins, the architecture, the different cultures and customs, and their history. I fell in love with Europe, and it made me fully realize just what a young country the U.S. is. And how hypercompetitive and intense we are ... one reason for our material success probably, but it did have its downsides, as I watched groups having coffee at tables outside of small cafes in small town after small town. And in Spain watched families walking to dinner at around 9 at night, tarrying until midnight talking and enjoying themselves.

One time in London we jumped a fence in Hyde Park and slept under a beautiful large willow tree whose drooping branches made a circular enclosure perfect to hide us from any authorities who might not want us there. Sure enough, at six the next morning, a bobby making his rounds with a German Shepherd police dog found us, the dog barking ferociously outside the willow branches. A bit terrified, we huddled together wondering what this park guard would do. Suddenly he gave a command and the dog stopped barking and lept through the branches towards us. We assumed we were goners ... until he went up to us and started licking our faces. Love those London bobbies.

After about six weeks of touring throughout Europe we headed back to London. When we got to London, Tom and I drove to the airport only to find that we had to pack our bikes in large cardboard boxes for them to be flown back to the states. We had no boxes. A quandary. We went to a supermarket, found the largest cardboard boxes we could find, cut them up, slapped cardboard on each side of the bikes and front and back, and duct taped it together and rolled these admittedly crazy looking contraptions back to the loading dock. Whereupon the same guy laughed out loud and told his crew, "Ok boys, load 'em up".

At LaGuardia, we picked up our bikes and I headed to Princeton where I was scheduled to start grad school and Tom went to Philly to start med school. A great trip.

Graduate School at Princeton

Riding up to Princeton in the fall of '68, I found my way to the graduate school where I had a room with a Japanese roommate named Nori Inagaki, a news reporter for NGK, the principal TV Network in Japan. He was a little older than I was, on a mid-career fellowship at Princeton. I was in a class of about 40 carefully selected graduate students in the Woodrow Wilson School of Public and International Affairs. (Just last year, Wilson's name was removed due to his racist Presidency. It is now known as the School for Public and International Affairs - SPIA.) I was thoroughly intimidated by this group, as they represented a far more talented and experienced group of people than I had ever encountered. Campaign operatives, authors, one Heisman Trophy winner (Pete Dawkins from West Point), TV and news people. Most were a little older than I and had been out in the work world a few years. This two-year master's program was fairly elite as all expenses were paid for all of us by fellowships set up by a donor (who I later learned was the MacArthur Foundation founder).

I buckled down and took the courses, doing fairly well, but was not happy there, and should have waited to go. I did meet a roommate during my second year, and future great friend Robert Cunningham, as well as a good friend in Greg Wilcox, a son of a Philadelphia Quaker who disliked the Woodie Wilson School as much as I did and made no bones about it. We hung around together, did goofy things like rolling down a long hill over and over one spring day. I spent the summer of '69 in Sacramento with Greg, doing an internship with the Legislative Analyst's office during the governorship of some actor named Ronald Reagan.

That summer started by us driving to California in four days in my Chevy Malibu tracing Rt. 66 for a time. We ended up along the Big Sur coast looking for any place to eat around 12 o'clock at night, and coming upon Nepenthe, a new age restaurant and exclusive enclave of cabins overlooking the ocean and Big Sur. One look at the hip clientele, and the open smoking of marijuana, told us that we were, once again, "not in Kansas anymore".

Arriving in Sacramento we got into our summer jobs and took long weekends during that Woodstock summer of 1969, pretending to be hippies, exploring the highlights of the West Coast from the Mexican to the Canadian borders. One Saturday in San Francisco we found ourselves dancing with the Hari Krishnas as they celebrated some holiday with an annual parade to the sea. This I think was the same weekend in 1969 that Woodstock was taking place in NY. It was a fun summer, ending abruptly by my returning alone to Princeton for my second year, while Greg took a year off and stayed out west. Greg was upset after I left him in California when our summer internships were over to drive back to NY. At the time I could not understand this, but which I now think he may have seen me as a father figure of sorts. He had a love/hate relationship with his highly successful and overpowering father, and he could have seen me as a surrogate ... or it could have been just the leaving of a friend.

I was happy to graduate from Princeton and get outta there in the fall of '70, as I never felt comfortable there, almost wordlessly passing through my small classes, doing the necessary work but not engaging with the faculty or benefitting as I should have. My fault. I learned that only half of my starting class of 40 graduated when I did. The other 20 either took a year off, dropped out, died (three Black classmates) or went back to jobs they had. But I had secured a job at the Ford Foundation as a Training Associate, whatever that is, in the Big Apple where my current girlfriend Melinda Woodward lived, so was facing a better future.

The Ford Foundation: A Night to Forget

My last exams before leaving Princeton were take-home affairs and I turned them in at midnight that night.

I immediately packed and left for my job. But it was not in NYC that first night, as my bosses were holding a conference in Carmel, California, and I was expected to be there. My friend Robert Cunningham drove me to Kennedy Airport at midnight to catch a one a.m. plane for San Francisco. My job was to monitor the seven universities involved in a program to train unusual professionals from a variety of fields to be school administrators, bringing innovations to schools in the U.S.

The flight was a red-eye and I got on the new (at the time) 747 with two levels. I happened to be one of only three people in the upper first-class level with the huge comfortable seats and a bar and piano music. (The Ford Foundation flew all their employees first class back then. Whoopdedoo!) One of the three was the famous football fullback Jim Brown who was on his way to California to start his career as a movie star. I remember that all during the flight, the female flight attendants and other passengers would come up the stairs to get his autograph. It was a beautiful night for a flight with a moon over gorgeous clouds and I was upbeat and happy.

I landed in San Francisco at four a.m., rented a car and began the drive to the resort in Carmel where the conference was being held. It was a conference of about 20 people from the seven universities (Columbia, Harvard, Stanford, University of Wisconsin, Claremont, etc.) which the Foundation was funding to train innovative folks from all walks of life to become secondary school leaders (superintendents and principals) in large city school systems. My college roommate Joe McKeigue was selected for one of these prestigious spots at Columbia Teacher's College. The directors and key staff from the seven programs were in attendance at the conference. I arrived at Carmel at six a.m. and immediately went to bed.

I got up at 7:30 to go to breakfast with my new bosses and associates ... my first job! After breakfast we started the meeting by introducing me and beginning to discuss the progress of each program at the seven universities. It was interesting and we met until noon when we all had a lunch, and then everyone went to the pool.

During the afternoon, at the pool, I noticed that one of my new bosses (who was not really my boss but a more senior associate who had been with the Foundation for several years and was about ten years older than I was) seemed to be looking at me strangely and told a few off-color jokes to the crowd. I didn't think much about it. That night at dinner over a long table with all 20 of us spread on each side, I noticed that this fellow seemed to make a point of sitting next to me. Everyone had wine but I only had part of one glass since I had had almost no sleep and did not intend to get tipsy my first day on the job. I did drink a lot of water.

Well, the dinner progressed fine, but all of a sudden, (and this is my memory of what happened) I woke up and found myself nude, in a strange bed with this fellow, who was actively fondling my privates. I pushed him away, leapt up, told him that I was not gay and what was he doing, and quickly left in a huff to find my room. It seemed clear to me now that this guy had targeted me all day but how did he get me into his room? I learned from others the next day that I had "fallen asleep" at the table and that this fellow had taken me in his arms to my room. This seemed very odd to me as I was excited, not sleepy, at dinner and in no way could see myself falling asleep.

Now the rooms in this resort were laid out such that there was a larger meeting room in the center with four bedrooms off it, one off of each corner. I had one bedroom in one corner, my real boss had another and this fellow had one as well, diagonally opposite from mine. It was obvious then, that he had taken me to my room, entered it from the outside with me in his arms, and then just gone out the other door carrying me through the empty large meeting room to his bedroom, stripped me and put me in his bed.

I was mortified … I didn't know what to do. The conference finished in two days, and the three of us, my boss, the molester, and I flew back to NYC, and I started work at the Foundation. When I got to the Foundation, I didn't say anything to anyone. Partly I didn't want to start my first job as someone who was causing "trouble", even though I was the injured party. Partly because I felt that it was likely that this fellow, who was highly thought of by my big boss, would dispute what happened and say it was voluntary and I was drunk and willing. And partly because, and this was the lamest, that I felt sorry for this guy that he had to get sex that way by molesting younger naïve men (and

I was naïve!).

This was a time in the fall of 1970 when there was considerable attention given to gay people coming out of the closet, and the bleak double lives they were having to lead because of societal pressure. I felt that the gay community was being treated unfairly and poorly. I did not hold the fellow's offense against gay people in general, as I could just as easily have been a young female molested by a nefarious straight male.

A small part of me wondered whether I had indeed fallen asleep at the table from the lack of sleep. But I immediately dismissed this as I knew I had almost nothing to drink at all, knowing that I had not had much sleep, and I was fully animated by the conversation during the dinner. And I was too excited to just "fall asleep". For I also knew that I would not have stayed asleep when he carried me to my room, then on to his, and undressed me. In my opinion, there was no excuse in any way for what he had done. I concluded that he had drugged me by putting something in my partially consumed glass of my wine, or more probably in my water, which I drank a lot of.

One day after work shortly after we got back, I confronted him about what he had done and asked why. He pled all innocence and said he felt I would not mind or something like that. However, I read in the *New York Times* days later a story that a new date-rape drug, Rohypnol, was making the rounds in the gay and straight dating communities in NYC, and it had the same effects that I had experienced, a rapid blackout only to wake up later with no knowledge of what had happened. I now knew what he had slipped into my glass in Carmel.

But still, I stupidly didn't say anything. While I was in no way traumatized by this experience, I was greatly angered by it. I didn't want this to mark my reputation in my first job, so I remained quiet. The trouble was that my job was to travel to the seven universities to monitor and help the programs we funded, and I had to travel, staying overnight. And this more senior associate would be traveling with me, at least once every two weeks and sometimes weekly. I didn't look forward to this, and I insisted that our secretary always book us separate rooms. Now she did not know that I had been molested by the guy but probably knew that he was gay, having worked with him for years. She, and probably others, assumed, since I was a white southerner and he was Black, that my demanding a separate room was because I was a racist or a homophobe who did not want to share a room with him, a gay Black guy. Thus, I started out at the Ford Foundation being thought of as a southern racist homophobe who could not hold his liquor. What a start, being molested on my first day in my first real job!

As I later thought about it, and as some friends whom I told about it advised me, I should have told my big boss and sued the Foundation to take action against the molester, settling for a large sum of money and moving on quickly to my next job. But I did not. This was 45 years before the "Me Too" movement. I gutted it out, and did my job, traveling with this fellow, but never trusting him again, leaving the Foundation two years later. This did give me a particularly sympathetic and empathic insight into the experience and feelings of women who came forward in the "Me Too" era.

I now regret my cowardice at not coming forward to call this guy out, as who knows how many other young men he molested or raped, in his largely successful career.

The New York City Experience

Aside from this wonderful start, NYC was fascinating to me, but overpowering and lonely. I would walk the 12 blocks from my apartment on 31st street over Marchi's Italian restaurant up 2nd Avenue to the Foundation on 43rd Street every day. At first it was a wonderment, taking in all the sights and sounds of a big city, senses alive. However, I found myself, after a few weeks, getting dulled to the stimuli and my senses shut down. After six weeks I just trudged to work, not noticing anything. I spent my weekends exploring the city, once walking the length of Manhattan in one day. I spent a lot of time in the parks and Central Park became a destination, as I loved nature and the parks were about the only places to find and experience it.

Legionnaires Disease, Maybe

One early morning in that NYC late Fall of 1970, around three a.m., I awoke, sweating and feverish. It did not get better, and I knew that I was sick. Around eight a.m. I called in to work to get the name of the Foundation company doctor as I knew no one in NYC. I called and told them I needed to see someone NOW as my fever was getting much worse. I took a bus up town to the doctor's office and almost nodded off on the bus I was so weak. I staggered into the doctor's office and checked in and sat waiting to be called. Now in NYC at the time heroin was in full bloom and it occurred to me that the receptionist thought I must be a junkie, nodding off, looking feverish, sweating, etc.

I waited and finally got in to see the Doctor who first checked my arms for track marks and finding none, then finally took my temperature. It was 106! He was shocked and immediately ran me across the street to Lenox Hill Hospital to check in. They rushed me to a room and iced me down to bring the fever down.

I was in the hospital for six days as they could not find what was wrong with me, giving me all sorts of tests, sending my blood to the CDC for analysis. I felt better after a few days, but they kept me there as a case study hoping to find out what was wrong. They never did. I finally went home and went on with my life, not knowing what it was other than an unexplained exceptionally high fever.

A year or two later, I read in the paper about the Philadelphia veterans convention of the American Legion and the eleven Legionnaires who had contracted some strange fever and died. The doctors finally associated their condition with bacteria developed in the circulating air conditioners on top of the building. I thought back to my apartment. My bed was up against a window two feet away from a circulating air conditioner above Marchi's Italian restaurant. I began to think that I had had one of the first cases of Legionnaire's disease. Until the Legionnaires had contracted it in Philly, the disease was unknown. I still don't know to this day, though 48 years later in 2018 I wrote the CDC about my experience and never heard back from them, as by then Legionnaire's disease was a serious but well-known illness. Oh well. I lived through it.

My experience at the Foundation for two years convinced me that, while the program managers were needed to dole out the dough to various worthwhile projects, the real exciting work was being done in the field, so I didn't plan to stay long. I also didn't care for the behavior that being a supplicant for Ford money brought out. An applicant could have spent a year developing a plan and strategy for a new program, bring it in with pride, and a Foundation manager might say, "Well, I think if you did it this way it would be better" and, of course the applicant/supplicant would change his plans to accommodate the manager's wishes. Didn't happen often but with some managers it did and was quite demeaning to both applicant and manager. Ah, the power of the purse! Charles Brown (my big boss) and Ralph Borson were managers who respected the applicants' work and dignity and rarely inserted their own judgements to alter the plans of a proposed project. Unfortunately, Chuck Brown had cancer and came to the Foundation for a short two-year stint just to run the seven university programs in which I was involved. And when he left, I left.

The Personal Growth Movements

During the '70s, it was a time of psychological exploration, with all sorts of ways of expanding one's consciousness and potential through experiential "new age" groups. There were sensitivity training groups, yoga, Tai Chi, meditation (my then roommate John Vail and I had some fun with a technique called the Primal Scream for a time) and all manner of weekend trainings that promised to make one a better person. I tried quite a few and did indeed learn some useful things. One such group, very popular and controversial at the time, was EST or Erhard Seminar Training. My girlfriend at the time, Fran, convinced me to take this two-weekend training.

It really was a well-designed, mind-based, pyramid scheme with participants encouraged (or indoctrinated) to proselytize the experience to others, after going through it themselves. It largely consisted of a leader berating the participants, maybe 75-

100 in a room, to break down their perceptions of themselves as capable free-thinking adults, by haranguing them about their false beliefs and hopes, and by keeping them up all night one night, weakening their defenses.

Although I recognized it as such, I committed myself to getting from it what I could and do indeed credit it with changing my attitude and response to negative events as they hit me. One lesson was not to take setbacks personally, whether minor, such as spilling a cup of coffee on an important paper, or major, the breakup of a relationship. As was said, "shit happens", and our attitude toward it helps determine its effect on us. The lesson was to expect accidents, mishaps, or negative happenings, not be surprised at them, and to train ourselves not to react traditionally to them with hostility or anger but to laugh at them as expected and to get on with the next piece of business without obsessing about the recent incident. This alone was worth the seminar as it changed my attitude towards minor misfortunes that would befall me.

There were several other lessons I took away which I noticed helped me in my approach to life. A small one was being able to set an internal clock to wake up at a certain time whenever I wanted. I have used this often and it works. Just by focusing internally in your mind's eye on a clock face or two, analog and/or digital, set at the time you want to get up. Focus for a minute or so and you will invariably wake up within five minutes of that time.

And I must say that EST helped me with the one problem I had for many years during school - colds and a stuffed-up nose. During winters, my breathing seemed to be constantly difficult because of nasal congestion in the extreme. On average I would go through about 20 bottles of nasal decongestant, such as

Dristan, my favorite, each year from the Fall to Spring. It seemed that every half hour I would have to take a hit of Dristan to keep my nose clear and to be able to breathe easily. As my nose became more congested, I would get panicky and never went anywhere without my bottle of Dristan. I chalked it up to having constant colds during the winter, or mold in the old house, as the problem did subside during the summer. Little was known then about the rebound effect of using these things.

Once on a sailing trip at age about 32, again with nasal congestion, I remembered something that I had learned in taking EST ... a technique for breaking through panicky situations. I was sailing with Jack Phillips up north near St. Michaels, MD. We were anchored at dusk watching the sun go down and the geese gathering, when my nose started to become congested, as usual. I, of course, had Dristan with me so I was not concerned about not being able to breath. But I thought I would try the trick I had learned in EST. So, lying on my bunk, I let my congestion get worse until I could hardly breath at all though my nose. I felt the panic rising but let it continue as I had been taught. It got worse and worse as did my panic (as usual I could fully breath through my mouth, but this did not seem to stem the panic at all).

The hippie year in Cambridge/Somerville

Finally, after letting the panic build and build, I was getting stressed and was about to get up and retrieve the bottle of Dristan

I brought (always). Suddenly, just then, in my head I flashed on a time as a baby when I was on a diaper-changing table, when a person, I think my father's mother, put her hand over my mouth, perhaps to stop me from crying or something. But she did not realize that I could not breath because my nose was completely congested as well, and I was struggling for breath. I was dying from lack of breath!

Just then on the boat, with this revelation or flashback, my nose cleared suddenly, immediately, completely, miraculously! I never had such a panicky situation again for the rest of my life. I say never, but maybe once or twice, but never did I have to use Dristan constantly and never due to the thought that I might die without it. This was a miracle to me, for without that experience, I suspect that I would be using a nasal decongestant to this day at age 75. I assume that when my nose began to become the slightest bit clogged, I unconsciously focused on the time I was being inadvertently suffocated and the congestion and panic just worsened until I had to use artificial means (Dristan) to free my breathing. What a relief that breakthrough was!

I took other such weekend trainings beyond EST, the cumulative effect of which was to help me be more open, non-judgmental and growth-oriented in my life. So, although most of the events overpromised, you could get something from them, and I usually did. (It was at one of these trainings, that I was befriended by a woman who brought me to her house, as a friend I thought, only to realize that it was to make her husband jealous, when he came home a bit after we arrived. Again, teaching me not to be so frigging gullible.)

I remember that during this time we formed a sensitivity training group or T-Group. It consisted of a group of Boston friends, which I started and led, because I was into group dynamics and learning how they worked. This was a disaster as the group consisted of friends, all interested romantically in different parties in the group. Thus, the focus was not on personal growth and learning new things about ourselves, or in revealing our true feelings about things, but on attracting one of the opposite sex.

While it was not a complete catastrophe, it certainly did not achieve its ends, and we soon disbanded. I, as leader, also was not well trained in being able to surface and handle these tensions so they simmered. It also did not help that the sought-after persons were not only already in a relationship, but also seeking a different person in the group, who was not interested in them. Oh well.

The Wandering Months

I finished up my two-year stint with the Ford Foundation and then went to Boston to work a short time with my old boss Charles Brown at the Educational Development Center. Chuck lived with his family, and I lived temporarily with George Fosque in a house in Arlington. I cannot even remember what I worked on for the two months I was there.

It was then that I rented a place on the Somerville/Cambridge line with John Vail and another fellow for $75 a month or $25 each, a ridiculously cheap price. And it wasn't worth it! It was a terrible place, with holes in the wall from a raid by the police of a drug dealer who had lived there prior to us. But we fashioned ourselves as rebellious hippies living hand to mouth and took a kind of distorted pride in living so simply. (I recall one time I awoke to a line of maggots coming toward my bedroll across the floor from the garbage towards some spilled popcorn ... it was that bad.)

I spent my days learning to play tennis and playing chess (world's greatest board game in my opinion) with John, who was suffering from depressive symptoms at the time. The depression drugs were just not as refined as today and had worse side effects. He handled it well though.

The Governor's Justice Commission

After about a year, George, who was in law enforcement as a planner, introduced me to two consultants who needed someone to run an evaluation program in Harrisburg, PA, evaluating innovative law enforcement and corrections projects funded by the Law Enforcement Assistance Administration. In 1973 I packed my bags and took a U-Haul to Harrisburg, PA to start as the Director of the Evaluation Unit of the Governor's Commission on Criminal Justice, which gave about 100 grants a year to criminal justice projects around the state.

I spent two productive years building a well-organized system of evaluation which covered about 100 projects. I hired consultants for each one, designed the studies and reported the conclusions, with a two person staff. It was a fun time where I created an evaluation system which became a model for other states. Quite proud of it. I also learned to play golf, a frustrating game (which I enjoyed, but almost wish I had not started, given the time spent on it subsequently). I threw myself into this work and lived in Hershey Park for a while before taking a beautiful apartment along the Susquehanna River in Harrisburg.

This was a remarkably successful effort, with an excellent small staff, working for E. Drexel Godfrey, a former CIA higher up who had become disillusioned with the CIA's efforts in the late 1960s to involve the CIA in gathering information on domestic protestors against the war ... FBI territory. A fine gentlemanly man.

One summer, in 1974, I was asked to come down to Washington and work full-time as a consultant for the Department of Justice to help other states build similar evaluation systems. While there I had my bike stolen, coming into contact with the justice system in a minor way, and had a conflict with my boss who asked me to hire a secretary, then demanded that I hire a specific one who was not at all as qualified, but who was Black and filled their quota. The Justice Dept. job was for a Republican administration with few Black people, and this was during the time of Watergate. (My first and only brush with being on the other side of racial injustice or working with Republicans.)

I worked as a consultant at Justice for about six months before my contract ended and I left to work at another organization in DC ... an organization called the Advisory Commission on Intergovernmental Relations (ACIR), a sort of think tank. My job at ACIR was again a short-term gig to monitor efforts in criminal justice evaluation across the country and write a report on the results. Traveled some, quite boring. One visit I made was to California and the Pebble Beach Golf Course Complex. Didn't play but picked up some nice bling which was later stolen from my golf bag piece by piece.

The 1976 Bicentennial Voyage

A short digression. In 1976 there were to be celebrations all over the country to commemorate the 200th anniversary of the

The Navigator

The Helmsman

U.S. Revolution. My friend Robert Cunningham had been doing an amazing job of fixing up and fitting out his new Westsail 32 sailboat for the trip and took three of us with him on a sail to Boston from the Chesapeake – Frank Wilson, Jim Sharf and myself. We left the Potomac, went down the Chesapeake and out into the ocean for the three day sail up to the Cape

Other good times on Mistral

Cod Canal on our way to Boston. I served as navigator. We were using an RDF (radio direction finder) and a sextant to navigate, mostly the RDF, for after I put us in the middle of Ohio on one sighting with the sextant my fellow sailors lost a little faith in me or my expertise with the sextant.

The first inkling that this navigator role may not be the best job for me was late one night, when another fellow, Frank Wilson, and I were on duty, just sailing very gently in a very light breeze, heading for a lighthouse which we had spotted on our chart to be our temporary heading, I heard the sound of traffic rushing in the direction of the lighthouse. Puzzled, I went up to the bow and listened closely. Sure enough, it sounded like the flow of fast traffic between us and the lighthouse. But it was four o'clock in the morning, so I knew it couldn't be! Then it hit me. It was waves breaking on the shore not far ahead! I immediately shouted to Frank to go about and head away, which we did, not too far I suspect from grounding Robert's new boat on the Assateague Island shore. What had happened was that the navigator…who shall remain unnamed to protect the guilty, had not anticipated the backward flow of the gulf stream where we were, and we had been making far less distance over ground than we thought. Thus, the lighthouse we were headed for was an entirely different lighthouse, and one mile inland from the shore, than the one we thought we were headed for. Oh well.

A second incident occurred on our return through the Cape Cod Canal in a blinding rainstorm, with thunder and lightning all around. At night. We made it through and laid up in shallow water in the only anchoring place we could find. Unfortunately, it was pretty shallow, and we spent a restless night bumping on the bottom until the tide rose sufficiently to float us completely. The next morning, we all took a swim and grabbed onto the stainless-steel bowsprit forestay and got a terrific electrical shock! Lightning had evidently struck the mast, run down the metal stays and somewhat electrified them. So it goes, we survived.

A tanker on the Inland Waterway (like the one at night in the Delaware Canal)

The third incident worth mentioning was

when, again at night, we were motoring through the narrow Delaware Canal heading back into the upper Chesapeake. I was awakened by my friend Frank, yelling loudly topside. I rushed up and Frank was looking almost straight up, shaking his fist at something dark. I thought he was raging at God, yelling obscenities. I looked up and lo and behold, Frank was having a "discussion" with the captain, 35 feet above us, leaning over the railing of a 140 ft long giant tanker, right beside us, passing slowly. I then realized what Frank was saying … to the effect "I've got the right of way here! I'm a sailing vessel, you $@#% f*&^%#!" or some such nicely worded phrase. Of course, this was not true. We had no rights as a motoring vessel anyway, sailing vessel or not, and the tanker always had the right of way in a narrow channel because of its size and limited maneuverability. We meekly then cut our engine and let the tanker slide past, glad that we had not caused a grounding and a massive oil leak.

We made it back to Annapolis after having a great time in Boston celebrating our nation's birth and surviving our sailing trials. The navigator was fired.

Arthur D. Little, Inc.

I left ACIR after a year or so, when in 1975 I was wooed by the Arthur D. Little Co., the original old-time consulting firm (the story went that the founder was charged—dared really—to make a silk purse out of a sow's ear, and did, starting the company which made its rep handling difficult projects.) I was brought on for my work evaluating other projects with the Justice Department and they thought I would be a rainmaker, bringing in contracts from Justice and other Departments. It was not a good fit, as everyone had to account for every ten-minute segment of their time, allotting it to some project or other. I didn't like this at all, for it was one reason I didn't go to law school.

Fortunately, after about six months with ADL, my friend Frank Wilson, who had worked on the Carter campaign, asked me if I would be interested in working on the Carter Inaugural Committee as a Security Consultant for the three months of the inauguration planning. I readily agreed as did my ADL boss.

The White House Years

The Inauguration

I started with the Inaugural Committee in the fall of 1976 and had some humorous experiences during the short intense (14-hour days) inaugural effort. I remember my first contact with the Committee was being invited by my friend to a Security Committee planning meeting (the first) across town in Southeast DC. I got held up in or misjudged the traffic and was late arriving. When I did, I walked into a room with a long table lined on each side with many older folks, all mostly men (I was 30), maybe 16 or 20 in all. There were several military Generals and Admirals, the Secret Service, the FBI, the DC Police, and other big wigs there to handle different aspects of security for the Carter Inauguration. There was one seat left ... at the head of the table ... clearly for me.

My friend greeted me by saying "Good, now that Mr. Miles is here, we can start. Mr. Miles, what would you like us to do?" I was stunned. I then realized that my friend, Frank Wilson, who had worked on the campaign, had billed me as some expert security consultant from Arthur D. Little who was supposed to lead the group, as the incoming Administration's key security consultant for the Inauguration. My friend only knew that I had worked at the Governor's Justice Commission in Pennsylvania, and subsequently as a consultant for the Justice Department. He had no idea what I did (set up evaluation systems for Law Enforcement grants), but assumed I knew all about SECURITY!

Flabbergasted, but not showing it, I sat down and welcomed

them all here and said something like "I know this is nothing new to you folks and you've all been through this before, know your roles, so my involvement will be limited". I then in turn asked them to introduce themselves and to tell the group the status of their planning for security for the inaugural. After they each went around the table and did this, I thanked them and stated that we were clearly well along with our planning and let's all get back to work. I then ended the meeting.

After giving my friend hell for putting me in that position, I began to plan my role in the inauguration, as a security consultant on loan from Arthur D. Little, who I'm sure saw this as their entry into many projects and grants in the future with the new Administration. This work consisted mainly of planning for Inauguration Day and the six inaugural balls, (the military was constructing the inaugural platform; the Secret Service was handling the security for the inauguration itself; and teams were planning the Carter policy steps in the first 100 days). So, I focused on the attendance and the security for the six inaugural balls.

I organized a ticketing system to determine how to vet and invite the thousands of people to attend the six balls inaugural night, all spread around the city. It consisted of building lists of those whom senior people wanted to invite to the events and allocating them among the balls, sending the invitations, tallying responses, getting people to vouch for them, etc.

I remember the day that the White House staff were to pick up their tickets at a table with me and an assistant finding their names on the list and giving out the tickets. I distinctly remember Jack Watson, a "Georgia boy" then unknown to me but a close friend and aide to Carter, wanting a ticket but not having his name on the list. He was indignant that he be given a ticket, but

I held my ground and asked him to get Hamilton or someone to vouch for him as he was not on the list (evidently Hamilton Jordan had an ongoing conflict with him and left him off his list of senior WH staff on purpose. Speculation here). Needless to say, he ultimately got his tickets. But curiously, I got a bit of respect for standing up to him, though felt embarrassed for not knowing who or how important he was to President Carter.

Another anecdote involved the distribution of the final lists of attendees to each ball the afternoon of the Inauguration. For each attendee we had to match the ticket they brought to their Ball with their name on the master list. Since names were being added up to the last minute, the final lists could not be distributed to the reception table at each ball until late in the day of the Inauguration.

I asked an assistant to arrange a car and driver to take me around to the site of each Ball at different hotels and the Armory. When all was ready, I went out and to my consternation the assistant had gotten a white Cadillac with fender skirts which looked like nothing other than a pimpmobile. Being so late, we took this, and the driver took off with a portable flashing light on the top, tearing through traffic lights and past puzzled traffic cops at very high speed (it was rush hour). I could see the headlines now "CARTER INAGURATION STAFFER RUNS DOWN FOUR PEDESTRIANS IN WHITE PIMPMOBILE ... TWO DIE!".

I finally got him to slow down, obey traffic laws and got the tickets distributed, but I learned the next day, that the police, having tracked the license plate of the pimpmobile to the Carter Inaugural, questioned the assistant. It turns out that the driver was J. Edgar Hoover's former driver, and he was trying to impress me with his driving, thinking that I could get him a job with the new President. Oh well.

It then was the night of the six Inaugural Balls, fancy affairs with tuxes, gowns and jewelry and cleavage galore. We had security managers at each site. I put myself in charge of the Armory, the largest and the rowdiest ball, with all of the Georgia crowd, about 500 to 700 invitees. Things went smoothly at first as the guests poured in, dressed in their finest, and we checked them in quicky. I remember Bert Lance, the new Director of OMB, coming in with an entourage as he was a big deal back in Georgia - head of a bank who had helped Jimmy get elected.

As the crowd danced to the Charlie Daniels Band and waited for Jimmy and Rosalyn to arrive after making their rounds to the swankier hotel balls, two Secret Service agents and I stood at the doors to the ballroom watching and making sure things were in order. Finally, when it was close to time for the President to arrive, the crowd started pressing up to the front of the lobby, which consisted of six glass panels each about three feet wide and seven feet high, holding the crowd back. As crowds often do, they creeped slowly forward from the back, pressuring the folks in front closer together, as they all wanted to see the President arrive.

Finally, it got so cramped that the ones in the front row were literally smashed against the glass, bodies and faces pressed grotesquely against the glass. More ominously, the glass panels started to bulge inward with the weight of the pressed crowd! We had a budding crisis on our hands. I saw more headlines … "DOZENS INJURED IN GLASS-SHATTERING MELEE GREETING CARTER AT ARMORY, AS SECURITY BREAKS DOWN AND ARRIVING CARTER LOOKS ON."

It was at this point that a Secret Service Agent lost it and started screaming from this side of the glass "Get back, get back!!" Now this had no effect at all as he could not be heard through the glass, and it would do no good if he had, because the people in the front rows were so pressed that they could not move anywhere, and the people in back could not hear him. He kept screaming and again I could see the headlines. I could think of nothing to do until I had a thought. I rushed to open one of the central doors and took a bullhorn and yelled, "OK, guys, looks like we'll have to bring the President in the back," whereupon the folks in the back of the crowd eased their pressure and ran to the back, letting the suffocating folks in the front out of their predicament. A close call.

I later learned that two fist fights had broken out on the expansive Armory floor among the crowds from Georgia, which neither I nor the Secret Service knew about. So much for effective security. One thing I did was to wrangle two invitations for my sister and her military husband to attend another swankier party at one of the hotel balls. Thus, it was not an unmitigated disaster after all, and the President was neither assassinated nor embarrassed.

The Executive Office Reorganization

After the Inauguration was complete, I was one of 13 people asked (me by my friend, Frank Wilson, who got me involved in the Inauguration) to work on the reorganization of government starting with the reorganization of the Executive Office of the President (EOP). The EOP consisted of 32 different offices and agencies including the White House staff, the Office of Management and Budget, the Council of Economic Advisers, the Council on Environmental Quality, etc. It was a collection

The White House Years

After a meeting

of agencies designed to carry out the policies of the President. This was to be a six-month project serving as a template for a later reorganization effort of the entire government. I left ADL, never having liked the ethos of billable hours in ten minute increments, and joined the budding EOP Reorganization team led by AD Frazier, a banker from Atlanta who Carter had appointed to handle this job. This group was situated within the Office of Management and Budget (OMB) the budget arm of the government and a part of the Executive Office of the President.

The 13 person staff chosen for this initial reorganization task was a disappointment. Several agencies of government were asked to assign one of their staff members to work on the project full time. And one glance and a week working with them told me that each agency had seemed to send us the weakest person, the most troublesome, or incompetent staff person they could find. I thought about this. It may be because Jimmy Carter had campaigned on the need to reduce the size of government, and of course the agencies did not welcome cuts to their staff. It may also be that he campaigned as an outsider and the agencies wanted to show him that they controlled the staffing assignments, but most probably saw it as a way to temporarily rid themselves of a weak employee.

Thus, the eight folks assigned from the agencies were a poor lot in terms of capabilities, personalities, or both. The remaining five were Frank's friends brought in from the outside, including myself, and we literally saved the project. We each were assigned the most difficult tasks. Rick Heuwinkle was assigned to restructure the administrative staff of the White House, a delicate job, but one with the most lasting effect; Robert Cunningham was asked to come up with a strategy for developing policy within the White House by consulting all parties, more of a policy job. He developed an admirable report, but by the time it was submitted the policy-development habits of the new Administration were already in place and few wanted to give it the attention it deserved; Frank Wilson, who recruited us all was assigned to look at the Department of Agriculture; and I was assigned the most politically sensitive of them all, the Special Trade Representative's Office (STR). The reason for the sensitivity was that this small office was headed by Robert Strauss. Now Strauss was not only the Chair of the Democratic party, but he was also principally responsible for getting Jimmy Carter elected, as co-chair of his campaign and his chief fundraiser. A quite powerful guy from Texas, long-time Democratic Party heavy, and close friend of Jimmy.

The President had made a promise (unwise I thought) to cut the government staff by 30% and he chose to start with the 32 agency Executive Office of the President as an example of what could be done. I think I had been chosen for the Special Trade Office because of the job I had done with the Inauguration as well as because I was considered a Washington insider who might know how to tell Robert Strauss, one of Carter's key people, that he needed to cut his staff; or maybe I was just put forward as a sacrificial lamb.

In any event, I started by studying the STR agency with the staff person assigned to show me the ropes. The agency, which consisted of about 30 people, was one of the smallest EOP agencies. I examined every aspect of their operations. And lo and behold I concluded that there were four positions of the 30 that could be cut. It just so happened that these four positions had not yet been filled, so they were the easiest to cut (my profile in courage!). This of course did not represent a 30% cut, but I figured it was the best that could be done, given who Strauss was.

The day came when I presented my findings in a study paper to Robert Strauss, meeting with him and the staffer who had been working with me. We sat down in his large office ... which was the size of a small stadium with surrounding windows on the top floor of the Commerce building. Robert Strauss sat with us on matching couches in one corner of the room, patiently listening as I walked him through the steps I had taken. After five minutes he stopped me and said "Son," (I was 30, he was 60 or so), "I didn't ask for this job. I didn't want this job. But ya know Jimmy wanted me to do it. So I said OK. Continue, I'm listening". I heard what he was implying, but continued on, describing my work and his agency. After another five minutes, he stopped me and said, "Son, I could call Jimmy and get on the phone about this right now. Just want you to know that." Whereupon I said that I did know that, but that the President had made his commitment to examine every agency within the EOP and I was just doing my job for him. And I plowed on.

At that point I explained that I had concluded that in order to fulfill the President's commitment to reduce agency staff I was recommending that four positions in the STR office not be filled, and that fortunately they are vacant at the moment. At this point Bob Strauss got up and walked over to one of the windows and, looking out, said "Continue, I'm listening", so I started to explain what each position was and why it was able to remain vacant. He then moved to another window way across the office and said "Keep talkin', I'm listening" so I proceeded to tell him what would happen. The report would be sent to the President and the Office of Personnel Management would reduce the STR staff by those four positions. At this point he walked a few more steps to the door, opened it, stepped just outside it. He then leaned back in and said "Continue on, I'm listening" then promptly slammed the door!

At this point both the STR staffer and I burst out laughing, knowing full well that Strauss had the power to negate any cuts in his staff if he wanted. Then I left the office leaving a copy of the report with the staffer for Strauss to read. And to his credit he did not protest the cuts, but accepted them, recognizing that they were less than half of the 30% asked for by Carter, and were empty positions anyway, and perhaps that he knew that the President would expect him to do his part. I just hope that Strauss did not take it out on the staffer. (I thought the idea of cutting the EOP staff by an arbitrary 30% was a bad idea to begin with when it should have been larger if anything, which Reagan promptly took care of when he came in.)

At this time, AD Frazier asked me to become his deputy, formerly being just one of the 13. I again made a dumb decision, this time out of loyalty to my friend Frank Wilson, who had brought me into the inauguration work which led to this work. I suggested Frank for the job and worried about what it would do to our relationship if I were promoted to a spot Frank thought he should have (more of that father-son, "can't be too good or risk losing a friend" dynamic).

I turned the STR report over to the heads of the reorganization, Harrison Wellford and Peter Szanton, and waited for the fallout from Strauss. It didn't come and they were so impressed with the work I did on the most politically risky agency that they put me in charge of organizing a reporting strategy for now reorganizing the full EOP and its agencies. No good deed goes unpunished.

I took to the task well. Planning first a report outline for describing for the President each of the 32 agencies within the EOP; their mission, tasks, structure, personnel, challenges, etc. It resulted in a good report that the President, who remember came from outside Washington and did not know the agencies within the EOP – could use to make decisions about their future, if we ever got the time to meet with him.

Unfortunately for me, a key architect of the report, I would miss the meeting with the President where we presented the report. My girlfriend, Fran, who had been patient with my 14-hour days during the six-month EOP reorganization, and I had planned a vacation but agreed to put it off until the Report was presented to the President. Unfortunately, as each date was set for the meeting with the President, it was delayed and put off to a later date, and thus our vacation was put off three or four times.

Finally, I agreed to go away for two weeks and sure enough the report was presented by some other team members while I was away. Evidently it was a great success as the President was fascinated by the various agencies under his direct control in the EOP and wanted to know all the details about each agency in the report. (This attention to detail was a fault of this President as he was distracted from other larger policy issues which he needed to focus on, rather than details that could be delegated. But I digress.) Anyway, I was congratulated for developing the report.

Wing And Feather

Just prior to my time in the Executive Office, I bought a sailboat, my Tartan 27 "Wing", in 1976 in Charleston after a month-long search along the southeastern coast from the Chesapeake to Key West looking at dozens of boats. I sailed

My Tartan 27 Wing

it up from Charleston and it proved to be the perfect boat to single hand, as it was small and manageable. However, it had no roller furling genoa, meaning I had to put up and take down the large foresail by hand.

I subsequently sailed it in weekend races with a group of identical Tartan 27s on the Chesapeake for four years, giving me a release from the pressures of White House work on the weekends. Some great times were had on that boat, as I usually took a girlfriend and another couple. I never once thought about work on those short trips. I rarely if ever won any races as I did not have a spinnaker and without one, I had little chance. But with an inexperienced crew, I could not have flown a spinnaker anyway. And frankly I was racing for the fun of it, not to win. (And to my discredit, I took some delight when, on the downwind leg of a race, running wing and wing, I would get behind a boat that had just passed me with spinnaker flying, and, stealing her wind, watch as the sail collapsed or corkscrewed, causing all sorts of problems … hey, all's fair in love and sailing!) We would sail over to Oxford or St. Michaels on the Maryland shore and go ashore for some carousing and a fine seafood meal. Then wander back to the anchored boat to watch the stars before hitting the rack.

I sold half of the boat to Frank Wilson, and we sailed the boat regularly for about five years. Dad built a small skiff of perfect dimensions which I named "Feather" and trailed behind. Every spring I would have a "fitting out" party to get the boat ready for the summer. We had some great times on the boat, with many friends enjoying the weekends.

On one of these weekend trips, we were blindsided by a fierce storm which tore across the Chesapeake just as we were leaving Eastern Bay on the eastern side when it hit. There was no mention in the forecast of this storm. I tried to tack out of the Bay to make it across the Chesapeake when, on one tack, I heard a "CRACK". The tiller, one of the few weak points on the boat, had cracked but not given away. I managed to jibe the boat around one more time but knew that we could not make it home that afternoon in this storm with a cracked tiller as the winds were gusting up to 40-50 knots. I checked the chart and headed for the only semi-shelter there was … a small indentation in the shore on the lee side of the mouth of Eastern Bay. I committed to set the anchor and wait out the storm overnight. I had no idea whether the holding ground was good where we anchored.

Unfortunately, the wind was howling, and the anchorage was not that sheltered, so there was a real danger of our being set against the shore if the anchor did not hold. Moreover, one of the ladies aboard had had a traumatic experience in the water as a child and was slowly going into shock, very afraid for her life. I tried to calm her down, explaining that the worst thing that could happen was the anchor let loose and we would be swept onto a beach whereupon we would just step out and walk to a nearby house. But to no avail, as she started to shiver violently and showed signs of hypothermia. I knew a little about both shock and hypothermia, so we got her wrapped up heavily in blankets and

The Spring Boat Outfitting Parties

The crew after the storm

fed her some very warm hot chocolate. Soon she came around and calmed down but remained quiet and vigilant all night.

However, the night passed slowly, and the wind continued to howl. The boat swung almost 160 degrees on anchor, and we had to keep someone on watch all night to make sure we were not dragging the anchor and getting nearer the shore. We prepared meticulously for what each would do if we started to drag anchor at night. We made it through the night, but the next day, the wind was even worse, and the radio forecast gave no hint that it would let up. So, we were marooned for another day and largely sleepless night. We had plenty to eat but knew that our friends would be worried sick about us as we could not communicate with anyone. No cell phones in those days and I did not have the money to put a radio system on the boat. However, we could hear the broadcasts on our portable radio and learned that there were over a hundred boats stranded around the Chesapeake, waiting for the unexpected storm to pass.

And pass it did the following, third, day. We limped back across the Bay and up the Severn to my home, nursing the slightly reinforced tiller and hoping that it would not crack under the strain. We made it back around one p.m., called our friends and reassured them of our safety.

Another sailing adventure, or something to be better termed a crazy feat, was my attempt around 1975 to sail my small Sunfish-type Laser sailboat across the Chesapeake from Fran's house, not far from Leonardtown up the Potomac River to my home outside of Onancock in one day ... a trip of about 40 miles. I prepared for it with water, sandwiches, life jacket, a make-shift harness to keep me on the boat, and sunscreen. I took off one Saturday morning at six a.m. I got out into the Chesapeake and the wind died, leaving me stranded. Fortunately, Dad came to meet me in his 37 ft Cormorant, as he knew how foolhardy it was to do this. He and Mom had set out to meet me, sailing across the Chesapeake to sail behind me about a mile or so.

We turned back when the wind refused to blow, and I decided to try the next day, a Sunday, and again Mom and Dad insisted on following me for safety. The wind was better on this day, and I made the trip in 15 hours, sailing into our creek and up to the dock at nine p.m. after leaving at six a.m. A true feat, very stupid and risky, but I wanted to do it.

Other than sailing, I hung around with a fine group of friends in Washington, Frank Wilson, Pat and Betz Saccomondi, Rick and Judy Heuwinkle, Robert and Rigney Cunningham, Leo Surla, Peggy Rainwater, and several others. We would arrange parties, the most important of which was the Thanksgiving get-together at a national park house in Harpers' Ferry. One of us, usually Frank, would have to get up at 4:00 in the morning to reserve it for the weekend, when we played touch football, went on hikes, and had fabulous meals. It was a good group of well-loved friends.

The Reorganization of the Government

The reports I did for the Special Trade Representative and the EOP became the template for the much larger effort subsequently planned to examine and explain the plethora of agencies that we were to study over the next four years. Each of the 300 reorganization staff members ultimately hired for this larger effort would use this template to essentially reorganize the government efficiently and structurally … an enormously challenging job, politically and managerially.

The D.C. Group

My role was assigned as the deputy to Peter Szanton, a RAND corporation thinker who was an expert in defense systems and reported to Harrison Wellford the head of the reorganization. Our job was to corral the senior folks brought in by Harrison to run the various staffs responsible for the overall government reorganization. And though we tried, I must say that this effort was largely unsuccessful.

Peter Szanton was a strong policy thinker, but was not a manager, coming from RAND as a strategic thinker about nuclear war, which perhaps is why I was assigned to him, to help him manage. And for a while we tried to get a handle on the numerous heavyweights who ostensibly reported to Peter. But Harrison, as Peter's boss, did not direct people to go to Peter, but allowed them to come directly to him with choices, decisions, and strategies, circumventing Peter. Not the best management style.

There was also a senior OMB person, who was Harrison's equivalent, handling the management side of OMB. He curried favor with Harrison's staff and in my opinion undercut Harrison when they differed on policy. For example, I was asked to weigh in on an issue which unbeknownst to me was in dispute between Harrison and this senior person. It was to be resolved by me studying the issue and giving my recommendation at a meeting with the head of OMB (where the reorganization was based) and all senior staff. I was told by the senior person to be sure my recommendation included a certain phrase, which I thought had been agreed upon by Harrison to feed to the OMB Director. I did this at this large meeting, and only later learned that I had with this phrase undercut Harrison's position, by seeming to side with the other person. (I actually thought the senior person was correct in this case so his direction was not needed, but I would have alerted Harrison beforehand had I known of their conflict.)

This was just one minor issue in, from my perspective, a somewhat failed experience. Peter was sidetracked and largely ignored, and Harrison and Peter were both thwarted by the senior official who had assumed some power in the project and had courted Harrison's senior staff while also undermining Harrison from inside (my judgement, admittedly possibly wrong).

Early on I made one of several decisions in my career that would turn out to be wrong, or that appeared wrong in retrospect. (I don't know why I seem to focus on some of the bad decisions and failures here, since there were a number of successes and triumphs. Perhaps because they gall me and stick with me so much.) I was asked by Harrison Wellford what I wanted to work on from among the many projects of this larger effort, perhaps because of my work on the initial Executive

Office Reorganization I was considered valuable and successful.

Harrison asked me if I wanted to lead the effort to create the new Cabinet-level Education Department, a totally new agency which had been discussed for years, but which no one had dared to bring into existence due to various political toes being crushed. Carter had declared during his candidacy that he would create the new department. I knew that this would involve a ton of political maneuvering with Congress to achieve the consensus needed to pass, working with lobbyists, interest groups, Congressional leaders. It was a real step up, and a plum assignment. But by this time, I was totally turned off by politics and quickly told Harrison to find someone else. A bit taken aback by my refusal, he asked what else I would like to do. I told him (and this was the biggest mistake of my career) that I had always wanted to work on the management side of OMB. Thus, he asked Howard Messner on the management side to take me on.

I started with Howard, who was a seasoned bureaucrat leading a team of analysts to operate within the management side of OMB. But Howard didn't know me from beans, and had nothing to do with the prior reorganization, with which he had felt competitive. Thus, I was a persona non grata. He stuck me in a back room with nothing to do. And for three months I did exactly that, nothing. Until another fellow who was also assigned to the sticks by Howard, and who sat by me in the back room for those three months told Howard that I was about to leave and was being wasted back there. Howard then gave me an office and a few minor tasks, one of which was to go present OMB's and the President's position on things to a town hall in NY where a fellow named Charles Schumer was running for his first year in Congress.

At one point I became a little frustrated that President Carter was not increasing his polling lead over this actor guy, Ronald Reagan, who I felt knew little about government and was not qualified to be the President. I still think that is true, but the Republicans put in a great staff for him. I wrote a "political" memo to Howard, outlining what I thought Carter should do. I can't remember exactly what the memo said and have no copy, but I do remember that it did not go anywhere. For this meddling in politics for one candidate was just not done at the Office of Management and Budget (OMB). It was supposed to be above the political fray, much like the General Accounting Office. Staff and officials were not to take political positions for or against one candidate or another.

At that point, Howard Messner assigned me back over to the Old Executive Office Building, next to the White House (now called the Eisenhower Building I think), where the more political staff of the White House had their offices. I had been there before when working on the reorganization, but this time I was assigned to a surprisingly large office nearer the White House itself. I think Howard wanted to shield himself from criticism in case I got in trouble for expressing political thoughts from within OMB.

At that time, I was told that I reported to Hugh Carter, the President's cousin. I was given the sensitive task of determining the source of suspected security breeches within the White House itself, as senior staff had asked Hugh to find out. Evidently some non-authorized personnel had been seen in the White House and folks wanted to know who was letting them in. Now security at that time was lax, as the attempt on Reagan's life had not taken place yet, no one had jumped the wall around the White House grounds and things were just much more informal than when Reagan took over and turned it into a formal place.

The thing was that some people pretty much knew who was responsible for the lax security, as it was the President's second cousin himself, Hugh Carter, who had a job at the White House in charge of White House administrative matters. In this job he had earned the enmity of several high-level staff for cutting the perks to the bone. He was known as Cousin Cheap - no more limousines, no more fancy lunches, no multiple TVs, etc. Now Jimmy Carter ran a pretty tight ship anyway, particularly compared to Reagan's, or god-help-us, Trump's palatial White House. But the few new perks that folks had were important to them, so I think I was brought in as the sacrificial lamb to investigate and show that Hugh was the source of the security breaches. Payback for them against Hugh.

I did my due diligence duty and checked the entries into the White House and indeed, Hugh had let in several of his friends not authorized to be there and let them roam around. I also found that security at the entry of the EOB was lax, as several times I just flashed my driver's license instead of my security pass (they looked similar) and was waved through. In due time, I wrote my report, a two-page affair, recommending that entry security be tightened and that all White House staff use recommended protocols when having visitors brought into the complex. I mentioned that some staff were lax in following appropriate guidelines but mentioned no specific names. Hugh was aware of the rumors that the lax staffer was him, so I suspect he did not like the report. In any event Hugh's only response to the report was that it should have been only one page long instead of two, as his time was valuable. What a joke.

The Camp David Run

Around this time, President Carter hosted a White House staff 6k run one Saturday at Camp David in which one of my roommates, Sharon Metcalf, and I participated. We all started off in staggered groups with Carter starting in the first group. Sharon and I started a few minutes later as we were in no way competitive runners. I paced myself easily but after about a mile, I saw a group of runners bunched ahead of me, running slower. It turns out it was President Carter and his Secret Service guards.

As I came up to them and passed, I saw the President staggering, partially held up by his White House doctor. Evidently, starting with the first group, Carter had run much faster than he should, or had ever before. Since he was running with the very fast runners put in the first group, he must have thought it would look bad if he fell behind. He had become drastically fatigued and was about to collapse. At that time, I was running with my friend Susan Zirinsky, who was working as a CBS News producer. She had a video tape taken by the pool reporters of Carter in distress. She handed it to me and asked me to take it to the finish and give it to her crew, which I did, since she wanted to stay around to report on Carter. After the race I was interviewed by her about what I saw, the interview ending up on the front page of the *Herald Tribune*, the international paper in Europe, along with the struggling Carter's picture. Not much of a claim to fame, but interesting.

I felt I was very unimpressive working for Howard, and with Hugh Carter, with little real work, and certainly not drawing on my skills. It was a laid-back White House. With my pass I could roam around at will and it was heady, going to watch the

President take off and arrive in his helicopter, Marine One, but I was certainly underutilized. Howard did get me into the civil service (having been a consultant up to that point, whereupon I concluded that I was wasting my time and decided in 1980 to quit the government and go sailing. I felt sorry and guilty for Sydney Greenspan, Howard's sidekick, who had worked hard to get me the GS 15 government position in civil service, not an easy thing to do.

The Camp David Run: Sharon Metcalf and me at the start, being eyed by the No. 1 ranked runner (Alas, he had little to fear from us.)

It was then, and only through this at times psychologically agonizing process, that I had to think about "what I wanted", what were my expectations for myself. And I began to realize that, perhaps because of my laid-back rural childhood, and having had so much success already in early life by conventional standards, some of which proved hollow, that I did not care much for a high-powered life of achieving monetary gain or professional fame just because it was expected of me. (There was also a smidgeon of worry that I did not want to get caught up in something that would take an intense 14 hours a day for an awfully long period of time. A bit of laziness I suspect.)

This came to a head when I decided to leave my work on the reorganization effort at the White House in the summer of

1980. People thought I was crazy. My bosses were afraid that I was leaving in a huff and sought to make sure that I received certificates of appreciation, photos, etc., as going away gifts, much as they had done when Jim Fallows had left earlier. But I was not leaving with bad feelings. When I left in Sept of 1980, Carter was ahead in the polls and looked to be headed for reelection and I held nothing but admiration for his intentions (although, like too many others, I questioned some of his actions and appropriateness as President). I just knew that politics was not for me, and to stay would just be following other's expectations for me once again.

So, I went sailing.

The Voyage

In 1980, about three months before the election, I ended my government tenure. I had decided to take my Tartan 27 sailboat down the Intracoastal Waterway to the Bahamas on an eight-month, single-handed trip (with a month break back in Virginia for Christmas).

I began planning in great detail for the trip south and started in mid-October in 1980. I left my job when Carter had a fairly good lead over Ronald Reagan, the actor, who most thought had no business running for President. I had an aborted start of the trip in very heavy winds when I found that I had poorly tied both genoa leads. My best friend Jack Phillips started with me in October 1980. Jack spent the first few days with me crossing the Chesapeake and getting the radio antenna installed in the mast in Ruark's boat yard in Deltaville, VA.

Jack then left and I was on my own, planning each day's journey meticulously, stocking with ice and food as needed. Going through Norfolk and entering the waterway and then crossing Pamlico Sound in NC, I quickly developed a routine of planning the day out and making sure everything I

On the Inland Waterway

needed was topside. Being alone you could not very well leave the helm to go below to get something in a 40-50 yard wide waterway, with huge barges and tankers, about one every hour or two, bearing down on you while trying to stay in water of sufficient depth near the center.

Nights were spent at anchorages marked on the charts along the waterway, or every four days or so at a marina to get a shower and supplies. It was a wonderful trip, listening to opera or folk songs, and reading books at night at anchor, and sailing during the day, cooking on a propane stove, and storing fresh veggies and meats in an ice locker.

When I put in at a marina on election night in Charleston in early November, I was shocked to learn from a bar TV that Reagan had beaten Carter in a landslide and would take over the Presidency. The hostage situation and a high interest rate economy had doomed a fine person, though a little ill-suited to the Presidency, for he was ahead of his time on many things.

I continued on my journey, too fast, as it was November and getting cold and I wanted to get to warmer climes as soon as possible. In retrospect I would have started earlier and taken my time traveling, as the beauty of the trip was worth relishing. To have spent more time in each port and at anchorages would have been very welcome.

But I proceeded south, through South Carolina, Georgia, and Florida, crossing Florida mid-state through the Lucie Canal and across Lake Okeechobee to get over to the west coast. I spent my time in the waterway looking for alligators from Georgia south through Florida with no luck. Then as I was leaving Lake Okeechobee, I saw a large log on my right on a small beach. I wouldn't have thought anything about it, but it had a funny bulge in the middle. So, I turned the boat around and sure enough, it was now in the water swimming toward me ... an alligator. It was large, at least 13-15 feet long with a head about three feet at least. I stopped the boat and let it come toward me as I went up on the bow to get a better look. It came right below me, and I stared and took a few pictures, all poor as it turned out. Then I realized that if he went under the boat and came up under me, he could rock the boat a little, perhaps enough to pitch me into the water and I would be dinner. So, I backed off and let him return to basking on the beach.

I continued sailing down the Gulf, past St. Pete, and ritzy Naples (where I was stopped by the police walking into town to get supplies, because I looked like an outsider in my cutoffs and tee shirt. They said they stopped all persons who did not look like they were residents ... clearly a "gated" city). Met a lady jewelry store owner there who took me to dinner and a nice evening, before retiring to the boat.

I journeyed down to the Keys along Florida's western shore in the Gulf, slowly making my way to Key West, and staying a few days there. I then sailed back to Marathon, FL in the Keys and left my boat there, at a resident's house on one of the canals, for about three or four weeks while I flew back home to Virginia for Christmas.

Returning in mid-January I carefully planned my jump off to the Bahamas, leaving from Dinner Key just south of Miami one late night (to arrive in daylight the next day - a 16-hour crossing). I was joined by Frank Wilson and his girlfriend, to help me cross, arriving in West End, Grand Bahama, at three p.m. the following day, exhausted. Thus started my two month long stay in the Bahamas.

The next day we took off across the flats of the northern Bahamas (about six-eight feet deep), enjoying the crystal water and warm breezes, to Walker Cay, the northernmost cay in the Bahamas. We almost missed it, as I had not counted on the strong current sweeping me northward. Had I missed it we would have been out in the Atlantic again, heading for South Carolina. Navigation was rather primitive back then, using RDF and charts and compass.

Frank and girlfriend left me in Green Turtle Cay after a struggle down the eastern coast of Grand Bahama in a gale. I stayed there a few days and sailed alone again, for Marsh Harbor. I hit a rainstorm which had me maneuvering between a small cay and a large set of boulders, with me blinded by the storm and my dingy "Feather" filling with water, in danger of sinking. I made it and reprovisioned in Marsh Harbor.

From there it was all fine, as I visited the ports in the Bahamas – Hopetown, Man O War Cay, etc. In the latter I woke up one morning and getting out of the quarter berth, my hand brushed against the obviously corroded water intake pipe, knocking it off. The intake pipe had broken off from electrolysis. Capping it with a shaped cork, I thought I was doomed. How would I find one in the Bahamas? But luckily, it happened in the best marine repair island in the Bahamas, and they fixed me up very quickly. Luck seemed to follow me on this trip.

My old roommate John Vail then flew into Marsh Harbor and joined me at this point, and we sailed for about two or three weeks before he had to go back. We sailed to a beautiful harbor, Little Harbor, in a race of about 25 boats from Marsh Harbor. The race, which had no rules (as some sailboats used their motors) was loads of fun. We skirted across a riskily shallow one mile flat (we had shallower draft) and finished third overall among much bigger boats.

The one resident on the island, a sculptor of some renown, Randolph Johnston, had brought his wife and son down to Little Harbor in the '50s. He had stayed and achieved international renown as a master of the lost wax bronze casting process, building a studio and home. His son hosted a cocktail hour for all the sailors in the harbor, calling us in around six p.m. every night from our anchorage by the blowing of a conch shell. He hosted us in an 8' by 12' pub shack on the beach, serving smoked octopus (the best!) and beer in a rowdy rustic setting as the sun set.

It was an idyllic time in the Bahamas, John and I getting tomato sandwiches in Hopetown, snorkeling, exploring the cays, reading many books. I enjoyed my time. George Fosque, Tom Nary and lady friends joined us for a while also, renting a cabin on Man O War Cay. In March it was time to return home.

I met a young lady sailing with her parents in the islands who agreed to sail back with me for a good bit of the 35-day trip back home in April/May. She was a big help. On the way back we took our time, enjoying the ports and the beauty of the marsh, playing Pavarotti's Nessun Dorma at high volume at isolated anchorages. It was a wonderful trip not to be repeated by me. However, Dad and Mom in their 37" Irwin sailboat "Cormorant" took three subsequent trips down for the winters, once going over to the Bahamas. Mom said it was the happiest they had ever been in their lives.

When I returned to Washington DC, the world had changed, politically at least. I contacted my friends, some of whom had remained with the new Reagan Administration, and I heard horror stories of meetings where racist jokes would be related, and very conservative policies were being proposed and implemented. It was a good thing that I left the government.

Drifting

I floundered around Washington for a while, and started a small consulting group with two friends, called PMG, the Performance Management Group. I bought one of the first PCs with another friend, Pat Saccomondi, one of the PMG group. It was an IBM with 64 k memory (k not MB or GB!) and a 10 MB hard disk for storage, for $10,000! We also bought a primitive database management program called Condor which we thought was magical. You could fit it all on your wrist today with much more power with $9,700 left over.

After several small consulting projects, my friends gradually dropped out of consulting, and I continued on my own. It was around this time 1983-84 that I was asked to do a job helping a small town prepare for the computer age by doing a needs assessment of their police department. This started me on a small career of working with about 45 different cities and towns, bidding on similar projects with police and fire departments. Many were funded competitively through a Connecticut State agency, similar to the Pennsylvania Governor's Justice Commission.

A little later I met Sandy Starr through Robert and Rigney Cunningham. She lived in West Newton outside of Cambridge. I packed up my things and in 1986 drove a U-Haul truck to Massachusetts to live with her for a short time. During this time, we bought an 18 acre property and house together in 1986 in Deering, NH, formerly owned by the famous photographer, Lotte Jacobi. After a year and a half, this relationship did not

The Deering View

The Deering House

prove to be made in heaven. Although we had some good times together (I remember a memorable trip to Canada from Boston), we split up and after a difficult split, I bought her half of the house in Deering, moved up to Deering in 1987 and ran my small consulting business from there.

The PMG business was easy, I would bid on small projects against two or three other large firms. Since I had little overhead and worked very inexpensively on site (cheap motels, and meals), I was able to win every bid as the larger firms always wanted more money than I did. But the main reason that I could do these jobs was that the police and fire departments were remarkably similar. I would accumulate all the forms that could be computerized and show them that by buying a small computer and using database software they could quickly become more efficient. Since most departments were similar, I could just use their forms (also very similar) and write a report by cutting and pasting from one report to another and changing the names of the towns (once I left a reference to another town in one report and was embarrassed when it was reported to me by a police chief).

Most of my projects could be done for between $6,000 and $10,000 where the large company competitors would bid $30,000 or $50,000. My clients were overjoyed and very impressed by the report I gave them for that much money. Much of my work was in Connecticut, but I did jobs in Tennessee, NYC, Massachusetts, Pennsylvania, and Virginia. I clearly should have charged more. I also did organizational studies, and other studies as the towns needed them, branching out a little from police and fire to other departments.

I once did an organizational study for a troubled police

department in Tennessee. The Chief was in competition with one of his officers who was backed by a strong local evangelical church. One incident exemplified the strife. The officer had found in a squad car he was about to take out on a shift that someone had left a loaded gun in the rear seat/compartment of the car, where arrestees were put for the ride to the station. A loaded gun would NOT have been helpful in that situation. Also, the police were reportedly involved in drug dealing which was prevalent in the rural city.

As I left the city to return to New Hampshire after completing my on-site work, the chief solemnly gave me a warning … "Son, be careful crossing those mountains east of town, bad things can happen there to strangers …." I took it as a clear threat. As it turned out my report was critical of both parties and the Chief left his position soon after. The other officer was not promoted to Chief either.

I continued with about 40 or 50 of these small consulting jobs from '85 to '92 and realize now that these were my prime high production years, from age 39 to 46, which I had largely wasted, making a pittance, saving what I could. Had I taken a high pressure job in finance on Wall Street for just a few years, I could have enjoyed a richer lifestyle and set myself up for the future much better. And with my resume I could have, but chose to make a much lower key life, living in bucolic Deering. The choices one makes! However, no real regrets here.

The Deering Experience

Living in Deering was about nature. I loved the area in the hills of Deering between the city of Concord and the town of Peterborough. I gardened (you can't take the father out of the son) and in Deering I had a large one, filling two freezers each year.

The house was old and funky and full of character. It had about ten rooms, but living alone, I used only three. I had a good wood stove and heated the three rooms with about four or five cords of wood each winter, though the house had a full heating system. Cutting, hauling, and splitting the wood was an experience to say the least. It would involve finding a stand of trees on the 18 acres that was near enough to the road to allow easy transport, hopefully downhill, and contained mostly small

Part of a winter's wood

trees that did not have to be split. I would cut the trees into 12 to 20 foot sections, pitchpole them down the hill to the road and over the rock wall (which enclosed all the land). Then load the trees onto the pickup, drive to the shed, and unload into large piles. After 8-10 pickup loads, I would then chainsaw the logs into 15-18 inch lengths, splitting those too thick, and stack into rows. Then, as needed, I would take about 15 wheelbarrows of the logs at a time into the house, about 50 yards away, and stack them in a vacant front room. Then I would, again as needed, use them in the stove. This would continue throughout the Fall and Winter, an elaborate process which kept me in shape, but always carried the threat of cutting an appendage off with the chainsaw. Very proud when completed.

I joined several Boards as a volunteer. On one, The Children's Alliance, I composed a Bill of Rights for Children which we used to promote the organization. I was proud of that.

The Children's Bill of Rights

"We hold these truths to be self-evident, that all children are created equal, and that they are endowed with certain inalienable rights, among these ...

1. *The right to enter the world loved, nurtured, and in good health ...*
2. *The right to be well-nourished and sheltered from harm ...*
3. *The right to live free of exploitation, abuse, and neglect ...*
4. *The right to grow and flourish in a safe place, among those who care ...*
5. *The right to cures for their ills, and comfort for their hurts ...*

6. The right to educate the mind, develop the body, and nourish the spirit ...
7. The right to be prepared to assume a productive role in society ...
8. The right to assume the responsibilities and just consequences of their actions ...
9. The right to participate in determining their own destiny ...
10. The right to the liberty, justice, and dignity accorded all.

And that whenever these rights are abridged or denied, it is the duty of a just people to protest ... in the name of the children."

Developed for the Children's Alliance of New Hampshire – June, 1990 by Keith M. Miles, Member, Board of Directors, (apologies to James Madison)

Wendy and I would take long walks during the summers and spend bright brisk days snowshoeing in the winters, through beautiful woods and around two ponds on the property, (which I expanded by buying 50 adjacent acres around the year 2000, more on that later). I dabbled in local town affairs, and wrote occasionally, mostly essays and whatever I had on my mind.

I composed a piece which better than anything captures how I felt about my life on the Deering property. Every word is true as it related to an aspect of the Deering experience and land. It was written when I thought I would have to sell the property in 1987, because Sandy, my previous partner, initially did not want to sell me her half of the property, finally relenting. Here it is.

The Worth of a Homeplace

(Spoken by an old codger with a Yankee accent, upon having to sell his farm)

"What's it worth?" they asked, walking up the lane past the sign.

"Well, now", I said, "that's a hard question, one I've been asking for about forty years. But it's a fair one, and I'll take a crack at answering it. Meantime, why don't you just sit down out here on the porch, and I'll pour us a cup a coffee. You got some time don't you, cause it'll take a bit of time to 'preciate the worth of this place.

There, that's better. Now, where to start. Well, this porch is as good a place as any I guess, sitting out here on a morning with a cup of hot coffee, watching the sun glisten on the dew over the meadow as it moves the shadows down those far trees ... now I suspect that's worth about five dollars every time I do it. Don't know for sure, of course, but that's a guess.

And if you look close you can see the path through the meadow where it enters the woods over a bit. That path winds around the east woods, filled with tall pines with clear ground below, so the sun's rays slant through real nice. That's worth a morning walk, and a little exercise for stiff legs, or about ten dollars if you need a figure.

And then that'll bring you to the treehouse I built with a special young friend. Didn't cost much, of course, just wood, nails and sweat, but since you want to know what the place is worth, I guess that treehouse is worth a good half-day's work and a bushel of faith.

And that brings you back out to the meadow. Now this

meadow has a lot of features, even though I cuss it a might every time I have to cut it. You can see it's on the south side of the house, which gives us a lot of light, of course. But it's also just the right size for breathing room, always giving you something to look at, and just big enough so the deer feel safe to play at the far edge. The nightly fifteen-minute walk around it to "check the property" is alone worth about a hun'erd dollars I'd say, just for the feeling of wellbeing that's hard to get anywhere else.

That peak? Ah, you noticed. Well, if you cross the road there, walk uphill for ten minutes, then turn right along the ridge for five-minutes, you'll come out on top of that little peak with a view for thirty miles in any direction. A short sit up there on a Sunday morning is worth a month of sermons, I'd say.

And on top of that peak you'll find a plaque set in the rock, dedicated to a young chaplain (used to be a neighbor of the former owner) ... one of four on a torpedoed ship in WW II who gave their lives so others could survive in the remaining lifeboats. That's worth a kick in the pants when you're feeling a mite sorry for yourself.

And if you look off to your right you'll see a path that winds through the tall pines down to the pond. That path has a bit of mystery about it, for it's always covered with an evergreen canopy, layered with pine needles and makes you feel like you're in another secret world. A walk down that path at dusk is worth at least one fantasy, maybe two.

And the pond at the end of the path. Heck, it's not much of a pond, not much bigger'n a wading pool. But it runs clear, and it's small enough for the kids to stretch a rope across high up in the trees to swing off'en. As for the worth of that you'll have to get them to put a price on it.

If you turn left at the pond, it'll take you down through an ancient gorge, cut out of the rock high up on either side by a million spring runoffs. Nobody goes there but the deer and me. It's a place for losing time, listening close, and putting things in perspective. Worth a lot when you're bothered by something petty.

And then there're the blueberry bushes by the pond. Well, truth be known, those bushes are just like that garden out front there on the edge of the meadow. Seems the birds and other critters get more blueberries and vegetables than we do out of them. But there's something about the ritual of checking the growth each day, watching life start up each year, and cycle through. Well, it's best we not try to put a value on that. Anyway, that comes free with the farm, courtesy of the real owner.

Of course, since we're talking worth, there's always the walk back up the path on an evening, with the soft light from the kitchen melding with the smoke from the chimney to make the world seem OK and home seem safe. That's worth about a gallon of peace of mind ... harder and harder to come by these days.

What's that you say? Gets cold up here? You betcha. Now you talk about worth ... just turn around and take a look at that old wood stove in the kitchen. Ain't much of greater worth on a cold afternoon when the first winter Northers are blowing in from Canada, and the wind's spitting sleet, than sitting in front of that stove, sipping some hot apple cider, listening to a cherry log simmer. Yeah, I guess those days are worth about two hundred apiece, three hundred when we have chicken and dumplings for dinner.

And speaking of those cold days, just being able to watch the snow slowly cover the full woodshed from inside this warm house is a feeling that's worth a good bit of peace of mind, maybe a thousand dollars worth if you need a price on it.

Now there's also the tall pines on the North, which anyone can tell you are worth a lot in breaking the cold northern winter wind. But the way they're situated, they cradle the house just about perfect I'd say, like they're standing guard. Worth a good bit to me anyway.

And there's the little things, of course. Like the deer's antler we found last spring over there in the south woods. I'd say that was worth about a dozen stories at least. And the beavers that take up in the pond for a week every spring, only to leave for bigger digs. That's worth a wish or maybe a sigh or two. And the clearing over on the west side of the meadow that it took all one summer to complete. Just looking at it makes my back sore, but it makes my pride soar too.

And the afternoons around this place ... watching the shadows lengthen over the meadow and creep up the birches on the far side, as the sun waves its goodbye. That's worth a dream.

But I must be boring you, for you want to know what it's REALLY worth, don'cha. Well, I wouldn't really know, I guess . The developers say the eighteen acres would make five or six nice lots. I don't see them that way when I walk along the rock walls of the boundary. For me they're a place to get away... to pretend that much of what happens each day in the world doesn't... a place to take a walk, to feel essential, and at peace.

Take that bedroom out back, with all those windows showing nothing but woods surrounding the room, with the morning light streaming through the trees. It's hard to get up in a bad mood with that kind of greeting. But then you can't put a price on that, I guess.

Just think about a thing like a tin roof... not much to think about, really, until it rains, and then a whole new world of sound opens up here in this old house. Sometimes the rains come so hard it sounds as if they'll beat the roof in. Other times a soft gentle rain can go on steady for a whole night, not varying in tempo or rhythm. That's worth a memory, or at least a perfect sleep.

I'll tell you something that's worth the price of a movie. You see that tall pine tree on the far side of the meadow. Well, once or twice a year the full moon will rise right over that thing and move by it with a grace and awesomeness that takes the breath away. Can watch it from right here on this porch. Good value all right.

But what this place really gives, that for the life of me I can't put a price on, is a home for your soul. It seems to make life whole, not just by the demands it makes of you, but by the wonders it offers to your spirit in return.

Gotta go? Too bad. There's a few more features that I probably could mention if I put my mind to it. Sorry I couldn't give you a better idea of what the place was worth. It sorta grows on ya over the years. Of course, it's just an old run down place really. Probably not worth much to most people. As I said, it takes time to appreciate it. You take care now."

So that's how I felt about the Deering place ... a very special place to me. All the things mentioned in the piece were true and reflected my experiences there.

I particularly enjoyed watching the bears. They would come around trying all sorts of tricks to get at my bird feeder, particularly in the spring when they came out of hibernation. You were supposed to take the feeders down when the bears were out, but I enjoyed the birds so much that I couldn't. (I've

On the deck checking us out

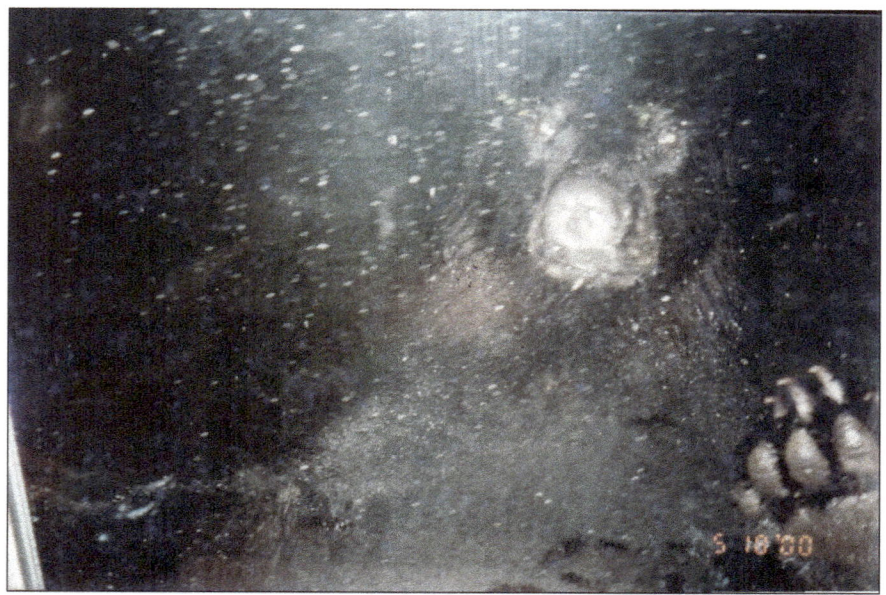

At Chess - look closely for the face and paw

always said that if there's a heaven, my treatment of my birds would get me in. Always had three of four feeders filled.)

One night when Robert Cunningham and I were playing chess at the table (we played 200 or so games over the years and were so even that after that stretch one of us was only one game ahead of the other…chess, world's best table game). Robert looked up to see a bear's face staring at him right at the window, three feet away. I pretended it was nothing and "Smokey" came around all the time. Both of us were a little shaken though as one paw through the glass would have been trouble. Almost always, they were very frightened of humans, and any sound or sight would send them scampering. When they had cubs, however, I was always careful not to go out.

Along about 1989, I decided that I did not want to continue doing needs assessments or organizational studies for small towns. But what to do? I had renovated a large portion of my house at that point, and funds were short, so I began looking around for things to do in New Hampshire. Slim pickings. I did a few small consulting jobs in New Hampshire, while sending out resumes to the few companies and organizations looking for help. Almost all came back saying "You're overqualified for this job", and I suspected, thinking to themselves "What is this guy thinking, with a background at the Ford Foundation, the Justice Department, the White House … what is he doing looking for a job in small town New Hampshire. He won't stay with us for more than six months." This was a dispiriting time but an intensely introspective time as I took stock of my life to date (I was 44 or so). I also felt for the first time what it must be like for others who are unemployed and feel the desperation about finances (although I did not, principally because I refused to dip into the savings I had accumulated). I did some writing, took long walks, and concluded that I needed to contribute much more... and could.

The Group

Now I must digress to talk about a group of about eight friends that I made before and after joining the fraternity at Trinity. The group of friends were roommates, almost all in Theta Xi except Tom Nary who chose Alpha Chi Rho. While we hung out with each other at Trinity (conducting endless and largely inconclusive discussions in our rooms about civil rights and the Vietnam War), the stimuli at college were such that we each had our own lives and interests and did not become a real "group" until later.

In the late '70s and '80s several of us in the group went skiing together each winter or took trips, but we did not do things

The group in Deering

together as a whole group until the late 1980s when I was living in Deering. I had invited the group and spouses to all come up and camp out in my meadow in Deering for a long weekend. We had such a great time that we vowed to get together each year as a group. After a few years coming up to my place in Deering, we decided to pick a different place each year to meet, almost always at someone's house or second home. We met for long weekends in Franconia, several times on the Cape and in Maine, in Vinal Haven, Rehobeth, and even in Onancock. It's been over 50 years now and we stayed in touch during the year and commiserated or celebrated through many marriages, divorces, illnesses, tragedies, deaths, births, and travels. We always got together once a year.

The group, somewhat expanded over the years, consists of a doctor, several lawyers, a carpenter/philosopher, an educator, a mental health activist, a criminal justice professional,

The group at play

psychiatrists, psychologists, an artist, and me. The spouses of the group became part of their own looser mini-group and put up with our "groupiness" steadfastly and played important roles in our yearly gatherings. They all remain among the best friends I have. During the pandemic of 2020-2021 we gather for a Zoom call each Wednesday night to discuss politics (these were Trump's presidential fiasco years), elections, social lives (nil), and our thoughts and feelings (on too few occasions in my view, being a touchy-feely kind of guy).

While my educational experience, research studies, and athletics and honors were important to me at Trinity, my friends were perhaps the most meaningful things I took away from college, aside from the credential and the eye-opening experience with politics and social causes (this WAS the mid '60s).

The New Hampshire Dartmouth Psychiatric Research Center

In 1991 I took a consulting job with the New Hampshire Dartmouth Psychiatric Research Center (PRC), a small group of psychiatrists conducting research projects for NIMH, the RWJ Foundation, and others. From 1992 until 1995 I worked with them as a consultant while still able to do a few other consulting projects. I took on increasingly responsible jobs for them and got a reputation as a skilled employee. I was acting as an employee but wasn't really since I had no benefits or secure wage, as a consultant. In 1995, I became a regular employee with them at an office in Concord where many PRC staff were located. It was interesting work, and I threw myself into it.

I was working with a young psychiatrist, who knew only a little about research but was ambitious. I worked incredibly hard to write his grants, hire the staff, and manage the projects when we won them, as he had the medical credential and I did not. As it worked out, as a consultant, I had been working three days on site in the office and two days, Monday and Friday, in my home office in Deering. It was a perfect arrangement as I also worked most weekends at home on Dartmouth PRC projects often pulling off impressive feats of production, in terms of writing, research, data analysis, etc. They were getting more than their money's worth, even though I was working largely unsupervised at home for those two days (really 4 days including weekends).

This continued for about three or four years. The psychiatrist's reputation climbed (in my admittedly not so humble opinion based a good bit upon my effort, and ideas, and his name, and of course his credentials). And his salary tripled while mine was less than a third of his, not being a psychiatrist or having a doctorate. The psychiatrist was elected president of the American Association of Geriatric Psychiatrists. He went on many trips to conferences, away more than he was in the office many times. I went on a few of these trips, but I usually stayed back at the office, doing the research. We published about 25 or 30 papers on the elderly and mental health.

This arrangement was ripe for resentment on my part, and I did become resentful. This came to a head around 2001 or 2002 or so when an AAGP conference was to be held in Hawaii. My boss for the first time said that I could not go, though I often begged off other conferences, I wanted to go to this one. It took an intervention by the financial officer of PRC, who knew a little about how important I was to the psychiatrist's success, to convince him to let me go. I went with Wendy, and we took another ten days of vacation on Kauai after the conference.

(Kauai is a wonderful island which we revisited for two more vacations over the years.)

Another issue arose around this time. There was an opportunity open in Massachusetts to consult on a small project to help another psychiatrist with her project. I wanted us to do it, and my boss did not. We made an agreement, I would do all the work associated with the project, sign his name to the work and correspondence as the one with the credential, but I would get $10,000 of the $12,000 fee. His role would be to make two site visits with me to the project in Boston to meet with the psychiatrist and discuss the project, which he did. I proceeded to do the work, draft the correspondence, sign his name which he okayed each time, and I completed our part of the project.

Well, the check for $12,000, due around June, never came. I would call the other psychiatrist in Boston to check on it, and she would say that it was not her bailiwick, but she would check and get back to me. Each time she said it was in process and these things took time, which I understood. I told my boss about these calls, but he was passive in all this as he stood to only receive $2,000 of the fee so he couldn't care less, with his salary, but I had to check with him every time I called her to see if he had received the check yet. And then after about three months she said the check had been mailed long ago. I waited and it never came. This began a process of monthly calls to check on the status, and each time she said it had been mailed and had not come back. I asked her to double and triple check and must have become a little pest to her, as she knew only that her financial office said it had been mailed. I'm sure that she was getting a little upset with me for calling about it.

Finally, after about six or seven months I asked her to check to see if it had been cashed. She did and said yes it had been cashed. I then thought that the check had been intercepted and fraudulently cashed. So, the next month I asked her to check the name of who cashed it. She said she would get it for me. I told my boss that she was going to check the signature and see who signed the check, and he suddenly said "Let me check my accounts, it may have come to me and I may have cashed it, not focusing on what it was for", (as if he got $12,000 checks all the time for his speaking trips, which he did not). The next day he comes in and says "Yep, it came last summer, and it's in my account, here's a check for your $10,000." I knew from our long relationship that my boss was extremely cheap, but I had no idea he was capable of this. The upshot of this was that I lost almost all respect for him.

It was later that I found out that my boss (who did almost nothing for the project) and the other principal investigator (PI) in Boston had had a paper published about the project (publishing is the currency in academia) and left my name off the paper. My boss did not tell me about it or argue for my name to be added to the paper, and of course the other PI did not know my role – one more nail in the coffin of my respect for him.

This respect continued to plummet. One final insult completed my disillusionment. Throughout the late '90s my boss said that he was pushing for me to be promoted to Associate Professor because of the PI (principal investigator) work I was doing, which was on the level of an Associate Professor. He kept making excuses and finally said it's "in process".

After several years of this, I learned from another source, that years earlier when he had first approached the head of PRC and told him about my wish to become an Associate Professor, the Director had said "No way, he has to have a doctorate to get that", again the credentialism focus of academia, and my boss did not push for me. He kept telling me that it was in process and there were a number of bureaucratic hurdles that had to be overcome.

I finally asked a peer of my boss's what was going on with my application for an Associate Professorship. He said this was the first time he had heard of it and picked up the phone right then and called the Dean of Faculty of Dartmouth Medical School. The Dean told him that he had never heard of my application and that no one without a Doctorate would ever get an Associate Professorship at Dartmouth as they had tried it once and it didn't work out. I confronted my boss with this, and he said he did not want to disappoint me all these years. I really suspect he did not want me to leave and was leading me on. I could accept the problem of my not having the credentials needed, but not being lied to about it.

Now I know this sounds like "sour grapes" and that I should have expected that the "credentialism" within academia would limit the rewards I received. And indeed, it is sour grapes. And you may wonder why I remained at Dartmouth while all this happened. (Frankly, I do too.) The reason is that Dartmouth would pay health and retirement benefits for the remainder of my life if I or any employee stayed on the staff for ten years, and I wanted that privilege. My three years as a consultant did not count towards the ten years, meaning I had to stay 13 years. And I did enjoy the research.

However, given these experiences with my boss, I began to slack off, by my standards, which meant I no longer always worked weekends. I would no longer feed my boss ideas for projects nor work so overly hard to manage the projects. In other words, I was just putting in time until I could reach ten years with the PRC and Dartmouth. At that point, I would soon be vested and would receive my health care and retirement benefits. This slower pace was fine with me now, as I had met and was going with, a wonderful woman who would become my wife, Wendy Nathanson Mansback. Now these events are my memory and opinion of what happened. I suspect my boss would have other interpretations. So be it.

But first it's important to know a little about my life with women up until then, as it had much to do with who I was and had become.

What Women Taught Me

It is difficult to know much about me, my development, my growth, and who I am now, without a look at the impact women have had on me and my life.

And it started early. I think it started with being doted on, by my mother and other relatives, as all new babies are to some degree. But as the only boy in the family, l received more than my share of doting.

Then I "went steady" in high school with Robin, from whom I learned the neediness and ultimate futility of jealousy. And the importance of respect and discipline in a relationship.

From there through several short relationships in college and after, learning tenderness, caring, hurt, the importance of feelings and truth and honesty in relationships. One of the most important lessons of all for me, was the unimportance of being "right" when it comes to feelings and relationships. Or perhaps better put, the need to subdue the need to be "right" all the time, which for some reason was, and continues to be, particularly hard for me. I do want to be "right".

I also learned that, unlike me, some women did not want a long term relationship, or did not want one with me, and would be satisfied, to my surprise, with a one-night stand, and thus, that feeling of being "used" was not restricted to the female sex. I also learned patience, and persistence, and a little about when to exercise each.

One of the biggest lessons I learned from my relationships with women is that attraction, to someone's charismatic personality or physical appearance, no matter how powerful, was insufficient for a long-term relationship. This lesson alone kept me from making some big mistakes ... and perhaps multiple divorces. It also led to some hurtful endings, on both sides in different relationships.

All this gives the impression that I had a number of relationships with women ... and I did. Perhaps, too many, though I'd be hard pressed to pick one I would have omitted. (Well, maybe a few on second thought.) I sincerely wanted to know about women, on a personal level. I could also share with them my own feelings, in ways that I could not with male friends. This was partly due to the typical problem of men not being comfortable sharing feelings. But it was also due to the fact that during my teenage years, when boys learned to bond in tribes and do male things together, I was almost completely absent, going steady with Robin and devoting all my time and attention to her and our relationship.

I found females more interesting and easier to talk to. And I listened to them with interest. I also came across as hopelessly naïve, which may have seemed refreshing to some women. This resulted in my being taken advantage of as many or more times as I took advantage of women. And yes, I too was no saint in pursuing relationships when I suspected there was no future with a woman. But these relationships did not last long, because I felt such guilt at not expressing or acting on my true feelings, or lack thereof.

I did seem to have the proverbial "fear of intimacy," perhaps stemming from observing my mother and father's relationship of practical necessity. They both worked so hard that they seemed to have little time for intimacy for themselves, certainly not in front of my sisters and me. Perhaps a symptom of the times.

I continued to seek a relationship of honesty, passion, and growth, and ended up finally getting married at age 62 after courting, and being courted by, Wendy Nathanson for 12 years from age 50 to 62.

Yes, I learned much from women …

The Longer-Term Relationships

The longer-term relationships were most educational for me, as they each were wonderful women with whom I shared much and learned a tremendous amount about myself and life. I debated including this section in the book as it's more personal. But I owe each of these women much and want to acknowledge them for being who they are, or were. Several have died by now.

Robin

Robin was the smartest girl in the class and pursued me from third grade on, until I became interested in girls and began pursuing her in the eighth grade. It was puppy love for sure, but it felt about as real as it could. We dated every weekend, in those formative teen years from the eighth through the eleventh grade. We were both in the Methodist Church choir, holding hands surreptitiously under our huge black robes all during the service, every service. We were bonded, as I would drive by her house numerous times when I would go out with my three friends, Danny Payne, George Parker, and Curtis Badger, whom I hung out with on weeknights.

A couple of memorable episodes with Robin. Robin and I had a favorite "parking" spot which we used regularly. Once, during one break up, she had made a date with an upperclassman, but then we got back together so she broke the date giving some excuse. On the night of our date, we forgot and went to the Forks Grill where everyone went after the movies and before going parking. He must have seen us, or someone told him. Afterwards, we went to our favorite parking spot, the cemetery across from the junction of Cashville and Savageville roads. He and a bunch of friends drove up with lights off, then suddenly putting them on bright to shine in the car. He got in the car and gave us both a ream of crap for embarrassing him. He was right of course, as we had totally forgotten about him, so we let him have his say, blow off steam, and then he left. Just an episode.

Another time I was backing out of a spot in the woods where we were "parking" after school and the car door snagged on a tree and tore completely off. I rushed around trying to find someone to weld it back on before Dad and Mom came home, finally finding someone to do it. Could not believe my luck, good and bad.

Robin was my first and thereby, in some ways, my most endearing and powerful love. We explored our feelings completely. That first puppy love relationship lasted for years. There was the eighth grade hayride where we first professed our love, the dances, the parking, the jealousy when she went out once with another senior who was her neighbor. It was wonderful, even the brief times when we would break up, as I remember to this day the sinking feeling in my chest and stomach when I would wake up in the morning after. And the wonderful rush when we got back together. Those memories stay with me today.

It was an intense relationship, which ended in our senior year through my immaturity and knowing that I was heading to college up north to Trinity and she was slated to go to a Virginia school. At the end of that senior year, I was named salutatorian and she valedictorian of our class. I later learned that a "B" in my final class that year kept me from being valedictorian. It was given to me by my algebra teacher, Mrs. Booth, a good teacher.

Robin went on to a good college. She began seeing a local guy and I heard that she left school and married him. When Robin returned to the Shore, she started a successful franchise with her husband. She had a fine son, whom she was immensely proud of and who was involved in running the franchise.

During college, I went out with women but had no significant long-term relationships. I began to recognize in college just how deprived I had been both financially and culturally. Others seemed much more worldly and sophisticated than I, about all aspects of life. My classmates mainly came to Trinity from fancy prep schools, with wealthier parents, fancier clothes (although this was the '60s and clothes didn't matter much). In college I began dating more in earnest, making the mistakes usually made in relationships, but I was learning a lot. I listened to women, and was interested in who they were and how they differed from me.

I majored in psychology because relationships, motives, social needs, biases, and the source of emotions and behaviors intrigued me. More than one woman would tell me that I was being too analytical in our relationship and should just let it happen … a fault of my introspection and curiosity about all things human.

One time a girlfriend and I visited her grandparents on the Cape. They caught us sleeping together at their Cape house when they - we thought - were supposed to have gone to church by ten a.m. As we came down from her bedroom together, they took it in stride and only made the remark "I guess those branches scratching against the window caused you to change rooms". Whereupon I, the dunce, did not take this easy way out they had given me, but said "No, I didn't even hear them." (Dense, dense, dense). Geez, the things you remember. Just another episode.

My reputation among my friends was of a naïve guy, who after a date professed that the lady was "a really fine girl", which was seen by them as the kiss of death for the relationship.

Melinda

In graduate school at Princeton, I met Melinda, a fellow classmate one year older, who was more mature than I (many of my women friends were) and certainly more worldly and less naïve. Melinda was a serious feminist and an intellectual who taught me much about women's status in life and men's and society's oppression of them. We dated for two years, one at Princeton and one, my first year in NYC, her second, when she had just begun to experience the attractions of NYC and the men there.

It was not a strong love or passionate relationship, but one built on respect and learning about the world, in particular enduring graduate school at Princeton and adjusting to NYC. This is when we stayed for a short time in Robert De Niro's cockroach-ridden apartment, and we all had dinner together as he and I were dating sisters. He was rude and less than nice as I think he wanted to break up with Melinda's sister whom he was dating. He soon did. Probably saw me as the country bumpkin I was. At the time I think he was making the movie "Mean Streets" with Scorsese, which put him on the map and gave him his start. A great actor, and almost certainly a better person than he showed me at the time.

During the summer after my first year at the Ford Foundation in NYC Melinda and I took a wonderful cross-country trip which brought us closer together (floating in innertubes down glacial rivers, camping all the way, doing crazy things). We learned to live and laugh at each other's foibles, but it was not love, simply good companionship. So, I left her in California, as she had graduated and wanted to stay on the West Coast, while I raced back to NYC (SF to NYC in 3 ½ days, one day travelling 950 miles in 18 hours).

There were other women in NYC. I remember one, Heather, who after going out a few times asked me "Are you for real?" Of course, I didn't know what she meant, until it finally hit me that she meant that I was so naïve and spontaneous in an unguarded sense, that she thought I must be unreal or faking it.

And I was, and continued to be, unrealistically naïve, or unwary and uninformed of the real world. And as such, I ended up being taken advantage of by some (not many by any means, but some) women who were looking for short-term or one-night stands, while I was always looking for Mrs. Right, it seems. Although to be honest, I did not turn down many one night stands … This was the "free love" era of the late '60s and '70s after all. It was not until later in life that I headed off some relationships by not engaging when I had the opportunity, knowing that they were not going anywhere. Caused some puzzlement and hurt there.

After leaving the Foundation and NYC, I moved to Harrisburg to take a job with the Governor's Justice Commission, and lived in nearby Hershey, PA for a while. The life in Hershey Park apartments was quite flooded with young professionals cavorting at all hours. I was probably the least active participant, but still had my fill of fun times at night around the pool.

Fran

In 1974 I was asked to move to Washington DC and the Justice Department from Pennsylvania to develop a model evaluation program for all states (what I had done for Pennsylvania). I had met Francine, who worked with the Urban Institute, on the same national program on which I was working. Fran was the third long term relationship I had.

Fran was a petite, pretty woman with a sharp wit, and we enjoyed each other immensely for several years. But something in me knew that Fran was not the one for me. Fran was a very good person and Fran seemed to need me. We went together exclusively for a few years enjoying each other's company, yet not getting too serious.

But one time around 1976, Fran went to a conference and came back and told me that she had met another man and might see him again. I was devastated, but more than that, it opened in me a release, which I recognized for the first time had been keeping me from truly feeling, and expressing, love. While I felt this overwhelming sadness that this had happened, I also felt a liberation and an exhilaration in allowing myself to feel fully, and express love without fearing the intimacy it entailed.

It was so powerful that I later wrote up the experience in a rather long description, "The Gift of a Transformed Heart", which captures my emotional liberation. I will offer this paper in a later section.

As a result of this transformation, I then gave Fran the love she deserved, and we continued seeing each other with me finally, and for the first time, being able to express the caring I felt. Ultimately, we stopped seeing each other, and went our separate ways. But I remained, and do remain, so thankful to Fran and the event for my "awakening" of the ability to give love without fearing the consequences.

Kristina

During my time with the White House, around 1978, I was sent up to the Hill to monitor a Congressional hearing and there saw a young woman who intrigued me, Kristina, an aide to Senator Cranston from California. I immediately asked her out and we began a short but very powerful relationship. Kristina was the daughter of a former Republican Congressman from California. She was named one of *People Magazine's* "Ten Women of the Year" in the mid-'70s for starting and running the Grey Bears Program in California, which involved gleaning farmer's fields at the end of harvest and using the leavings to give food and vegetables to elderly folks in need, who also helped with the gleaning.

Only 28, Kristina was a wonder, full of whimsy, and the most insightful person I have ever met about people and their motives. She knew what I was going to say before I did, whereas I never knew her next move or statement, as she was free, unpredictable, and totally fascinating. I cannot say I loved Kristina, but had an enormous respect for her intelligence, authenticity, and honesty. She taught me so much about the importance of being oneself, and not bound by society's expectations and rules. I lived with her in Southeast Washington on I St. for about a year. We lived in an apartment and, among other adventures, went through the big snowstorm of 1978, for which I was docked a vacation day for staying home with Kristina a day too long after others had returned to work.

Heading back from a trip out of DC one long summer weekend, after stopping at a roadside rest area and sunning ourselves in the nude a short distance from the rest area (that was the sort of crazy thing she, and we, did), we saw a shooting star. Whereupon suddenly she asked me to marry her. I agreed.

We took a trip out to California to meet her mother. (I had had lunch with her father in DC already and told him of our plans to marry.) The trip turned out to be a disaster as she spent a whole day with a former boyfriend, I suspect checking to make sure she did not want to be with him. I spent the day with her mother, who was a sophisticated artist who did not like me very much (perhaps seeing me for the straight rube that I was, unworthy of her daughter). She liked the ex-boyfriend. We also took a trip to the farm in Virginia to meet my parents who did not take to Kristina, nor she to them. Soon after both trips, we decided that marriage was not for us.

Kristina had it in her head that she wanted to go to Harvard Business School, so I wrote her a glowing many-page reference, which described her well, and that, despite her grades (she did not take school seriously), but with her outward success with Grey Bears, she got in that choosy school. It may have helped that I had hand-written it on White House stationary, which I should not have used.

We decided to part before she left for Harvard, and I never heard from her again except one weekend a year later she asked to see me when she visited her father in DC. I did, and suspected that she had met someone at Harvard, and wanted to just see me one more time to make sure that I was or was not the one for her. I did not try to impress her at all during that short visit, and she returned to Harvard. I learned she had gotten married and had several children with a fellow I think from Harvard, and was living in California, starting a small, successful healthy juice company with her husband.

Sadly, I later learned that Kristina died around 2003 from breast cancer. I always felt that Kristina and I greatly cared for each other for who we were but were not in love and would probably not have stayed together had we married. I have never respected anyone as much though, except for Joan and Wendy.

Joan

I met Joan around 1979 through two friends who then worked as news bureau producers for CBS News, Susan Zirinsky and Joe Peyronin. I heard recently that Susan is just now retiring after a two-year stint as the head of all CBS news operations, the first woman ever chosen for the job. I was living with two roommates in the American University Park section of NW Washington, DC - Sharon Metcalf and Lisa Strasburg. Sharon worked in the White House communications office and Lisa worked as an ABC News producer who covered the White House.

Joan is an elegant, dignified, intelligent and sophisticated woman about my age from Beacon, NY. Joan and I dated for a short period, feeling out our relationship until we decided we were better as friends. We did dozens of things in DC, mainly movies and parties. Indeed, we became lifelong soulmates, a relationship I treasure to this day. With Susan and Joe, we got a taste of how the other half lived as we took trips with them, once to the Hamptons to hobnob with the Washington and NY glitterati, and went for a long weekend to the Homestead, then a fancy resort in West Virginia, and went to the annual White House Correspondent's Ball, a big black-tie do back then where all the media big wigs and major personalities gathered to congratulate themselves on making it. (I had a private side conversation with Walter Cronkite at that event and discussed our mutual love of sailing. What a nice guy.)

I remember one remarkable 60-person party at Sharon's house (Sharon owned the house we shared) after the Carter Inauguration, where several famous TV folks in tuxes ended up skateboarding at midnight on the street outside our house, while one or two others indulged in cocaine upstairs, (Sharon and I were furious at this when we later learned about it.)

Joan worked as a producer of independent films for National Geographic for a while and then a small production company. She would take trips to Cannes, or Robert Redford's Independent Film get togethers in Utah to scout out the best new documentaries. We had a great friendship, going to movies and events regularly, and sitting in the President's Box at the Kennedy Center several times letting all of the people wonder "Who are those people ... must be someone important?" Little did they know that anyone who worked at the White House and knew about it could ask for tickets to sit in the President's Box if some other dignitaries weren't using the tickets. Few knew about the perk though, so it was rarely used.

I moved out of Sharon's and Lisa's house when I got back from my eight-month sailing trip. They had become good friends with a replacement roommate during that period and would rather him stay than me. (I suspect their lack of desire for my presence was also affected by my desire to take Carter's energy use suggestion seriously and keep the temperature in the house at 68 degrees.) I moved in with Jay Beck, a Georgia fellow who worked on the White House Reorganization Project with me and was close friends with Hamilton Jordan. I think Jay just retired after a career working with the Carter Center in Atlanta.

Joan and I to this day are best of friends and communicate regularly about life, news, and mainly the absurd political scene (Trump years). As a good soulmate, she and I share views on many things. I think the world of her.

Sandy

It was about this time, around 1985, that I met Sandy Starr through my Princeton roommate Robert Cunningham and Rigney, his interesting wife - a strong, fun, woman with a mind of her own. Robert and Rigney have created a good life on Cape Cod and have a one adult child, Caitlin, with a son-in-law and granddaughter.

After meeting Sandy, I moved to the Boston area and lived with Sandy in a house in West Newton, Mass. Sandy ran her own small but relatively successful design firm. Sandy was a mercurial, creative, dynamic woman who essentially took me for granted, until I left her, and then she called me and said she realized that she had loved me all along. I suspect a realization or "awakening" of the heart much like the one that I had had with Fran. In my opinion, she, much like me, was unconsciously withholding from relationships for fear of losing them, only to find that once lost, you do not die or collapse, and this realization freeing or liberating you to express and feel love. Just speculation here.

Sandy had a son, Garrett, who was going through his early teen years with great difficulty. Sandy did not seem to like being a mother and seemed to treat Garrett more like a suitor than a son, and possibly resented the responsibilities of being a parent (my opinion here). On the other hand, although I tried to be a moderating force and understand what Garret was going through and help him, I was really seeing him as a chance to experience a son. But it was Sandy whose love he needed so he resented me for being her love interest I suspect. It was complicated and did not work out.

Eventually, Sandy and I split, with difficulty. I bought her half of the house in Deering, NH that we had bought together and moved up there in about 1986.

All this time I was doing my consulting, but now from Deering. It was a lonely experience, traveling alone, with few options for romance or much of anything except square dances in small town Deering. I had a good friend, Marcus, a nature-lover like myself, and we took walks and had great talks about life. My chess partner Robert also came up to play endless games of that wonderful test of skills.

I became a mentor in a program called Junior-Senior Friends (much like Big Brothers), and took on a junior friend, Matt, for a few years. We did various things a ten-year old would like -bowling, drag races, hiking, skiing. We came down to the Virginia farm once, he caught a fish off the dock, something which I have rarely done. But eventually I could not keep him from his more suspect peers, and he drifted into a little trouble and ended the weekly activities

Matt

relationship. I guess it was my attempt to have a son, and so I probably came across more as a father (with whom Matt did not have a close relationship) than a friend, which was the purpose of the Program. My fault.

Robin

Melinda

Fran

Kristina and me

Joan and me

Sandy and me

Joan

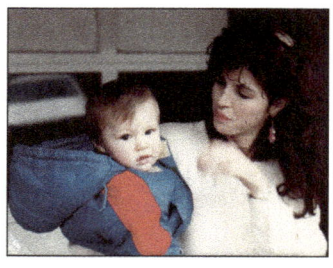
Rose and Vinnie

Rose

I was enjoying the beauty of New Hampshire, gardening, and renovating an old Deering house. It was at this time (1988) that I met Rose, a divorced young woman with a small two-year-old child, Vinnie, and a baby, Rose. She was ravishingly attractive, and once again troubled, in need of me, or so I thought. Because of what I had gone through with Fran, I was able to give her my love unbound and did so.

Unfortunately, I think Rose found it hard to get close to anyone, and the closer we got the further she moved away. This relationship did not go well, and, ultimately, I asked too much of Rose, not marriage, but love, she moved to Boston for a job.

I was not too devastated, realizing that I could not have married her. But I genuinely cared for her … very deeply. It showed me once again that one could love someone but know, in your heart, that they would not be good for you. I saved myself much heartache and several bad marriages with that realization.

Lessons

So those were my major relationships before Wendy, very fine women all. Each of the relationships taught me important things, of which I am so appreciative.

Robin taught me the power of feelings and the importance of self-discipline, restraint, and the futility of jealousy.

Melinda taught me that intellectual compatibility is insufficient as a basis of love and that I am capable of hurting another without fully realizing my effect.

Fran taught me that protecting myself from love is a losing

proposition both for me and for my loved one. And she gave me the opportunity to give love unconditionally and without holding back.

Kristina taught me that incredible respect and admiration were not love, and that love might be best expressed by letting go.

Sandy taught me that charisma, and attraction and fun times are an insufficient basis for love.

Joan taught me that friendship can bring lasting joy and trust and can be so rewarding.

Rose taught me that I cannot "fix" or make a person love me, and that no long-term relationship can come from trying to "help" or "save" another.

And all these relationships helped prepare me for finding and winning Wendy's heart.

Wendy

The final (I hope and believe) and true love of my life is Wendy. I met her in 1995 through an outdoor social club. She was a young, separated and almost divorced mother with two young girls - Leah age eight and Adena eleven. Wendy was a bright, attractive, devoted mother around 42 and I was 50. Wendy had separated from her husband a year earlier and was in the process of getting divorced. Her mother, so close to Wendy, had died of cancer a year earlier as well. Wendy had a wonderful father, Ben. Ben got to know me and forgave me for not being Jewish as he said I had "Jewish values" (Ben was devout, though not Orthodox.) Wendy's religion made no difference to me, and I respected her for observing the holidays and have tried to participate with her.

I was attracted to Wendy because she was honest, endearing,

and quite sexy, under a veneer of motherliness. We enjoyed each other immensely and laughed and had fun together. She was more "normal" than most of my previous relationships.

Wendy, who lived in Manchester, NH's largest city, and I fell into a pattern of her coming to visit me on Wednesday nights and every other weekend when her ex-husband had the girls, and me going to be with her in Manchester on the other

Wendy

weekend when she had the girls. This was a troubled time for Wendy, losing her mother, just divorced. And raising two children on her own, while working as a paralegal for a large New Hampshire law firm.

I think Leah, the youngest, saw me as the reason her mother did not get back together with her father and resented me greatly, doing everything possible to make our life miserable on the weekends I was there. This was very difficult for Wendy because Leah was her baby and Leah had trouble believing that I had nothing to do with keeping her father and Wendy apart, even though they had parted a year before Wendy met me.

Although Leah was more of a problem for me, the real problem for Wendy at the time was Adena, who was entering puberty and a time when she was rebelling against her mother's

Wendy and the kids

Wendy and me

wishes and breaking all the rules of the house ... much like a normal teenager. Wendy and I spent many hours on the phone, with Wendy worrying about the latest drama with Adena, my giving her advice about being firm with Adena, and Wendy finding it difficult to carry out disciplinary actions.

The result was that Wendy and I grew closer over time in the weekly intervals we spent together, but could not really have a "family" relationship with the girls. I felt that if I moved in with Wendy, or she with me, or we all found a new neutral place, it would not work at all. I could see me having to be the "bad guy" in the relationship, arguing for a more disciplined matter-of-fact approach with the girls when they misbehaved and Wendy wanting to, soon after a punishment was imposed, make everything all right by lifting or ignoring the punishment.

This led me into a push-pull relationship with Wendy where I felt it would be the end of our relationship if we lived together as a family. Yet I longed for that, as with Wendy it would be the only family I would ever have. We continued in this once-a-week-and-on-weekends relationship for 12 years, having wonderful times on vacations, weekend trips or in Deering and tense times at her Manchester house on Wednesdays and every other weekend. (Looking back, my troubled experience while living with Sandy and Garrett probably made me gun shy about living with Wendy and the kids.)

Wendy's and my relationship seemed to change over time as she became more enamored with me, almost too enamored, and I with her. To her I was a wise soul who had had many experiences in life, and we grew to love each other very much. So we persevered, and are so glad we did, and today we have two mature and wonderful children and five fantastic grandchildren.

I also have a brother-in-law and sister-in-law, and two nieces (on Wendy's side), and two sisters, two nieces, three grandnieces and two grandnephews on my side.

And finally, Wendy is still teaching me ... and I her ... that differences are OK, that compromise is essential; that we cannot (and should not) be made into the perfect mate; that marriage does change a relationship; that love can grow with appreciation of who the other is; that surprise is important to keeping a relationship fresh; that the mundane must be shared; that growth brings change and that's a good thing; that surface anger often hides a more complex feeling; and that life is better fully shared. A lot of lessons.

There was much more that I learned, from age 15 on, from the many other women I "dated" or "hooked up with" - today's term. (Remember this was the '60s, '70s, and '80s, the years of liberation and the sexual revolution.) And I cherish the time spent, experiences shared, and feelings explored with each. And the many who have taught me more about honesty, naivety, courage, self-awareness, empathy, fear, and love than I ever could have learned otherwise.

The Surprise Trips

During the years with Wendy, and for the first time in my life, and in Wendy's, we took long ten-day vacations, once or twice a year, mainly to the Caribbean, trying seven or eight different islands. We had a ball.

But also, one of the hallmarks of Wendy's and my relationship was treating each other to "surprise" getaways for a long weekend. In these, one party did not know what the other party was planning, and indeed, at times did not even know there was a surprise planned. I enjoyed immensely the planning and execution of such surprises and did it often. Wendy did indeed plan several getaways but being more honest and embodying less of a mischievous streak than I, did not enjoy planning them as much and was not as skillful at carrying them out. She would sometimes inadvertently give away the surprise and would be bursting with enthusiasm to tell me what they were halfway through execution. In any event I will relay some of the best ones, because they gave us a lot of joy and adventure, and still do.

The Little Palm Island Escape

We were on vacation in the Florida Keys one time and Wendy said to me, "Don't plan anything for Friday evening as I have a surprise." Friday came and Wendy told me to get fairly dressed up (for the Keys) in a blazer and slacks and we headed from Little Pine Key toward Key West. Well, about halfway there, we turned off and came to a small boat landing, spiffed up with shiny life preservers, new lines and decking. Several other couples were waiting there, all turned out as well. Puzzled, I wondered why we were dressed up to go on a boat ride.

Well, in about ten minutes, this classic old time motor launch pulled up, all decked out in bright brass and mahogany with a skipper dressed to the nines in his naval blues. Wendy told me to ask no questions, so I didn't. We took off and after a ride of about 20 minutes at a decent speed, we came upon a small island. Turns out it was Little Palm Island. I had read about it as it had shown up on many lists of best resorts and getaways in North America, which I look at all the time. I was impressed! We were to have a fabulous dinner there and then return (to stay there would have cost us about $800 a night in 1999, maybe $1500 today).

We disembarked and were told that dinner would be served in 15 minutes, but we could roam around the island until then. We did, walking down well-groomed narrow torchlit paths through palm trees and palmettos, past snug open-air bungalows with plunge pools and such. Upon returning we were seated in an open-air setting at a gorgeous table with fabulous place settings in a private section. We proceeded to have a scrumptious six course superlative dinner, selected from an exotic menu, and served impeccably by a fastidious waiter (in a tux, of course). It was quite the do and I was surprised. After dinner (paid for as was our custom, by the person giving the surprise) we were carried in the launch back to our dock and we returned home sated and quite pleased. A fine surprise.

The Cheerleading Getaway

The girls were slated to go to Portsmouth NH for a state cheerleading contest one Saturday. This seemed to me to be the perfect time for a surprise getaway, as the girls were going to be going there and coming home by bus with the other girls and staying over at friend's houses Saturday night.

Wendy and I got in the car when I said, "Oh, I want to take the trash to the dump on the way, and popped the trunk, and told Wendy I was going to get the trash from inside the house. Whereupon I went in, came out with the trash, and put the trash in the trunk. But I also picked up two suitcases I had surreptitiously packed earlier for each of us and snuck them in the trunk, Wendy's view blocked by the open trunk lid.

At the dump I told Wendy I'd take care of the garbage (she usually helped) while she stayed in the car, and with the overnight bags hidden. We went to the state competition, and the girls did well, and we saw them off on the bus. I said, "As long as we're here, let's have dinner". Wendy said she'd like to go on home, but it was beginning to rain, so I convinced her to stay for dinner. Then we "discussed" (I call it arguing) about where to eat downtown as I maneuvered us towards a restaurant where I had made reservations. As the rain was pouring, I found a parking spot near the restaurant and said, "Let's try this one". So, we went in, and I said "Why don't you hit the head while I see about a reservation (which we already had). Returning, I told Wendy we were in luck, and they had a table.

Now this was the tricky part. I had not been able to get away from Wendy before the trip to make a reservation at an inn. So, during the meal I told Wendy that I had left a window down in the car and had to go close it because of the rain. I got to the car, retrieved a travel book on NH listing all the places to stay, returned to the restaurant and secretly called and made a reservation at one nearby for that night… got their best room, which luckily was free.

I went back to the table, told Wendy that I thought we should stay the night as it was pouring and the two hour drive back to Deering would not be fun. I said I had retrieved the travel book, and let's call two or three places to check as to availability. She still argued strongly for going home, but I said we can at least check. So we picked three places, and I got up, and pretended to call each place out of sight of Wendy (this before cell phones). I came back and said, that no, nobody had any openings, so we should just start home and if we see a place we could stop and check on the way. Wendy started to complain again, about not having any of the things she needed for an overnight stay, making good arguments. I said it would just be for one night and we'd make do if we found a place.

We sprinted for the car in pouring rain, getting soaked and started home. Now to say that Wendy has a poor sense of direction would be understating things by a factor of ten. She's terrible at directions. I knew this and was glad, as the Inn I had booked upon returning from the car was in the exact opposite direction that we would have to go home. Little worries, Wendy did not catch on. As we started the car and pulled out the rain was worse than ever, and I again said we would try to find a place to stay, warm fire, soft bed, a cup of tea or Baileys (which I had secreted in the trunk too). As we drove slowly along, Wendy continued to argue, and I batted back her arguments and asked if she wanted to drive, which quieted her somewhat as she, like me, did not like to drive in unknown places at night, particularly in the rain.

After a few minutes we were coming up to pass the Inn where I had made reservations and I said "OK, what about trying that one, but if they're full we go home, agreed?"

Whereupon she said, "Deal." We went in and I asked about a room without giving my name and the desk person said, "I'm sorry but we're full" with Wendy breathing a sigh of relief. Then I said, "But I'm sure you could find a room for the Miles's from Deering." (Wendy rolling her eyes here) … and being in on the gag he said, "Why yes, we do have a small room on the third floor you could have." And proceeded to show us to it. It was perfect, with a gas fireplace, a huge bed, and a nice bathroom (always important to Wendy). So we took it. Then I said, "I'll be right back, I forgot to lock the car," and went down and retrieved the overnight bags from the trunk. Returning, the gig was up, and the surprise was sprung. We had a wonderful night laughing about all the subterfuge.

The Cambridge Surprise

Another surprise came when we were scheduled to attend a birthday party for Stu Edelman with the Trinity crowd near Boston one Friday night. After the party we were supposed to stay at George Fosque's place, but I had secretly made reservations at a hotel on Storrow Drive at the end of the Turnpike as a lark. As we left the party, I said, let's make a night of it and get a nice hotel somewhere and stay, instead of burdening George (which of course we wouldn't be, so my argument was weak). All the way down the pike from the party, we "discussed" the issue. She saying that George will be disappointed, it's wasteful when we have a place to stay already. While I played my romance card, describing having a drink in a nice bar, while listening to a quiet jazz pianist and having a romantic night away. We already had our bags, etc.

Finally, she gave up, as I was adamant, and as we approached the end of the Pike she said, "Well where would we stay?" And I said, "We'll just pick a place and try it." Whereupon, she said, "Well how about that one over there?" pointing to a tall hotel at the end of the Pike which just happened to be the hotel where I had made a reservation! I couldn't believe my luck, her picking the exact hotel. So, I started to unpack our bags and Wendy said, "No leave them, they're probably full on a Friday night", so we left them and went in. I coolly said to the desk person "I am Mr. Miles and I have a reservation for tonight". At this Wendy jabs me in the ribs, rolls her eyes again and gives me the LOOK as she knows I am just pulling the man's leg, playing one of my usual inane jokes, pretending to have a reservation and getting the poor attendant all confused. Then of course, the desk person says, "Why yes, Mr. Miles, we have a reservation for you and your wife Wendy for one night in the Bridal Suite and have a wonderful night". Which we did. The next day we had a beautiful view of the "Head of the Charles" annual crew races.

The San Francisco Caper – The Big Kahuna

One time when we had planned to go camping in Maine, I told Wendy we were going to another island for a week, and it was a surprise. I told her to pack a couple of nice outfits because on the way up and back we would be stopping for a nice dinner. We left and almost immediately Wendy said, "Where's the canoe?" as we always took the canoe with us. I told her this place already had canoes for guest's use. Going down Rt. 93 we usually took Rt 101 over to pick up Rt 95 going north to Maine. When I passed the usual exit, Wendy was a little perturbed, and I just said I forgot to take it.

At the next chance to take a road over to Rt. 95, I maneuvered to be on the left of a car and pretended that I couldn't get back to take the exit. Wendy was really mad then as it added a good hour to our trip. Then when I passed the around-Boston-beltway exit, our last chance to get on Rt. 95 before Boston, she turned to me and said, "We're not going camping after all, are we?" To which I said, "You'll just have to wait and see." As we headed into Boston, she tried to guess that we were going to dinner in Boston, that we were going down to the Cape to see Robert and Rig, our friends there, that we were going to a play, and I kept saying "You'll just have to wait and see."

When we got into Boston there was a sign and exit for the airport, and I took it. Now she was getting more upset, so I said, "OK, yes, we're flying down to Virginia to a resort, the Greenbrier", which was a very fancy resort in West Virginia. "But I thought it would be nice to pick up mom and take her as well, so we'll stop by Onancock to pick her up". To Wendy's credit, she took this very well, not that spending the long weekend with your mother-in-law to be, was any real treat, and a very controlling mother-in-law at that.

We headed into the airport, parked, and went in. I looked up at the flight board listing all the flights arriving and departing and found one that had a Norfolk flight and our San Francisco flight both among the listings. And before Wendy could check the times or gates, I whisked her away and took her to the ticket counter to check in. I gave the attendant my paper reservation info, and she checked it out and started entering the info and printing out our tickets, when she said, "I wish I were going to San Francisco", and Wendy replied with a sigh, still not getting it, "Yeah, I wish I was too". Of course, the attendant, puzzled, said, "But you are". And I had to tell the truth.

I had hoped and planned to get Wendy on the plane and after three or four hours, I figured she would say something like, "This is taking a long time to get to Norfolk." And I would pretend to get up to check with the hostess and come back and say, "They had to divert to North Carolina because of weather over Virginia but we should be there soon, just go to sleep". I wanted to get to California without her knowing where she was. Anyway, we had a great five day getaway in California at several places along the Big Sur coast in the surprise of all surprises.

The Remote Camping Experiences

In 1995 I stumbled across a beautiful wood canoe for sale in a yard sale and bought it. I immediately began taking long weekend trips to remote islands, at first without Wendy. In 1997 Wendy joined me and we began taking longer weekends together, many in Maine or northern New Hampshire, some in New York and Vermont. We would canoe camp where we would pack up supplies and find a remote island or campsite to canoe to and set up camp for four or five days.

Upper Pierce Pond and Mayor's Island

This soon turned into a week or ten days when we found the ideal island, Mayor's Island in Upper Pierce Pond in Maine. It was 23 miles from the nearest town along a sparsely- populated hard surface road into northwestern Maine, and then a turn onto a winding dirt logging road for another 15 miles. Then a walk with gear and canoe 150 yards down to the canoe put-in, and a one-mile canoe paddle to Mayor's Island where you are just about completely alone for your entire stay. Oh, then you canoe back that mile to pick up your second canoe load for the ten days stay. Owned and managed by an old sporting camp, Cobb's Camp, we went to the island often. We took my faithful dog, Eddie, or Big Ed, as the little dachshund was named. I had inherited him from the relationship with Sandy, who did not want him. Loved that dog, a most loyal and faithful friend.

I know I enjoyed the island camping trips more than Wendy, since she was more of an urban girl, but she pitched in and made

Cobb's Maine Sporting Camp

The first of two canoe loads to Mayor's Island

Upper Pierce Pond rock feature

Mayor's Island campsite

it fun as we enjoyed the isolation, the beauty, and the wildlife - loons, moose, eagles, and deer. She came to love it too, (though she never truly appreciated the pit toilet).

The routine was for me to get up at dawn, with fog on the lake, and canoe quietly for two hours around the pond looking for moose and other wildlife, returning around eight as Wendy was getting up and coming out of the tent. We cooked breakfast, went off together exploring in a canoe trip around the pond or down five miles to Cobb's Camp. In the afternoon we napped, fished (very little luck as I am the world's worst fisherman), gathered wood and prepared dinner. In the afternoon we watched the sunsets and had a nice fire at night to talk by. We had eight or nine years of blissful vacations each summer. I loved the place. We only stopped going when I had a bout with atrial fibrillation in 2007 and Wendy was afraid that if I had heart problems while camping in this remote area, she could never be able to get me help.

Mayor's Island moose

Our camp at night

It was on this island after 12 years of being together exclusively, that I asked Wendy to marry me, having concluded that this was the woman I loved and wanted to spend my life with. It was a bit uncanny. We had not discussed marriage at all for a long time, but one evening at sunset, I routinely suggested it was time to go over to the other side of the island to watch the sunset, as we usually did around 6 p.m. As we were leaving the campsite for the 50 yard walk to the other side, I slipped a long piece of grass in my shirt pocket. Seeing this Wendy said, "What's that, my engagement ring?" which of course it was, as I intended to weave it casually into a ring as we sat watching the sunset and then propose, which I did, but with Wendy somehow suspecting me all along. She's intuitive that way. Couldn't believe it!

Wendy laughed and readily agreed and on the way home we stopped by a fancy resort in the mountains of NH, the Balsams, and arranged to get married the next weekend. Wendy had had a small wedding before and she and I both did not treasure the trappings of a big wedding. After getting the license and paperwork completed, we drove up to the Balsams the next weekend and got married in a two-person wedding on a sunny August day in 2007.

Our Wedding

Back to the Five Miles Farm

Since the girls were now in college, Wendy moved into my Deering house on a more or less permanent basis. She still had her job in Manchester as a paralegal for a top law firm. Since I was planning to leave my job in a year, we planned to go back to my childhood home in Virginia. It had been my lifelong dream to go back to the Five Miles Farm on the creek and rehab the old house into much more modern and livable model of the old structure. We both had qualms about this move as I feared "you can't go home again" might prove true as friends and times had changed. But I recognized that the lure for me was the nature, the land, the water and pace of life on the Five Miles Farm and on the Eastern Shore. Wendy for her part wondered about the amenities available, the social life, making friends, and the cultural opportunities.

We decided to make the move, but I promised Wendy that if she did not like it there or if I didn't find the life I wanted there, then we would move somewhere else. During 2007 I designed the changes I wanted to the house and in early 2008 I hired a contractor to gut and redo the house according to plans an architect and I had drawn up, and it was started in May of 2008. In June of 2008 I left my job at the Dartmouth Psychiatric Research Center and Wendy and I moved down to Virginia. While the house was being finished, we lived first with my kind cousins, Jo and Kim Penland, for three weeks and then moved into one portion of the new house for several months while the rest was finished in November of 2008.

One surprise while redoing the house was the finding of a

cannonball lodged in a four-inch beam. This is how the worker who found it tells it:

The Five Miles Farm Cannonball

In April of 2008 when working for DDP Construction on the renovation of the house on The Five Miles Farm, I, J.D. Hogge, discovered a small 1 ½ inch cannonball lodged in the rafters. It had been fired from the direction of the water and had blasted through a 1" board, passed cleanly through one 4" thick beam, and lodged in a second 4" beam. I found the cannonball as described during demolition of the interior of the Five Miles Farm house in 2008 and turned it over to Mr. Miles.

— J. D. Hogge

I took it over to the Mariner's Museum in Newport News and I learned a lot from the curator and a staffer. The cannonball was identified by the "Associate Curator for Things That Go Boom" (self-titled) of the Mariners' Museum as most probably fired into the home either in the 1780s by British raiders roaming the Chesapeake, or during the War of 1812 when the British were stationed on Tangier Island in preparation for their attack on Baltimore. It was believed to be not later than 1812, as the swivel, or rampart, gun it was fired from was not used in subsequent wars. However, he speculated that it could have been used by pirates who occasionally visited the Chesapeake and regularly raided homes during those times.

They gave me a picture of the boat and gun, which was the kind that fired the cannonball. I learned that the British, from their big boat, would let over a longboat with the cannon mounted on the bow. They would row up a creek and fire cannonballs into the farm homes along the creek sending the occupants to the woods. Then they would ransack the house taking the food and items they needed back to the big boat. This is how they were able to survive as there was little food on Tangier where their 5000 troops were based. An interesting story.

Life Now in 2021

Which brings us to the present day. We share two daughters and I thankfully have a good relationship with both now. They each have fine husbands, good jobs, and live in northern Virginia and Massachusetts. We now have five incredible (of course) grandchildren, and we get them down to the farm as often as they can make it. The grandkids call me "Sea Daddy" which was a nickname for my father. They seem to like their time on the farm, and we try to make it fun - boating, kayaking, swimming, and sitting around the campfire.

Andy, Adena, and the kids - Jordan, Laila, and Benette

It turns out that Wendy fit right in on the Eastern Shore. Being a social person, she joined the YMCA and was introduced to all by Sonda Dawes, a former neighbor and friend. I finished the house, and started a garden, and with Wendy, filled the

Lukas, Leah, and the kids - Oscar and Otis

Our two daughters' families at their best

The renovated house and Wendy at lesiure

house with our things (We had a ton of stuff. Even after two big yard sales up in New Hampshire, it took three trips in those 21 ft U-Haul trucks to get our gear down from New Hampshire.) In 2009 we added a dock and bulkhead around the property and in 2010, added a large 400 sq ft glassed in porch and an outdoor shower on the end of the house, both of which are the most used features of the house now, at least during the summer.

We both started volunteering, Wendy with the Literacy Council and the Eastern Shore Coalition Against Domestic Violence. I threw myself into volunteering in the effort to build a new $5 million library, joining in 2012 the ES Public Library Foundation, the fundraising arm for the library. I devoted incredible hours, ideas, and effort to this endeavor.

Meanwhile, Wendy and I built a fairly idyllic life on the farm with her putting up with my messiness and me putting up with her five o'clock rages (which I ascribed to a touch of obsessive

Wendy's favorite pastime

Goofing off in the canoe

compulsiveness and menopause, and which after perhaps eight years finally tapered off). Wendy clearly began to see me as a normal human being and took me off the pedestal, which I knew would happen and which we both had to get used to. But in doing so, Wendy blossomed, and made a wonderful life for herself on the Shore, having many friends. We developed a group of friends with whom we hung out and have dinner parties. We now, in the time of the pandemic, meet every week or two for socially distanced gatherings on the lawn of each house.

Each hunting season, my cousin Stuart harvests two deer for us from our field (deer are so abundant down here - 32 in my fields one day, while in NH it was rare to see more than a dozen deer a year). Between my gardening and farm keeping, and Wendy's cooking, walking with friends, and flower gardening, (funny how we fell into traditional roles, something that I had never done before) we had plenty to keep us busy. We kayak, our favorite pastime, and go to the International Films, the farmer's market, and we acted in several plays at North Street Playhouse.

One time when Tim and Kitty Croke were away, Wendy and I took over for them in running the International Film one Thursday night at the Roseland Theater. This was their baby, and I knew they were worried about how it would go, so I emailed them a follow-up after the film night was over to reassure them that all was well in their absence. Here is the email…

A Night to Remember at the Onancock International Films

"Tim, Kitty, all in all I think it was a successful night…me manning the ticket booth and Wendy checking for passes at the door. Although I think it was a good night, there were a few

glitches. Well, at least there were no serious injuries. Things were going swimmingly until half-way through the ticketing process, (about 7:45) when I realized that I had been charging $5 a ticket instead of $7.50.

Then Wendy, right before closing at eight, had an altercation with a tough lady who would not produce her ticket. Just before Wendy was about to take her down with a patented kickboxing move, I, being a reasonable man, moved out to break it up, whereupon, her husband, being an unreasonable bigger man, cold-cocked me... not to worry, I bounced back up, waited until there were several people holding me back, then called him some frightful names. The police came but no one was arrested after a few Chicago payoffs were made (Tim taught me that). Finally, the police and fire departments left.

Oh, I forgot. The popcorn staff came out to watch the tiff and the popcorn machine caught fire producing a lot of smoke, scaring the already seated patrons. We all calmed them down and got the fire department to finally cut off all the sprinklers. What a mess! They left and things were just getting back to normal when I noticed the money bag was gone. But whew, the good news is I found it just outside on the ground... the bad news is the money and next season passes to sell were all gone. But not to worry, it was well past time to start so I didn't have to make much change.

With all seated at 8:22, Jeanne got laryngitis and Wendy, quaking in her shoes, went down to face the increasingly angry crowd, whereupon she promptly peed in her pants from anxiety. Luckily, I had some of my mother's Pull ups in the car and I brought one down the aisle to her just as she was finishing her stuttering speech. (In hindsight I think she would have preferred

I hadn't.)

Well, we were all ready to start and then... the projector jammed. After 30 minutes of trying, we couldn't get it to run so we offered the patrons their money back. Since we had no money, it having been stolen, all pitched in to help make change, including the projector man. This proved not to be too wise and the projector, motor silently humming but not running, if that makes sense, overheated, caught fire and well, the fire dept. had to come back, (after a delay because they thought it was a call about the first fire). We continued to provide refunds to folks on the sidewalk as the building continued to burn (amazing what all that movie reel tape smells like). There was only about $5000 damage to Runnigers next door as their building was brick, but a couple of expensive cars outside were damaged.

It appears you owe various of us about $450 for pitching in to make refunds with our own money and keeping the horde from getting physical as they chanted "We want our money! We want our money!" while rocking those cars outside! The nerve, some were demanding $7.50 back rather than the $5 they paid. Hruumph.

Anyway. Around ten p.m. the fire died down; a new building is on the way in eight months with insurance money (you did have insurance, right?) and we all went over to Bizotto's to commiserate. However, unbeknownst to me, Wendy had dared the woman she had had the altercation with to meet her after the show at Bizzotto's and she'd show her who's tough, so there we were. Police again. Bizzotto's' bar mirror was smashed (Wendy has a remarkable high step with that kick boxing move.) But, good news, still no one had to go to the hospital, as I kept the tough husband at bay by posing an ethical dilemma which he *had to think a long time about.*

You had indicated that if Wendy and I did too good of a job at this, we might be asked to do it again. Well, I think we done OK, and even acted heroically, with Wendy facing down the cheating tough lady (she really didn't know it was the Eastern Shore News Editor's wife), even though my own interaction with Mr. Tough Guy was less than sterling as I think back. We calmed everyone running out from the smoke, gave the police and fire folks free goodies from the refreshments bar (oh, that's another $122 the concession owner says you owe him). Some folks were talking suing from, you know, smoke damage to clothing, pain and suffering, etc. but I think I put the quash on that as I told them that the real guys who run this show were "connected" in Chicago and N.J. and they better think twice if they value their knees and small children, so I think you're off the hook there. However, one of the detectives overheard me making the threat. I went over and introduced myself to him as Tim Croke, so when he comes he'll see that you're not me and I'd appreciate it if you said you hired me as a drifter who was just passing through heading for Maine, and I probably stole the dough from the money bag (when in reality I just skimmed $50 bucks off the top.)

Well, anyway, anytime you need us (after the smoke clears and the new building gets built) just give a yell. Oh, by the way, I have your money bag. Wendy and I are heading for France for a week or two to lie low.

Best, Kim

Kitty said she had read half-way through before she realized it was a spoof.

I enjoyed writing ditties such as this, seeing them as much

more humorous than others do (like Wendy, who sees them as terribly corny and silly). I also enjoyed writing poems for the birthdays of my co-workers and friends. And, I have compulsively written essays about current issues and events and other incredibly wise ditties over time, some of which are enshrined in a notebook which, I'm sure, will gather dust and deteriorate into unreadability over the years.

The Library Experience

While I would join the occasional non-profit Board to help out, my main charitable contributions were financial. That is until my boyhood friend Curtis Badger asked me to join the Board of the Eastern Shore Public Library Foundation in 2012, just as he was leaving it. (I write about this in some detail here because it consumed much of my time, resources, and emotional energy for eight years. Feel free to skip ahead if you are familiar or bored with this.) The goal of this small Foundation was to raise $5 million to build a new main library for the Shore, a herculean task for a rather poor 2 county area of perhaps 45,000 souls.

Yet I threw myself into this effort in 2012, becoming a lead organizer of fundraising efforts, as Committee Chairman for some committees, and then the President of the Foundation. For several years from 2012 to 2018, I devoted at least 20-30 hours a week to building the case for first the county supervisors (whose responsibility it was in other regions and states to fund a library, but not a clear priority of our supervisors at that time), and then taking the case to the state of Virginia for supporting the new library's funding. I naively first thought that data would convince the supervisors and prepared and made several presentations to the county asking for their aid. I documented how it would be a crucial investment in the county's future at less than half the cost of a paperback book annually per adult taxpayer over 20 years.

We were forced by the supervisors to have a referendum asking the public for the money - the supervisors knowing all along that rarely more than 20% of the public had hardly ever voted in favor of a measure involving tax dollars, much less the $3.5 million we were requesting as the county's part of the $5 million project.

We went into this campaign whole heartedly, organizing publicity, developing letters to the editor, distributing hundreds of yard signs, doing radio ads, everything we could think of. There was an amazing effort by a team of dedicated volunteers devoting hour upon hour to a campaign to convince the public to support the library funding in the November referendum. Then, in the last two weeks, one supervisor went public on the radio advocating against the referendum funding with a suggestion of alternative funding (which we had already explored and had led nowhere). This hurt us.

We ultimately lost the referendum by an astonishingly close 52.4% to 47.6 %. I say astonishing because the supervisors all thought we would lose big and were majorly surprised by the fact that we had come so close. And a little scared, because, being politicians, elected by the people, they did not want to be seen as ogres by 47 % of their public.

In a ridiculous (my opinion) auction-like meeting, the supervisors discussed various figures ranging from $2.5 to $3.5 million to give to construct the new library. Finally they settled on $2 million ... $1.5 million less than we had asked. This effort ultimately left us with $2.5 million left to raise, as the efforts of several folks had already convinced the state to give us $500,000.

Our next step, and this was my idea and effort almost exclusively, was to go back to the State and request an additional $1 million to build, attached to the library, an Eastern Shore of Virginia Heritage Center to house the wealth of historical documents, newspapers, photos etc. which were both held in the old Library and which many residents had in their possession without a place to donate them (this idea was not mine initially but had been batted around by others earlier with no way to fund it). I say it was my effort, not just because I thought of approaching the State again, and pushed the idea through the Board, but because few thought the State would agree to it, having given us $500,000 already.

Thus, it was left up to me to take it on. And I was doggedly determined to convince the State to do it, because 1) it was eminently worth doing to preserve Shore heritage through valuable documents, collections and photos; 2) it could generate enthusiasm among the moneyed crowd on the Shore; and 3) because I felt the Governor, being a native son of the Shore and my neighbor in childhood, would be interested in the project.

I first organized, with Curtis Badger, an ES of Virginia Heritage Center Committee made up of the most prominent historians on the Shore, some of whom had personal connections to the Governor (like Dennis Custis, having taught him in school for example), while others, like Miles Barnes, had enormous respect in the community, and MK Miles, a recognized world-wide expert for his Eastern Shore genealogical research. I then made the connections with the Governor, calling his Chief of Staff weekly to make sure it got into the budget, and to check on the status as it passed through the various approval stages. Others, such as Dennis Custis, also contacted Governor

Northam. We finally saw it ultimately approved by the state in the spring of 2018. This gave us only $1.5 million of the $5 million remaining to raise, which the Board has worked incredibly hard in a variety of ways to achieve.

Since the supervisors felt they had given the $2 million, (despite the Library Foundation having to find the remaining $3.5 million), they immediately took over the building project, hiring the architect, selecting the builder and project manager and oversaw the progress, or lack thereof, of the effort (for this was during the COVID period and the project did indeed experience several substantial delays). And they took possession of the old Library, which the Library owned but had planned to sell for about $500,000 toward the funds we had to raise. We had little leverage.

Since Wendy and I had given a ton of money (for us) and me a ton of time to the library project, at this point I was pretty much burned out and stepped back substantially from active fundraising efforts around 2019, just serving on two or three committees in a more passive way.

As I write this in mid-2021 we need about $70,000 to complete the construction with the library well over half built after a number of COVID-related and other delays. An additional $500,000 or so will be needed to outfit it internally. I have devoted this space and time to writing about this library campaign because for eight years it was my chief "hobby" and an effort for which I was proud. There were political and personal conflicts and struggles throughout the project, which are quite normal in long term efforts such as this, but the result was worth it.

There were, and are, a lot of heroes (and one or two villains) in the 12 year struggle to raise funds for the new library, very deserving folks, but sadly far too numerous to cite here. And it's too bad, for some devoted, and still devote, many hours to the effort and deserve the thanks of Shore residents.

The Trips

For fun Wendy and I continued to plan and take trips during retirement ... to Europe for five weeks in 2014, across the country during a six week journey in 2012, to more islands (Kauai three times for ten days each in recent years), and two Regent cruises to Alaska and the Far East. (The Far East cruise being the cruise from hell as we call it, as we both were sick for two weeks aboard the boat from a COVID-like illness, in mid-December, 2019, a month before COVID was transported from China.)

I took great pleasure in researching and planning the trips in fine detail. Wendy was better in deciding the day-to-day activities on the trips and getting my aging body walking all over the cities. I enjoyed driving all over a country and seeing new places, so we travel well together.

Wendy's relationship with her two daughters has grown closer and more of a friend/mother relationship with Wendy being more independent and less needy of their love. They call her about every other day with information about their lives and the kids and to seek advice. They both know how happy their mother is and know that I am a big part of that happiness. They no longer resent me, and I no longer try to see them as my own kids to whom I can give lectures on life. And after 25 years, we get along well, and Adena is over her rebellious youth, and Leah realizes I did not cause the breakup of Wendy and her father.

Wendy's wonderful father, Ben Nathanson, died in 2018 at the age of 93. Back in 2012, I sent him a long letter about his daughter, and her happiness in making a home on the Eastern Shore. Ben was one of the finest men I have known, as was my father, who died from a heart attack at age 76 in 1996. My mother died peacefully at age 98 in 2017.

In terms of illnesses, Wendy has had some minor ailments, being quite healthy overall. In 2007 I had a serious bout with atrial fibrillation leading to an ablation procedure. I had two pulmonary embolisms, one in each of the last two years, from a condition called hypercoagulation or "sticky blood" resulting in hospitalizations with dangerous blood clots, which moved from legs to lungs. I also have developed the usual high blood pressure and take multiple eye-drops several times a day for glaucoma. But all in all, at ages 75 and 67 in August of 2021, during the pandemic, we are doing fine, and life is quite good for both of us. We often tell ourselves how lucky we are.

Ben, Ruth, and the Nathanson clan

Cozumel - 1996

Vieques - 1998

Key West - 1999

The San Francisco Surprise Trip - 1999

Kauai - 2000

Bermuda - 2000

St. Lucia - 2001

St. John - 2002

Tortola - 2003

Rincon, Puerto Rico - 2006

Marbella, Spain - 2005

Cross Country Trip - 2012

European Trip - 2014

Kauai - 2018

Alaska - 2019   *St. Kitts/Nevis - 2019*

Singapore-Southeast Asia - 2019

Now, as I look back on my life, I have to delve more deeply into several aspects, so I will end the chronological play by play and become a little more reflective and philosophical about the things that have shaped me and who I have become. From now on it will be even more egocentric and self-centered, and considerably more boring, than what has gone before, if that's possible. Proceed at your own risk.

Who Is Keith Mathias Miles?

Looking back from the vantage point of 75 years, I can see that several personality themes have characterized my life. I know a person is much more complex than some fundamental underlying characteristics that he or she might possess, or be possessed by, but for a start at describing who I am, several stand out. The main ones are: 1) a naive approach to the world; 2) the need to empathize and see others' points of view; 3) the need to understand people and events and to be understood; 4) a strong sense of the importance of fairness or justice in the world; 5) an awe of, and need for, nature; and 6) a mix of introversion and extroversion. All of which stemmed from either my childhood upbringing or my core being, I don't know which, though I have suspicions.

Naïveté

Perhaps because I was brought up in relative isolation on the farm or sheltered from most things evil or harmful in the world, I approached everyone and every circumstance with an innocence that bordered on the humorous. Like the time already mentioned when the NY sophisticate asked me after knowing me for several dates "Are you for real?" seeing me as so unworldly and innocent as to be acting or pretending.

I also had little awareness that there were people in the world who would take advantage of my lack of worldliness or knowledge. I remember when I arrived at Trinity, coming from a small school of grades one through twelve with a total of 500 students. In the first week I was asked by an intimidatingly sophisticated classmate, from a large urban area, whether I had ever read any books by George Sand. I, of course, said "No, I haven't read his work", having only a passing knowledge of Shakespeare, not to mention George Sand. Then he asked me about George Eliot, and once again I said I was not familiar with him. Only to then learn from my friend that Sand and Eliot were noms de plume for female authors. I, certainly, was embarrassed by my ignorance. I certainly had a lot to learn, about literature… and people.

Similarly, but in a different venue, on several occasions in my life I had been "used" by women who I thought of as friends, to make their real mates jealous and perhaps thus more attentive, by asking me over on some innocent excuse and having their boyfriends or husbands arrive while I was there helping with some homework or task. It only occurred to me later, when I either realized it on my own or was told by a friend, that that was what I was being used for. Or sometimes being used sexually by a woman who had no interest in spending more than a one-night stand while I saw it as a budding relationship. Yes, I was, and to a substantial degree remain, naïve and gullible about things many people would recognize and take for granted.

But over time I came to see such naivete as not all bad, since it made me fresh and less cynical, less jaded and suspicious of others, and perhaps put others with no evil intent more at ease with me, to trust me. I have retained this trait for much of my life, with some leavening over time so I don't get totally taken advantage of. But I still cannot recognize until well after the fact when I have been insulted, or made fun of, or taken advantage of.

Another offshoot of this naivete, is the outrage I feel when someone misinterprets my motives for doing something as selfish or to gain a personal edge or goal, when I feel I am doing something noble or selfless, only trying to help. This infuriates me. I recognize that this suspicion may come from their experiences with others or the world (see empathy below) but to have them think ill of me for only trying to do what is right makes me very angry, as there seems to be nothing I can do about this misjudgment of me. In their eyes, what I did was a normal selfish act, with no altruistic element. But people are different, and long ago, I learned that I rarely can alter their worldview. Indeed, after all, I WAS gaining something for myself from my act, a feeling of nobility or righteousness in doing the right thing. So, I was being in that sense selfish, just not for the crass reasons ascribed to me.

Empathy

This is something I noticed in myself from an early age, and I think it came from my mother, who, whenever I did something not so nice to Sammie, or a friend, would say to me, "Think how you'd feel if they did that to you?" and try to put me in the shoes of another emotionally. This, coupled with my naivete, led me to always try to see the other's point of view or to make reasonable excuses for bad behavior by another. This led me to not get as angry as I sometimes might have or even should, but also to not carry grudges or lose friends over small incidents.

And, of course, at times my conclusions drawn in attempts to empathize, have proven me wrong, as I misjudged why others have acted the way they did. But when my attempts to empathize with another have been in error, I usually err on the side of thinking better of the person than is justified, misjudging ill intentions as otherwise.

However, my experience suggests that this empathy be tempered if a friend rages at a driver who cuts her off in traffic. It is not helpful to say, "He must be having a bad day" or "He must be late for work or rushing to the hospital". This misguided attempt to empathize with another, just doesn't work in these situations. Better to empathize with your friend and say, "Why that arrogant prick, who does he think he is cutting you off! You must be pissed!"

This trait of being able to empathize with others I judge to be one of the characteristics I treasure most, as it relieves me of much stress, and helps me understand others rather than judging them ill. And since I find I am correct about their motives or thinking more often than not, it allows me to align myself with them rather than take offense or get angry when it is not necessary. It does leave me somewhat open and vulnerable to being taken for a fool, but such is life…my life.

One of the clearest expressions of empathy that I have been able to muster was expressed in an article I wrote in response to a letter to the editor in a NH paper around 1990. Here is the letter from a fellow from Connecticut, followed by my response. The letter:

"My wife and I moved from Francestown to Connecticut eight years ago. Recently we came back to visit friends in the area.

We were pleased to find that Francestown had not changed drastically. How I wish that I could say the same about West Deering and Hillsborough. We traveled to Hillsboro by way of the 2nd NH Turnpike and were appalled at the degradation of the two towns.

Many homes have sprung up in the lovely countryside, our favorite campground, complete with about 20 buses, campers, and assorted low lives.

Hillsborough is filled with young punks who seem to have nothing better to do than hang out.

I don't know why the two towns don't clean up their act and go back to the beautiful, respectable towns that they were eight years ago.

We were sad to see such tragic changes, and our summer trip that we had planned is now cancelled. I could not spend a whole summer in a place so changed in such a short time.

Why don't you people wake up and take a closer look at your towns?"

That letter provoked my response in the following article published in the local paper:

"On Low Lives and Other Men's Shoes

A while ago in the paper, a Gentleman from a nearby state wrote a letter in which he earnestly...and a bit angrily... complained about the "degradation" in two local towns. He cited the fact that along a certain road running through those towns, in the eight years since he had last visited "many homes have sprung up in the lovely countryside, our favorite campground, complete with 20 buses, campers, and assorted low lives."

He went on that one town "is filled with young punks who seem to have nothing better to do than hang-out." Finally, he indicated that, with these tragic changes, he had cancelled his plans to spend the whole summer here for his vacation and wondered why the people of the two towns didn't "wake up, take a closer look at their towns, clean up their act and go back to the beautiful respectable towns they were eight years ago."

Now this is tricky. I don't want to argue with the Gentleman, you see. I mean, who hasn't had some of the same impulses upon seeing some favorite place change over the years, in ways that we judge to be "worse". And the man could be a nice fella, just crying out for people to care a little bit more about their home and their environment. Again, not a bad idea at all, and one which I heartily endorse.

But I think there was a good bit more to it than that...and it bothers me...and not just a little. (To be truthful, I think it was the "low lives" bit that triggered my dander.) Which is why I'm writing this letter. It's more of a plea, I guess. A plea for a small opening of the mind, a little broader understanding, and not just on the part of the Respectable Gentleman (who shall remain nameless, for I may be misjudging his motives with only his short letter to go by, and he may already regret labeling the people who live on that road as just a bit lower than the rest of us.) No, this is a broader plea to others who may share a certain view of "campers, buses, and low lives" who should be "cleaned up" by the town.

Now I admit, it would be nice if everyone could afford to live in a nice white house with a picket fence and green grass...and maybe have a big red barn to hide those campers and buses. But alas, that's not the way it is now, is it? Nope. According to the people who keep the numbers, it seems there's a lot more not-so-well-off people today than there were years ago when the Gentleman was last visiting the area. (I know...there are more real rich people today too, but I suspect that the Gentleman is not too concerned about their homes spoiling the landscape.)

So, if you would indulge me, Mr. Respectable, I would like you to close your eyes, step outside what I imagine to be your quite comfortable world...just for a moment... and give a little thought to the people who might live in those homes which have cluttered up your favorite area in such a way as to incur your disgust.

I'll bet there might be a divorced mother or two with small children living in those less-than-immaculate houses, probably working two jobs to make ends meet to pay for daycare; or maybe a lumberman who's working long hours and hoping his daughter's recent fever isn't serious because he can't afford health insurance; or maybe a young couple trying to make enough to fix up their home a little...but just haven't been able to find the money or time...what with one child already, and another on the way; or maybe one little place is owned by an independent elderly woman who's lived here all her life and is just trying to scrape together enough to pay the taxes so she can stay in her home, which may not look like much, but it's hers.

I'm sure that these people would love to be able to afford a nicer home or take a whole summer's vacation as you had planned. After all, most of them can probably only afford to take that beat-up camper (the one you object to) for a week up north. Now I don't want to romanticize these folks, because the truth is I don't know a soul in the area you're speaking about. And I also suspect there are some people living in those homes who just don't care, or who've given up. And maybe there are even one or two living on the edge of the law (just like there are everywhere else... even in the suites of Wall Street).

But it seems to me you've got to be careful when you're classifying people as "low lives" by the quality of their homes or what sits in their driveway. For where would you want them to live? Thanks to rising land and housing prices (due in no small part to people from other states buying NH land so they can work or vacation here…ears burning, Sir?), many people must live wherever they can.

My experience is that people are pretty much the same the world over, and I suspect that the lovely back roads of your state have people just like those you're classifying as "low lives"… many good, some bad, and almost all doing the best they can. And what's more, I suspect that if you were to meet some and talk with them, you would find them to be pretty normal folks. And miracle of miracles with a little broader view, it just might be that you'd get beyond mere tolerance of these "low lives" to a real respect and appreciation for them, at least for how they've survived in the face of life adversity which might easily have humbled you or me. And do remember, you probably buy your firewood from them… and they might plow your driveway…or maybe wait on you at the local store.

And as for your remedy…"to clean up our act and go back to the beautiful respectable towns of eight years ago"…why is it that I think you have more in mind than picking up the trash along the roads? To tell the truth, it sounds like you would have us prohibit certain kinds of homes, buses, campers, and "low lives" from lovely country settings. Ah, were life so simple. Perhaps, as you seem to imply, we should allow only high quality, attractive homes in rural areas, preferably out of sight. Heck, we did it to the Indians and it worked out just fine for us, now didn't it?

And I won't even discuss the obvious dilemma of who's to decide what is an attractive home and what is an eyesore, except to say that I'm thankful for the honest, selfless people who are willing to serve on town planning and zoning boards and take the inevitable heat in an attempt to save us from our own selfishness. (And for those few on those boards who are dishonest *and self-serving…you deserve all the heat you can get!)*

And if it were just you who felt this way, Mr. Respectable, I would not be writing this letter. But you are not alone in this impulse. We all lament the fact that some things just aren't the way we'd like to have them…not as beautiful, not as refined, not as orderly or simple. And with increasing growth, more people, and greater development, the tensions and conflicts among values are going to get worse before they ease.

So, my plea, Mr. Respectable, is for a little tolerance and appreciation of diversity, to walk awhile in the other man's shoes, even the shoes of your "low lives." Take a little time to understand things from another's perspective. Might surprise you.

And for all you "low lives" out there (What? No volunteers?)… we all could do with a change of shoes occasionally. So don't judge Mr. Respectable too harshly. Change is scary and sometimes sad. And besides, he's probably just doing the best he can too.

Now…as for the "young punks who seem to have nothing better to do than hang out", I have some thoughts on that too. But I'll let that one go until next time."

Yes, I can get upset when someone looks down or deprecates another without understanding the struggles they have or obstacles they face in life. I enjoyed writing that letter to the editor and received some good feedback for it.

To Understand and to Be Understood

All my life I have tried to understand myself and others and what is happening around me. Associated with this was a keen need to observe what was going on. I relate this to my having to be a bit of a mediator in my life between my mother and father, who rarely argued, but who I felt were in some tension, perhaps brought on by their need to provide for their kids with little money, or the dynamic between Dad and Mom. It's complicated. For whatever reason, I always wanted to know what made others and myself tick. This is I am sure what led me to major in psychology in college and being an armchair psychologist.

I also got myself in minor trouble in relationships as I have been accused, rightly, of often being too "analytical" and not just "letting things be and flow naturally". However, I grew able through this trait to see beneath the explanations of myself and others, to what was really motivating myself and them and to get to the true cause of an argument or feeling (which sometimes the other person did not want to see in themselves as I often don't in myself). This gave me easier insight into people and allowed me to empathize more easily (see above), to judge less harshly and often, and diffuse situations. Likewise, my goal in life was "to understand and to be understood" (an inscription that I thought I'd want on my grave marker… in about 30 years).

This part of wanting to be understood, is critical to who I am as well, as I always wanted people to understand my motives and actions. This has led me to be accused of being too open with others, an accusation that is sometimes warranted, particularly when my openness exposes others as well as myself, when they may not wish to be as open as I. Others have sometimes been astonished about what I reveal about myself. (The contents of this book might be a prime example as Wendy often tells me.) On the other hand, sure that what I am revealing is not much unlike what others either are feeling, thinking, or have experienced, I say, "What's the big deal?"

This need to understand and the curiosity about others, and

the need to be open and transparent about what I am feeling or thinking, is a big part of who I am. Unfortunately, it is a source of repeated embarrassment for Wendy, who is a much more private person and is often shocked by what I reveal about myself (and at times, unthinkingly, about her, thinking that she could not possibly object, only to find otherwise. Indeed, Wendy would have preferred that I not have included any of the personal information about myself in this tome or to have referenced her at all. But she has become resigned to living with a transparent fool).

A Need for Justice

Another core trait of mine is a sense of, and need for, fairness or justice, which I touched upon earlier. It seems to permeate my life. I could be called, in my early years particularly, the straightest "straight arrow". I had high moral and ethical standards for myself and often expectations too high for everyone else. (More than a wee bit self-righteous there for sure.)

But for me there was no choice, I had to be the noble one, the one who took the hard road, made the difficult choice, because it was RIGHT! However, few people like a righteous prick to whom they inevitably feel they are being asked to compare themselves. They might respect it, but they sometimes don't wish to have the hard choice presented so blatantly. Or to be asked to take the high road, for themselves, or to be reminded that they aren't choosing the noble path. Far more fun, lucrative, or self-rewarding to go another way, the easier and sometimes more selfish way.

But for me, I had to be the Arthurian knight, the idealist, tilting at windmills, doing the right thing.

Though there was never any discussion of race in the family, there was an endless emphasis on "fairness". My mother stressed this mainly. Mom was always asking us and telling us what's fair between us, demanding that we treat each other fairly. Always making us ask ourselves "How would you feel if ..." (the empathy lesson again).

I totally internalized this lesson of fairness, and it became a driving force in shaping my views and attitudes, about circumstances, events, competitions, politics ... everything. I think, more than anything, this concept of fairness in life, and its importance, was what seemed to make me sympathetic (or perhaps empathetic) to the underdog, who has not had the opportunity or success of another.

I remember having a short 50-yard race with the second best runner in grade school. I got a quick start and shot out ahead. Realizing my quick-start advantage, I slowed a bit to let him draw even, assuming that the real test was a head-to-head running competition, rather than the start. But with his momentum picking up, and mine slowing in this short race, he won. I never forgot after that, that a quick start is part of the race, and rarely lost (he says modestly ... OK OK there WAS Doug Morrill in College, a REALLY fast guy).

This contributed somewhat to making me a loner in high school, and reinforced in others the impression of my naivete, a person apart from the crowd or the gang who all hung around, joked, made small talk. I looked for damsels to save, rights to wrong, and righteous causes to win. In one of the few job interviews I had with a business, I was asked if I was particularly religious or spiritual. I was not traditionally religious, but I could be called spiritual, in the sense that I believed in a standard of right and wrong and followed it, even though it was my standard, not ordained by any religion (of course, it had to come from somewhere. I assumed it came from parents with their own strong values inculcated in and adopted by me, at least early on, and probably from a Methodist upbringing, lax as it was).

The result was my always asking myself, on political issues, moral issues, job selections, behavioral decisions… what is right, what is the most noble course … for me. And it sometimes separated me from others, making different choices. And I had to learn fairly early, and repeatedly, not to expect or judge others harshly when they chose a difference course from mine. Empathy helped a lot, as it led me to see from the perspective of others how they viewed situations in which we differed. But it brought into question the dilemma of means vs ends, as sometimes to achieve righteous ends, I soon learned that one is tempted to adopt, and often did, less than admirable means or strategies. Thus, the idealist is brought down to earth by the practical… the perfect end is tempered by what is achievable. Alas, the need for compromises is learned and accepted. The perfect cannot be the enemy of the good.

An Awe of Nature

Perhaps because I grew up on a wonderful Eastern Shore farm, in the woods, on the creek, raising animals, watching crops and critters grow and die, the natural world was my world. It was where I was most comfortable, at peace, and alive. Some of the most idyllic times of my life were spent just sitting against a tree in the sun in the woods after school. Sometimes waiting for a squirrel to return to their nest at sunset, checking out the change in trees and foliage, listening to the birds, which soon came accustomed to my presence. But killing a squirrel, goose, or duck never gave me much satisfaction, except for the pride in showing Dad that I had gotten something this time.

Anyway, in nature was where I am at peace. It restores my soul and gives me a sense of my place in the world, among all other living things - plants and animals. Curtis Badger expresses it much better in many of his numerous books and I can't match his eloquence in describing a love of the natural world, so won't try. But watching living plants emerge from seeds and grow every day gives me pleasure which is hard to describe. I was never the survival gardener my father was, always striving to find the most productive tomato or corn to plant. To him the garden was a means of feeding the family, while to me it was a way to watch and appreciate nature. (I'm sure it was for him a little as well.)

In line with my feelings toward the natural world and stemming perhaps from my history on the farm and watching my father grow a vegetable garden every year, everywhere I have lived (maybe 10 - 12 places), I have almost always, NYC the exception, scratched out a vegetable garden. It gives me much pleasure to see seeds germinate and plants grow each day though the growing season. It also puts life in perspective to see them wilt and die after a long summer, and dissolve into the soil.

I am not a scientific gardener, deploying methods or soil additives to help plants grow or reading all about different varieties of seeds. And while I weed my gardens and keep them somewhat neat, my discipline in this regard is less than perfect (fortunately, Wendy likes to weed the garden and is great at it, much more meticulous than I – that's if the sun is out, and it's not too cold, and she has her IPhone charged for podcasts, and there is no mosquito within a hundred yards … you get the picture).

We now have a big 3500 square foot garden in the same place

that Dad had his and have four freezers (two refrigerator freezers and two full freezers). And luckily Wendy enjoys, or at least puts up with, helping with the canning, and mostly freezing, of our annual produce, which is a big job. My main job is to trap and relocate the raccoons who can decimate a plot of corn in about three days if they can get over the electric fence, and into the garden, which they invariably do. I relocated seven last year.

Now about living things. As I mentioned I have become a softie in my old age. While I went hunting in my blood thirsty youth and did not shy away from killing a squirrel or rabbit or ducks, I cannot do it now. Soon after I turned 40 or so I found that I could not kill anything. I now have Wendy call me to capture and take spiders, bugs, or even hornets outside rather than smash them. My refrain is "They're just trying to get a little food to take back to the family". Wendy pooh-poohed this but lately I seem to be getting to her as she is less blood thirsty when she sees a critter in the house. Ants and water bugs are another story for Wendy … around her they're history.

And, while cutting the grass gives me no qualms, if I see a small plant or tree, alone, I will often let it go, marveling at its persistence and endurance. I also get great satisfaction from feeding the 50-60 bufflehead ducks and an equal number of geese that come up to the bulkhead at a certain time every day to get their daily ration of corn and am sorry to see them go every spring.

I have become enamored with two osprey who have made a nest on a piling I set up to attract them. They have come back for three years in a row and had three offspring each year which I take great enjoyment in watching hatch, grow and ultimately leave the nest. I love watching the stages they go through, from the female sitting on the nest for 40 or so days then pecking at the eggs to help the babies out and then them peeking above the nest after about a week. And finally, after about six-eight weeks flying south with their parents. One was killed by an eagle or by hitting a power line on its first flight from the nest last year, just before the parents flew south for the winter, so I, as of mid-March, am waiting anxiously for their return this year. (YES! The male showed up on March 21st, like last year, and the female showed up on the 28th a day later than last year. They now have another three offspring born after the female sat on the eggs for 44 days this year. Makes my summer.)

Perhaps because much of my childhood was spent outdoors, I now find it important to get outside and experience whatever the weather is as often as possible, (though I'm no more tolerant of the raw windy winter days than most are). I love seeing the changing moods of the weather as reflected in the wave action (or not) on the creek and track the direction of the wind and the highs and lows of temperature associated with those changes. And to see and recognize the many changes brought about by the coming of the seasons and the movement of birds, deer, ducks, and geese gives me pleasure and a sense of stability and continuity that I treasure. Just seeing buds come out on trees is a pleasure for me as I watch them develop. Many others share this feeling, I'm sure.

I relate this also to finding beauty in a tree winding to find the perfect or only route to catch the sun, the rock made smooth by rushing water in a stream, flowers opening to the sun, or hearing grass grow, as on a warm spring day very soon after the snow melts, it pushes up through brittle leaves matted down by winter snow. This last I have heard only once, and it was an amazing peak experience in Deering. I was coming up a south-facing hill on a very warm spring day from the pond and suddenly heard things dropping from the sky and falling on the dried mashed down leaves after the snow had just melted. I couldn't figure out what was falling until I got down close to the earth and realized that it was thousands of blades of grass growing towards the sun and pushing from below through the brittle dried leaves. Together they made a soft crackling sound incredible to hear. Amazing, hearing grass grow.

I also enjoy watching the tides rise and fall and the storms and fronts form and pass. These make my days rich, and it is where I see beauty in its rawest form.

When I have felt most numb, and out of touch with myself, is when I have lived in a city or urban area where symbolically or literally, I could not step out of the house and take a piss in the backyard, could not walk among trees, or gaze upon water in all its various moods. This too is who I am.

Introversion and Extroversion

Perhaps associated with this love of nature, either as a result or a cause, is my introspective self. For I definitely am partly an introvert, who finds being in a social crowd often draining, energy-wise, and challenging to me to fit in. A disaster at small talk, I have never liked or been adept at making normal conversation about what seems to me as not very insightful or meaningful observations about daily tasks, schedules, happenings, or "doings". I recognize that these make up the gist of normal life. I'm sorry I don't appreciate it, as others seem to thrive on it, and it makes up a good bit of social interaction. This focus seems to keep things at a level which I do not find interesting or important, so I withdraw.

Yet at times I thoroughly enjoy the extrovert in me. At these times I can crack jokes (mostly quips, I'm terrible at remembering jokes), introduce meaty thought-provoking subjects, pose questions for friends to help me answer them, dance. (I love to dance, and I enjoy it.) Often, I find myself dreading going to a social gathering, but surprise myself by finding that I enjoy it once there. And I like nothing better than having a group of eight or ten friends over for a night of dinner and discussion about meaningful issues or questions all are wrestling with in their own lives or the political or social arenas. I find that ever so stimulating and worthwhile. In fact, the more personal the discussion the more I find it interesting. Others, my wife Wendy for example, find that kind of personal discussion to be overly intrusive and revealing, a sometimes humorous (sometimes contentious) difference between us.

I have this balance between the quiet introvert, drained by social interaction, and the outgoing extrovert, energized by people. I recognize it much more now and therefore don't reject the invite to a party out of hand, recognizing that it might be fun in the end, largely depending upon how comfortable I feel in the mix of people, activities and discussion (a whole subject in itself).

Touch, and Physical Intimacy

Perhaps because Mom was not too affectionate with us kids, all my life I have loved to be touched. Even as a child, I loved light touches and caresses of the skin. Once, at about age ten, I tricked my friend Hal's six-year old brother into scratching my back repeatedly using the rabbit-in-the-briar-patch ploy of "please don't scratch my back, do anything, but don't scratch my back" where upon he would sneak up and scratch my back squealing with delight, and me, protesting all the time.

But touch has always been important to me, both the giving of it and the receiving. Fortunately, I grew up in a time where it would not get you in trouble if you casually touched the arm of a girl or woman to show friendship, connection, or affection. Lately of course, in 2021, you must be careful to whom you show affection in that way, lest it be misunderstood. I find myself still wanting to give a gentle touch to show connection or friendship but having to hold back.

To me, to caress and be gently caressed is the mark of being loved and a way of showing affection and love and I still cannot get enough of it.

Now sex is a different story, all of which must be excised and deleted here, by order of, to borrow a phrase, "She-Who-Must-Be-Obeyed" – my wife, Wendy. She is much more private than I am, even though in this section I had not been planning to discuss our sex life. Yes, she asked me to take this section out, which talked about my sexual maturity (and immaturity in the early days) and what I learned as I progressed through my teens to my 60s. No names were involved, of course, just thoughts about lost time, learnings, and what is necessary for achieving strong physical intimacy. (Psst…it's COMMUNICATION!)

But alas, these pages will have to be added to the XXX rated version (available in brown paper wrapping at all disreputable news outlets for $59.99, or for three easy credit card payments of $20, plus $9.99 for shipping and handling - heh, heh). So, I leave you to your imagination here, and move on.

Image

I took a course in self-empowerment and understanding within the past five years given by a friend, Claire, here on the Shore. As part of the course the participants took a test to find out a little about who they are and what is important to them. It turned out that one of the things that was important to me was my image. This puzzled and angered me, for I took it to mean that I was caught up in projecting an unreal image of myself as more successful in the things that others or society thought important - money, status, achievement, etc. I equated it with shallow people who were pretentious, bought flashy cars and homes, and tried to put on an image of success to cover their insecurities. And I always thought of myself as striving to be authentic, not needing to be pretentious or dishonest or to project an "image "of myself as much more than I am. And I was often criticized by Wendy for being too humble, as not asking for or demanding the credit I deserved. So, I was confused by this finding.

But the more I thought about it, I realized that in some ways I WAS concerned about my image ... just a different image than what I was equating it to. For one thing, as shown above (and throughout this self-serving book!), I wanted to be seen as generous, kind, caring and willing to stand up for what is right. I realized that this may be the source of my outrage at having my motives questioned in instances when I was acting out of the goodness of my heart, and others suspected a motive of personal gain or selfishness. I realized that it WAS important to me that my image be one of a "good" person, and that even when done anonymously, doing good deeds, and being very honest with others about myself and my foibles (transparency) was important to me. It bolstered my image of myself to myself as a good person. In that sense it was also selfish, but at least to good effect. Yes, I indeed care about my image, just not the image I had in my mind when I was told I did by this test.

Ethics

Coupled with this image of being a "good" person was that of being an ethical person, who had a sound and ethical approach to life and took the ethical way of behaving and living. As such I was on occasion seen and accused as being self-righteous by others who felt that I had acted in a way that they would not and was in some way judging them for their behavior. I did and do take a strong interest in ethical issues, particularly when they put me in the uncomfortable position of being tempted to act less than ethically.

I remember when my friend Paul, in college, called me to tell me that he had found the correct diagnosis and case in a text for a take home exam in which we were asked to determine the condition and diagnosis for the person described. Thus, we knew the answer. I suspect he called me to ask me, without asking, what I would do with knowing the answer to the exact case we were being tested on. We each made our own decision, and I did not know what he did, but on the test I put down what I originally thought the condition and diagnosis was, and then qualified it by saying that it could also be what was listed in the text, but without saying that I had seen this correct diagnosis earlier.

I justified this by saying to myself that we were allowed to use all outside resources to find the answers. But I recognized that this was not truly ethical because I did not state in my answer that I had seen the correct answer to this exact case. I implied that although I thought differently, "the diagnosis could be … blah blah blah", suggesting greater knowledge than I actually possessed, since I would not have put down the qualifier had I not seen the answer. I can pinpoint other instances in my life when my ethics have been challenged and I have come away wanting. Ah, regrets. Can't dwell on them for long.

My interest in tricky ethical dilemmas and moral quandaries, led me to run a workshop on this subject as part of the Academy for Lifetime Learning here on the Shore. I think up subjects or circumstances which tax our ethical boundaries and then toss them out to the participants for all to discuss "what would you do". The differences are stark on occasion and the discussion is illuminating at times about human behavior and choices. This has been going on twice a year for eight years now and I love it. I'm proud of it.

My Values and How They Developed

Respect for and Appreciation of Differences

During my early youth, I didn't think very much about my "values" and certainly not my political beliefs stemming from those values. I grew up in a highly segregated rural part of Virginia. The Black folks I encountered were always either a farm hand who helped us bring in the crops, or a lady (Virginia Paddy) mom hired for $5 a day (in the 1950s) to do housework for one day every other week after Mom took a full-time job. My first brush with racism was when my father forbade us as 12-year-olds from watching a Black fellow on a neighboring piece of land running a backhoe and bringing him water during the day. I didn't understand it but began to realize it was because of his being Black. Or it could also have been about the danger of the backhoe.

And again, at Princeton when I offered a Black classmate a ride and to stay at the house for the night as he was hitchhiking from Princeton, NJ to Norfolk, right past our place near Onancock, halfway to Norfolk. He declined repeatedly, perhaps knowing more about my father's type than I did. When I casually mentioned it to my father later, he said it was a good thing he declined because he would not have let him stay at the house. I was appalled, not because I didn't know about racism by then, as I did, but because I had not realized the depth of my father's racism and fear of the other.

Yet my father changed in his later years, and while never the model citizen, he once was appalled himself. He visited my uncle in the hospital, and while walking the hospital halls, my great uncle, seeing a Black man on a gurney in the hall, suddenly punched him in the stomach, and said "You don't belong here". My father was shocked.

The first time I noticed my own moral development was an incredible experience. In the tenth grade during one boring government class, I was thinking about race. All of a sudden, I had an astounding experience … a revelation! In an instant I realized fully the equivalence and thus the equality of all people. This was accompanied simultaneously by an extraordinary physical feeling of an "unfolding" in my brain as if a new side of my brain expanded. I was astounded, sitting there in class!

Then, as I focused upon this "revelation", it happened again, as I then realized that not only were people equal, but that some were superior and inferior on various characteristics in equal measure across races and ethnicities. This was also accompanied by that physical, and astonishing, feeling of unfolding in my head.

Several minutes later, my brain seemed to "unwrap" again as I had the revelation that not only were folks equal in their rights and variety of talents and internal differences, but that we could benefit from what these differences were to teach us and offer us and society the true benefits of diversity.

It was an astoundingly sudden new dawning of appreciation for differences and diversity, and how we could all learn and benefit from this diversity in human beings. All of this happened in ten minutes sitting in class, and it literally blew my mind. I felt the world and my view of it had shifted permanently. What was mysterious was the physical feeling of "unfolding" in my brain which accompanied this. Can't explain it. Would love to be able to understand it. No longer try to.

From this moment on, I began to notice the differences, economically foremost, but also the housing segregation between Whites, and Blacks and migrants (we were a big summer farming community with a large itinerant migrant population) and the educational differences. For even then I was aware of the inequity of having our old, used schoolbooks sent to the Black school when we, the "white" school, got new books. This was the time of the Freedom Riders in the South, a group dismissed and disliked intensely in my white community, particularly when they drove through the Shore in the buses. I saw the images on screen of the demonstrations in the south, the beatings and hosing of Black marchers and secretly (because sympathy for the cause was not only not popular, it was also not tolerated by most) felt for them.

My mother was less racist, but also had the usual (for the times and our local society) belief in inequality. Yet she gave to the poor, Black and White, continuously. Being a Christian church goer, she seemed to recognize the hypocrisy and wrongness of racist beliefs. To their credit, my parents never (with the exceptions noted) showed my sisters or me manifestations or evidence of racism. No speaking of "niggers", just "colored people", the accepted and universal term at the time among Whites. And no demeaning talk about "colored people" (other than the term itself). I never noticed it because it just wasn't done in our house. Dad treated our farm hand John Bill, as he treated us in the fields, picking corn or getting in hay after work and on weekends.

Political Values and Thought

My introduction to politics was really in college, although I was beginning to be aware of race and the civil rights movement in high school. For some reason, I was chosen to give the address at graduation usually given by the valedictorian. I prepared a talk about the key to the race question being education. Of course, at that time, in the south in 1964, I was talking about educating the "Negro" race at the same resource intensity as the White race. Pretty tame stuff for the times. At that time, I certainly was not talking about the real problem… educating the White race about their own racism and the needs of the Black race.

My independent political thinking and growth started in earnest in my college years, when confronted with discussions about civil rights and Vietnam, and thoughts about culture, life and lifestyles in the 1960s. But my political thinking was firmly based in my values, which I had given much more thought about prior to that time. As I have discussed, the important principles of my political thinking were founded in such values as:

Fairness and Equity, meaning the equitable division of resources and opportunity to allow everyone the opportunity to live the life they wished.

Empathy and Compassion, meaning the willingness to picture the plight of those who, either through fortune or talent, had not achieved that life, and to help them achieve it. I naturally took the side of the underdog in life, having been one.

Economy and Efficiency, meaning I wanted a system of governance which achieved its goals as economically and efficiently as possible, without wasted time, talent, or resources. (Perhaps a bit of the Republican in me.)

International Equity. The equivalent importance of all nations and national interests in international affairs, regardless of their state of development, resources, might, or economic status, or the color of their citizens' skin.

The Value of Peaceful Coexistence, respect for sovereignty, and the limited role of war.

Democracy, with a small "d", meaning the need for, and equal right of, each person to participate to choose the kind of governance they felt could best achieve the ends they saw as important.

The Value and Importance of Diversity in thought and people to bring fullness to life and society.

These values bent me politically towards the Democratic way of thinking quite naturally. I say "bent" because this was not achieved without an examination of the alternative, and at times I thought I could best be described as an independent, with Democratic leanings. I often frustrate Wendy when I point out the motives, flaws, or unintended consequences likely to flow from some Democratic initiatives which she thinks of as mostly perfect.

Attending the Woodrow Wilson School of Public and International Affairs at Princeton taught me much about the workings of the governmental and the political systems, particularly their flaws and weak points, as well its necessity and fragility as a model for democracy.

Working in government also taught me how the best of intentions and priorities can get twisted and bastardized by the desire for power, influence, and resources, even for well-intentioned ends, and by both parties. I am far from a "knee jerk liberal" who will take the Democratic policy position no matter what. For sometimes I take that position reluctantly, feeling that it is better than the opposition's position, but not without its own dangers or limits.

My work in the government gave me insight as to how government programs can grow large, unwieldly, and intrusive, even through good intentions, foregoing for the moment the negative effect of greed, the pursuit of electoral power, and money, on government policy.

I have seen small programs, with admirable goals, grow into quite large programs which drive out other worthy programs by the resourcefulness of its managers, the power of its political backers and sometimes the cowardice of those charged with examining all programs and choosing priorities (listen up, Congress). It is often much easier just to let all programs grow than to make the hard choices among different desirable programs or choosing among the positive elements within each program.

This is most clearly seen at the local level, where elected officials are in power for only a few years. Why fight the police or fire departments over large, expensive pensions which might tarnish your image or jeopardize your reelection, when you will never be there when the chickens come home to roost and the bills must be paid on generous pensions well into the future?

Thus, importantly, there is little push to limit the program, just expand the funds for the programs being pushed out, meaning there is no real prioritization among the many "good" programs and the budget expands. And thus, the Republicans complain loudly about government overregulation and the need for limited government, while the Democrats challenge them to single out the "good" programs they wish to eliminate, and again no one wants to be seen as the killer of a program popular with their backers. Few chances for reelection with that stance.

And then the table is set for an egomaniacal demagogue like Donald Trump, the President for the previous four years. Recognizing that others will vehemently disagree with this assessment, in my opinion he is the poorest excuse for a leader or a human being that I can think of legitimately elected to such a high public office. I can write a separate book on why I think he was elected, the damage he has done, and how he did it through narrow-minded minions implementing many self-serving short-term damaging policies in just about all agencies. But others have already done that, and I can't get started on that or will lose focus (and certainly a sizable portion of potential readers of this book).

One of my dilemmas is that having been born rather poor, but having been educated and informed about, and lived, how the system rewards the "elite", I can empathize with the feelings and plight of those who have been left behind. I also can understand why they voted for a maverick like Trump. I castigate the Dems for not seeing how they appear to the common man, who most of us are. And for not articulating a down home message telling how Democratic programs benefit them and Republican programs are usually targeted for the rich, settling for trickle-down economics to serve the poor and middle class.

Suffice to say that I bemoan the state of our Republic, as money for re-election is the coin of the realm and longing to stay in power drives partisanship and policy votes in both parties, which common sense (admittedly MY common sense) would dictate should go the other way.

Thus, I see the faults of both parties, but since my values lie with much greater equity (mainly international equity given the resource inequities among countries, but of course within our country as well), removing the power of money in elections, improving people's lives, and the earth's and our own chances of survival, I bend Democratic. But I reserve the right, policy by policy, to independently look at the ends sought against the costs and benefits and unintended consequences. And I also see some of the excesses of the Left and the consequences of some of the questionable policies they propose in efforts to achieve equitable outcomes for all.

When I was considering a political career way back, I viscerally knew that I would never be elected because I could not bring myself to promote Americans and "America First" as more special or needy or deserving than the people of other, much poorer, less lucky, nations. Thus, whenever on the news I hear of an airplane crash, I lament that invariably the focus is on the number of Americans killed. A very recent example of this was the news that 13 servicemen had been killed in a bomb blast in Kabul during the evacuation process following the Taliban's victory. It was four hours and repeated broadcasts before it was mentioned that 60 Afghans had also been killed (subsequently found to be 200). While I understand the concern for Americans, I see this as a problem, for rather than identify with the humanness of a person, we identify first and primarily, with their being an American human. Understandable but lamentable. I would have preferred if the news led with "73 people were killed by a bomb in awful carnage in Afghanistan today, and among them 13 were US servicemen."

Similarly, I knew that I could never pursue a harsh immigration policy that kept all refugees out of the U.S., even though I clearly see the need for limits. My whole philosophy and world view is there must eventually be a leveling of economic disparities, and opportunities, and that it was the duty of the wealthier nations like us to enable and promote that striving toward equivalence, and certainly not to exploit them with our might and leverage. I'd never get elected on that platform.

But it was in college that I was introduced to ideas and concepts that became central to my thinking. It was there that my independent views were formed … I say independent because until then my views had not changed much from the views of my parents and those of the people I grew up with. But change they did, as I began to be forced to think through what I really thought about the key issues of the day.

Vietnam was particularly difficult for me. As I learned more about the history of the country and first the French and our involvement, I began to see how we were rather blindly caught in the mindset of the domino theory … let one country fall to Communism and they all will in sequence, without understanding the independent history and wishes of the Vietnamese people. But what was equally important was the question of what I would do about my own situation vis-vis the war.

So, I hit college unformed politically, but knew from day one that I had a lot to learn. And I did. Fortunately, I met a group of friends who accepted this hick from the sticks. We became friends and formed the group of friends I have described, who decided to go to the same fraternity, Theta XI.

Theta Xi was considered the "intellectual" fraternity on campus, different from the jock fraternity (Sigma Nu), the party fraternities (Alpha Delta Phi) or the rich boys' fraternities (St.

Anthony's and Psi Upsilon). This decision, and this group of friends, made all the difference in my development politically and educationally in college.

As mentioned, we had bull sessions (and they were BULL sessions!) as we hashed out our views on the civil rights movement and the Vietnam War, our plans to protest, or avoid having to support the war by joining (and possibly dying as the death toll rose day by day through our graduation in 1968). But the sessions also focused on income and racial inequality, and some, but less so, gender inequality (as this movement was just beginning in earnest as we left college). These discussions with my roommates helped me in the development of my own opinions and values, finally separate from those of my parents and upbringing.

Also, classes that I took in history, and psychology under George Higgins (my psych teacher and assigned faculty mentor) clearly helped me understand authoritarian and racist societies. And particularly one I did not take, with Ed Rabil, made a huge impression, as most of my roommates and friends came away talking about the ideas and concepts discussed in this class. So sorry I missed out on that class.

The Essentials: Beauty, Truth, Love, and Courage

I've on occasion thought about what the essentials of life and living are, as a human being for me. These four elements seem to me to be the essence of what is important in a person's life. I certainly will not do them justice here, but they are worth noting, as they are things I value greatly.

Beauty

To me, beauty is, you guessed it, best expressed in nature. I can be humbled by the grain in a piece of wood, the texture or color of a stone or rock, a stunning sunset, the dark sharp edge of a storm cloud coming in over the water - all have the power to raise me to awe.

I often even now sit for an hour or so several times a week in the woods, listening to the sounds, examining the trees and wildlife, or watching the growth or death week by week of the vegetation around me as the seasons change. It's my form of meditation.

Some human creations, particularly finely wrought pieces of sculpture or a beautiful piece of music can move me. Certain paintings (some portraits, still-lifes and landscapes) can also inspire me, though I have never been trained in what to look for, and perhaps that's best. And I have little appreciation for abstract or modern art, except as a puzzle to solve.

Some learned things, perhaps not natural, can be beautiful to me, such as the lines of an attractive classic sailboat or a field of planted wheat. Acts of human kindness also have a beauty all their own, and the calm, forgiving nature and behavior of some people seem beautiful to me. For me, beauty enlivens life and gives it fullness.

For me, to experience beauty is to be open to it, to be aware, and to stumble upon it in unexpected places. These are but some of the things I find beautiful, but, alas, beauty is indeed in the eye of the beholder.

Truth

I rank truth up there as one of the key elements of life, as it underlies all that we know, or think we know. To find truth and understand life is a largely unconscious goal and effort, undertaken daily. It is elusive, as often what I think is truth turns out to be rational enough, just not true. But the pursuit of what is real and factual is worthy and often fundamental. Particularly in relationships, as often what we think is going on is but a veneer we adopt, often unconsciously, to disguise the underlying issues driving behavior. Getting at the truth of those issues can be the key to resolving conflict and opening oneself and others to love. The pursuit of truth requires honesty, with oneself and with others. And this perhaps is the hardest truth to discern.

Now this pursuit of truth does not mean that it is necessary to be truthful or to express truth at all times. ("Of course I like what you've done to your hair, dear.") But the curiosity that it takes to always be open to hearing different "truths" expressed and trying to resolve in your own mind what is real vs what is false, is extremely important to me. Coming to some accumulation of what is true in the world forms me and my worldview as a person. And to be able to live with not knowing with certainty what is true about something.

While what is true has always been important to me, I have learned that it is not necessary (and often not possible) to convince others of my truth, for they see their own truth. To always seek truth is yet another basic element for me, and what life and being truly alive means.

Love

Love is perhaps the most elusive, and yet the most powerful element of all, at least for me. It so often hides under layers of fear and insecurity such that love can sometimes be so difficult to tap, and once tapped, to keep alive, to keep it from going back under that rock, to protect oneself from the hurt of not having it returned.

Yet, love, once unleashed, is so powerful that it makes meaningless much of life around it. And Wendy taught me that love can grow and can be expressed in wanting to give all you have to another ... with honesty being one of the most important and most difficult gifts. For honesty requires letting down barriers, being vulnerable, and having sufficient self-love to risk another's rejection of you because of feared weaknesses or inadequacies.

Love can also be most easily seen and experienced with your children, and even, it seems ridiculous to say, with your pets, perhaps because it is so unconditional, with no threat of loss. Yes, for me love has been the most elusive, and ephemeral, yet the most powerful and sought goal. It is mysterious.

But as I mentioned earlier, I fortunately had a powerful experience while seeing Fran which transformed my ability to feel and express love. Here is my description of that experience, written sometime after the fact:

The Gift of a Transformed Heart

The following incident happened to me during the fall of 1976. It changed my life and how I live it. I give thanks often that it happened. I am writing this for others who might exist under the same burden of not being able to truly love.

In October of 1976 I was thirty years old. To that point I had had numerous relationships with women, most short-term, two to four month affairs, and two longer term relationships (two-three years). At the time of these events, I was seeing no one exclusively, for that summer I had broken up with a woman after going with her for two and one-half years.

The reason for the breakup with this woman was similar to my reason for leaving the other relationships that I had ended prior to this one: I was unable or unwilling to feel the same depth of love for the woman I was with that she came to feel for me. The feelings leading up to the ending with this fine woman were similar to those I had felt before. As the relationship progressed and became more intimate, I drew back, became "numb" in my feelings, and found myself having to draw away. I did this by explaining to the women that I did not know why, but that I was not feeling the same love that they felt for me ... but was feeling more and more "suffocated" or "trapped" by their increasing love and "dependence" upon me. I would explain that it was clear that to continue the relationship would mean that they would end up getting hurt, and since I did not want that, we should not see each other anymore.

I might add that during all of these relationships, I had had terrible difficulty saying, "I love you" to a woman, not because of a macho avoidance of the word, but because I never felt that the somewhat lukewarm feelings that I had were "love". I am ashamed that my leaving hurt some very goodhearted and wonderful women.

This syndrome had repeated itself enough times by the time

I was thirty that I was worried about my ability to love another person wholeheartedly and feel deep feelings. It seemed to me that I might very well be afraid of love even though I wanted it to "happen" to me desperately…since I knew about such syndromes from my psychology studies.

However, fear of intimacy was not at all the feeling that I had when feeling the need for more "space" or "freedom" from an increasingly loving woman. It was just a feeling of not caring as much about her as she did for me and needing to end the relationship to avoid hurting her and ending my own guilt at not feeling love for her. I sometimes explained it away by telling myself that this relationship was "just not right" or that this must not be "real love", or I would feel it. Yet because several of these women loved me greatly and were very accomplished and dynamic women, I suspected that the fault must lie in me rather than in "us" or them.

This is the quandary that I once again found myself in during the summer of 1976 when I broke up with this woman, with the thought of each of us seeing other people. It was a mutual agreement as she was tired of waiting for me to love her, and I also. But since we still cared for each other more than anyone else, we would still see each other regularly.

In October I went over to her house to pick her up for the movies one night and she broke the news to me that she had become infatuated with a new man on a visit to Kentucky the past weekend. She had spent the weekend with him, had begun to feel real love for him and wanted to devote her time to him.

I was shocked to put it mildly. That night we held each other closely and I cried. I felt totally bereaved and I grieved heavily. I was happy for her yet totally forlorn for myself at having lost a love that I had assumed. In my grief and through my tears I did not know what to say or do. She had never seen me show such emotion nor had I. We talked and talked about her needs and my lack of feeling, all the while I was feeling a great grief. I felt that it must come from having lost something that I did not know I had counted on so much.

I left her late that night. All during the next week I found myself rarely going through a fifteen-minute period both at home and at work without tearing up. I slept very poorly as emotion came in floods. Frankly I was totally puzzled at why this should strike me so hard. I knew this woman was seeing other people and wanted her to. I knew that it was likely that she would fall in love eventually with someone else. I also knew that just the week before I was happy that we broke up and I did not think I loved her, at least in the way I want to feel love.

Yet now on some deep, uncontrollable emotional level, love was pouring out of me unrestrained and free flowing. During the week in which I was constantly grieving, I examined what I was feeling carefully. Almost from the night that she told me of her new love, I had become a different person. I COULD FEEL! Raw emotions came from me. No longer was I concerned about "losing" something by showing love for her. No longer was I afraid of being vulnerable through showing feelings of love. It was in feeling this release of emotions and being aware of losing these fears, that I came to realize what fears had been holding back my emotions. I was never aware that I was afraid to show love, until I wasn't.

During this week of emotion, I would find myself suddenly laughing in the midst of my grief. Laughing at myself for feeling all of this emotion for no apparent reason. And laughing from joy at being able to feel such intense emotions. It was as if these feelings represented a lifetime of emotions blocked by the fear that I would lose love if I let it touch me or if I submitted to its allure. Thus, I had remained aloof and loveless.

Now…the feeling of desolation and grief came from the realization that I had lost love anyhow, in spite of my protective aloofness, and I assumed the world would fall apart. But it didn't … and that led to my laughter and wonder. Instead, the feeling was one of a strange liberation … a "What have I got to lose … the worst has already happened?!" kind of feeling, which gave me license to feel and show the love that I had been blocking. Make no mistake, this was no neat intellectual process as it might seem as I describe it now. This was a mixture of strong emotions rolling over me for a week … emotions that I knew had less to do with the current loss than my fear of loss originating way back somewhere in my childhood. The fears that I did not even know that I had, I began to recognize almost as they disappeared, and in their absence gave evidence of their former control over me.

The result of this transforming experience was that I became a truly loving person for the first time in my life. I showed affection openly, by touch, word, and deed, not only to this woman (she stopped seeing the new guy after a few weekends), but to all my friends and those that I cared about. The feeling was wonderful! The change absolute. Although never a really selfish person, I was definitely self-absorbed and self-protective. After this experience I became mush more unselfish, empathetic, and caring. I showed affection through touch and words

This experience was a powerful, world-shaking, eye-opening event for me. I became more open about my emotions and expressed love for others in a variety of ways – through tolerance, understanding, empathy and caring. I became a transformed person who could finally feel the emotions that I had seen others feel and had longed for. I became much more courageous in showing feelings, where before I had not realized I was even being cowardly. I could now leave myself open for hurt, be honest about my feelings, and show vulnerability to people I cared about, knowing that I could survive the hurt if it came, and that expressing feelings was far more fulfilling, and alive, than to suppress them and protect myself.

The nature of my relationships also changed dramatically. I became a giver, instead of a taker. I enjoyed giving love, showing affection, and expending effort on behalf of those I cared about. I became much less self-centered. It was as if a whole dimension of life and a new level of "knowing" had opened within me and there was no turning back or wanting to. It has made me able to relate to people in a more direct "real" fashion with honesty and trust. It has made me more fully human and compassionate in a way difficult to describe.

This is not to say that all my troubles ended with this new-found gift. Not at all. It seemed than an air of "mystery" and aloofness that had seemed to make me attractive to some women had gone, replaced by a boyish enthusiasm which I was no longer afraid to express or able to suppress, but which was sometimes not as beguiling to some women as my earlier "inaccessibility".

A second possible result of this transformation was that I became a little too indiscriminate with love. It was as if I could now find the ability to feel love for almost everyone and did. I found myself in several relationships with women who themselves were where I used to be ... afraid to give love and running from love. (I could now see this protective fear more clearly in others who suffer from it.) In these relationships, I now became the "giver", feeling great joy in loving them and showing them love. They were the "takers", not appreciating my affections and almost wanting a less available, more challenging man. The result was that I too often did not look out for my own needs and interests as I should have, feeling that "I'm a big enough person" to give love and emotional security sufficient to turn these women into lovers themselves. It didn't work. In pursuing their growth, I was taken advantage of and hurt at times.

However, the trade-off has been well worth it, for seeing these women who cannot love, and being able to feel the joys of loving and showing love, there is no comparison between the two states. Even when experiencing terrible emotional pain of loss, I have thanked the heavens for the ability to feel that pain, rather than the numbness that I felt for so many years, and the lack of deep loving feelings. And I recognize much more quickly my own propensity to be attracted to women to "help" and the ultimate frustration and lack of fulfillment for me with them, when only they can help themselves, and only when ready.

The reason I am writing this is because I see far too many people, particularly men, but a surprising number of women also, who suffer from this same incapacity to love. Knowing how quickly I was transformed through my experience years ago; I often wonder if there are ways of replicating this transformation for others. For the power of loving, not just one person, but all life and the living of it, is immense.

Courage

Of these four elements, I suspect courage is the most essential. Without courage, neither truth nor love are possible.

I know I am not particularly brave in some ways. Physical confrontations scare me. I have had them, particularly with bullies. But it has been because I have been forced to.

I remember once, in Crewe, Virginia, I was about 11 or 12. Our family was visiting when Dad had left the Naval Base in Chincoteague when it closed, and was wondering if he should take a job managing one of my grandfather's (Big Daddy) or Robert's stores, this one in Crewe, VA. For some totally unknown reason, this much bigger bully confronted me daily outside of the store and threatened me, with great anger and hostility. Totally unexplained. He engaged in some minor pushing, and shoving, and finally said he was gonna kill me. He would give no reason when I asked him. It got to be so bad that I couldn't sleep and feared even going to the store, for fear he would be waiting.

Finally, the fear became so great that I went to Mom and Dad in bed one morning and told them that no matter if I died, I was gonna end it. (This was the first they had heard of it.) I was quite sure I was going to die, as he was much bigger. But for once in my life, I realized that dying was better than living in continual fear and humiliation. This was incredibly liberating.

So, the next time he confronted me next door to the store in a yard of Christmas trees for sale (it was near Christmas) I decided to act. When he tried to push me, I gathered all my energy and with all my might, shoved him back into a row of Christmas trees, knocking him off his feet. With all the rage I could muster I yelled at him, "If you ever, ever, come near me again, I will kill YOU!" and walked away. He never did bother me again, but at that point I learned that some things, such as the freedom from fear, are worth risking dying for.

One other experience stood out in my youth, at about age 14

or 15. We were playing keep away by kicking a ball around the playground at school. I was running for the ball when a much bigger boy ran up behind me and slammed me hard in the back, knocking me to the ground, saying "Outa my way little man!". I was incensed! I got up, ran after him and came up behind him and with all my strength, pushed him in the back sending him to the ground and said, "Outa my way big man!". Whereupon he got up and we went at it for a minute or two until someone broke up the fight. It felt good. So, it seems that rage at unfairness or extreme desperation seem to be the main motivations to get me to fight physically. But otherwise, I try to avoid physical confrontations and rarely have had the experience of engaging in one.

However, what courage I have is usually shown in matters of principle, in which I do act with courage, often at the risk of sacrifice.

For example, I will (and often have) admit to wrongdoing if I did something wrong. Or I will stand up for a friend if he is being falsely accused. Or I will make a principled stand for something I believe in (the takeover of the admin building to get more Black students recruited at college). Or to tell the truth to a friend or lover when it is necessary but may be hurtful to us or the relationship. This is more like moral courage rather than physical courage. I feel a sense of nobleness or responsibility when confronted with challenges to do what I think is right, even though the consequences to me may be serious (getting kicked out of college two months before graduation was a possibility). It seems easier to put myself at risk in such situations, and the payoff, and personal risk, are usually more consequential than engaging in physical altercations where the only outcome is to physically "win" or lose, or psychologically prove to myself that I am not a coward.

I can also imagine (and fortunately it's all I've had to do) risking my life to save another or others in a wartime battle (e.g., crawling to an injured buddy, storming the bunker). This is noble and self-sacrificing for a greater good, and you never know how you would react in situations such as this, until you're there. Though I fully recognize that acting on this "nobility" would probably result in my death, most certainly if I made a habit of it. But I can easily imagine myself doing it. And my sister Sam would say, and be correct, "Dumb shit!".

But most of my demonstrations of courage are not in the physically risky domain, but in relationships where I try to be courageous enough to expose myself to another, making me vulnerable. Or in telling the truth (as I see it) when it is needed to avoid greater hurt. Or to "let go" when it will hurt me greatly, but it is the right thing to do. This kind of moral courage and self-sacrifice comes more easily to me. And perhaps that's why I see it as more important and lacking on the whole, in society's self-focused, individualistic imperative today.

So, to the best of my ability now, that's who I am. Or at least the major themes. You may wonder about my negatives … my selfishness, defensiveness, laziness, self-centeredness, self-righteousness, impatience, jealousy, need to be right, etc. I could go on but, hey! … this is MY book, so I'll focus on what I want! I'll leave the negatives for all my friends and enemies to list in some other tome, or this book would double in size!

Whose Expectations? Whose Success?

A little here about the burdens of achievement: overcoming and shedding the expectations of others; rising above mundane expectations: the college years (1964-1968) of broadening, politicization, wonder, maturity, honors, and burdens – and coming into one's own.

From early childhood, I was the product of expectations. Mostly, my mother's I suspect, as she was a strong, judgmental figure with specific images of what a successful young man was to be. And that was to be me. This was never displayed directly, but subtly, through conditional love, such as the frown or the withholding of praise at a less than stellar outcome. Also, by way of the expectations for behavior worthy of merit and praise, though this could not be given too effusively or often, or it would lose its power. For this was how my mother was raised, as the good girl in a family with an older brother and an older sister (who turned out to be the rebel). And succeed we both did.

Now this set of expectations of success was not all bad. I succeeded as a young man by all measures, academically, athletically, and extracurricularly. And with this success came awards and honors, and a feeling of achievement, which got me into a good college with an excellent scholarship. And I, too young in high school to understand this dynamic, seemed to achieve every milestone seemingly effortlessly, without too much analysis or angst about what I was doing. As it seemed normal to me and was certainly not something that I saw as harmful.

And then came college. Partly because of my psychology major, where I learned about unconscious motives and forces directing behavior, and partly just being away from home, I began to see my style of upbringing as having negative effects. Being expected to not choose my own path, but to plod along the path set by the expectations of others. Also, this was the 1960s, 1964 to be exact, and new ideas and energy were in the air. (For example, my first night on campus, upperclassmen led a march down to the Capital of Hartford to protest a new policy of no drinking on campus. My friends, classmates, and I joined, and I loved it, as a lark more than anything, but as a break with authority. No, I was not in Kansas – or Onancock – anymore! Everyone was questioning assumptions. Vietnam was afoot, and civil rights were being fought for and granted grudgingly.

I absorbed it all, just sucked it up. So much so that in my sophomore year I was asked back to my church on one vacation to preach a sermon one Sunday (an annual practice of asking one of the students who had gone away to college to come back and lead the sermon). By then I had my eyes partially opened about the evils of segregation and Jim Crow. On the Sunday in question, I suggested to my parents that they not attend this, showed my mother an outline of what I was going to say, and left on a bright Sunday morning to give my sermon.

It was more like a harangue. I lamented the ways of some in the congregation, as only a repentant and reformed sinner can do, giving outrageous examples of racist and unfair events that had taken place on the Shore that in my eyes were inexcusable. And tying it to the teaching of Christ, who I said I knew would not have condoned such behavior.

You can imagine the reception I received. As I stood with the minister at the door greeting all the congregants on their way out, most would at least shake my hand, but some didn't and only a small number talked to me. However, a few ladies (no men) in sotto voice thanked me and whispered that it was "finally time that these things were said" or similar. I, of course was headed back to college and did not catch the fallout or opprobrium that I'm sure my mother and father felt.

Perhaps as many do, during my early to mid-20s I began to examine the way I had been raised, and to blame my parents for creating a little successful automaton who met all the expectations put in front of me. This caused a mini rebellion in me, and I began to not conform to expectations when home on vacations. I distinctly remember someone saying something about me to my mother in my presence and her responding "Oh, Kim would never do anything that I didn't approve of." My upbringing in a nutshell.

Now Dad I'm sure had hopes for me, and admired and appreciated my success, but he rarely put pressure on me. He did not praise me much either, though, and he took my achievements in stride. Which perhaps made me want to earn his praise and look up to him even more. This made me work harder after school so he would be impressed when he arrived home to see whatever job on the farm I had done.

Now this emerging realization of how I had been living by the expectations, and values, of my parents and society set the stage for my participation in the takeover of the administration building at Trinity to protest the lack of recruitment of Black students. This was the ultimate break from following the expected path of the "good boy".

My parents were very upset, not understanding my actions, which they saw as ingratitude to the College which had given me so much. A sympathetic faculty member (George Higgins), had to write to them, explaining my motives and the reason for my actions. This seemed to help. But as a "Big Man on Campus", as it were, I received the wrath and truly angry letters of several Trustees, who also had expectations of me, and were outraged by my actions.

So, I spent a good bit of my 20s going through a rebellious phase. But it was in the late 20s that this changed. Partly through the experiential "new age" experiences of the '70s, I began to realize and accept that my parents, particularly my mother, was only doing what she thought best for me, and being her, could have done little else. I began to forgive, having achieved a measure of independence from having to live up to society's expectations of me. I, frankly, was also getting bored with the "victimization" story and saw it as limiting my life. So I stopped worrying about it. In my 30s I began to come into my own, shed both the expectations of others and the need to rebel against those expectations, and start living by my own values, standards and expectations.

Money and Me

When we were young, I had little concept of social class or wealth differences on the Shore since everyone seemed to be within a range of everyone else, though some did have newer and bigger houses and first-hand clothes rather than hand-me-downs. I guess I knew there were differences, as I went over to my friend Hal Lassiter's and could tell that his house and style of living was a step or three up from ours.

But it didn't seem to matter. We played together, hunted together, and were on teams together. One time I foolishly thought I could hit a baseball over his mother's car and smashed the driver's side window. I dutifully paid for my hubris, and the damage out of my meager savings, $25 dollars I recall. These savings as a 12 to 13-year-old came from my winter's wages of $50 for meeting Dad's challenge to cut all the small trees and clearing out all the brush to the right and left of the Shatterhouse Path. This was all small growth between the ditch on the corner and the field using a small axe alone, leaving a park-like setting. It took me most of the winter after school to clear the two or three acres. I was immensely proud of that work, and it looked great, until the weeds and trees inevitably started growing back.

I knew that money was scarce. Mom put linoleum in our shoes when they got holes and most of our clothes were hand-me-downs. But this was little different than many other kids, and I knew we were much "wealthier" than a few kids who rode the bus in almost rags and smelled from having no running water. I felt deeply sorry for them as they had no friends and seemed very shy. I feel guilty for not making friends with one in particular as he seemed like a shy, but nice guy.

I learned to save for those things I wanted from an early age. I used to pick apples out of our orchard (bushels of different types of apples, mainly golden and red delicious) and when Mom would go into town on Saturday mornings to do shopping (before the strip mall took the business away from downtown), I would open the trunk and sell the apples out of the trunk, maybe making $5 or $10 a morning … big money for a ten-year-old then, which I saved. It seems I have always been a person who delayed gratification all my life. Eat desert last, do the hard tasks first, anticipate for later rather than indulge now.

My first real job was as the attendant on a private truck weighing scales in Tasley because Dad knew the owner. I was 15 and legally had to be 18 to do the job because of the danger from the big rigs. But nobody checked or cared. I worked 12 hours a day, six days a week for $48 dollars a week, which came out to 66 cents an hour. But it was easy work which consisted of siting in my car where I would read books until I heard the truck's air brakes, then run into the scales shack and weigh the trucks as they drove onto the scales. Sometimes I'd weigh about 100 to 120 trucks a day during high potato season. They paid a dollar for the weighing, trying to make sure they were legal when they hit the official State scales 23 miles north.

Sometimes when they were overweight on one axle, they would hire us to move the bags of potatoes from one axle to another … dirty work up in the truck body shoving 100 lb. bags of potatoes around. Once, a guy bet me a dollar that my scales were wrong and challenged me to follow him up to the State scales to prove it. I followed him and sure enough he was a little over. But they let him move the bags and he gave me the dollar and asked me to move the bags for him for another dollar. I then knew his strategy, to get me to follow him up to the scales so he would have someone to move the bags, thinking it was worth the $2 loss to have someone to move the bags up at the State scales if he had not used that much heavy gas to get up there and was still illegal. (The weight of the gas used was a big factor sometimes when their weight was close, and they were trying to figure if they would be overweight on an axle.)

When I hit college, money was more of an issue. I had gotten a Baker Scholarship which was prestigious and helped me get an $1800 financial aid package, which sounds like truly little as I write this in 2021. But the cost of college then (1964) was only about $3200 total while today it is $75,000, so I had a decent scholarship. I did not do much that cost money, with a budget of $5 a week in college. I did have a campus job, giving tours of the campus, for which I would receive $5 each Sunday from 3-6, plus any tips offered. It was a honey of a job since I wasn't doing anything else on Sunday afternoons. And sometimes no one showed up and I still got $5 for waiting around. I did a great job, memorizing all the facts about Trinity and its traditions and the gorgeous Chapel. I sometimes had praising notes sent to the Dean about my tours.

But money was tight, and Mom and Dad thankfully paid the dues for me to join Theta XI fraternity my sophomore year. Don't know how they did it on their meager salaries, but they did it, and it made a huge difference in my life.

When I graduated from Trinity and lost out for the Rhodes Scholarship, I was accepted and received an all-expense paid Fellowship to the Woodrow Wilson School at Princeton, doing graduate work in public policy, so money became less of an issue during those two years. Also, I earned money doing an internship with the Legislative Analyst's Office in California during the summer of 1969, so I was OK.

But when I entered my first job in 1970 at the Ford Foundation was when I truly made big bucks ... $12,000 a year! It was enough to live on in NYC at that time and have a $250 a month studio apt. And lunches were provided in a sumptuous dining room at the Foundation. As I moved through a series of jobs with the Governor's Justice Commission '72-74, the U.S. Justice Department, ACIR and Arthur D. Little in 1975, and finally the Executive Office of the President (EOP) ('76) I received higher and higher pay until I was making about $45,000 a year living in DC in 1980.

At this point I had enough to invest, even after buying my Tartan 27 sailboat WING for $15,000 in '76. I bought a home on the waterfront near Annapolis but sold it too early during my sailing trip to the Bahamas after leaving the EOP (on the advice of an unscrupulous real estate agent). So off I went into the world of investing, promptly losing about a quarter of my small pot of investable money through trying options. Lesson learned. In the early '80s I settled down to investing in low fee, dividend paying, stable stocks and mutual funds, and later, ETFs. Thus, began a rather lucky and small-scale lucrative career in the stock market. Investing in the '80s in two budding companies named Microsoft and Intel didn't hurt. But I really had little money to invest because this was the period when I was making peanuts working for myself as the head of my one-horse consulting firm, PMG.

But I did OK, slowly building a small portfolio of stocks, learning more and more about the tricks of making money in the market, and keeping it when paying taxes. There really is no mystery to it ...

1. Buy bundles of stocks (formerly called mutual funds, now I invest in lower cost exchange traded funds) ...
2. Choose funds holding solid stocks with ...
3. Low total fees (expense ratios) in ...
4. A diverse array of cyclical and counter-cyclical stocks covering widely varying sectors of the market. And ...
5. Stay with them, don't jump in and out of the market except to lighten up a little when it seems too high after a long run up, so you have some free money to invest when it takes a sharp dip (admittedly this last trick is a little more difficult so should include only a small portion of your assets).

During the later time in DC, I had a roommate, and then lived in Deering, New Hampshire from '86 on, with its low taxes and minimal living expenses, I began to build a sizeable nest egg to invest and did fine, particularly after I joined Dartmouth and worked my way up to a more decent annual salary, plus sometimes another $10,000 in consulting.

The Windfall

Around 2000 I bought a section of about 50 acres of land adjacent to my 18 acres of Deering property, with about a third of a mile of pond frontage. I had had my eye on this for some time and had asked the absentee owner to let me know if and when he wanted to sell it. In 2000 he agreed to sell it to me for $50,000. This was not that much of a steal because it had no road access and to reach the large pond would require that a half mile road be built through someone else's land and forest at a substantial cost. I just held it and enjoyed long walks through it and snowshoeing with Wendy on the large pond.

When I was thinking of leaving New Hampshire in 2007, I had planned to keep the 50 acre pond plot and sell my house and 18 acres. I contacted three realtors to see about realistic selling prices for the house and 18 acres. They all suggested about $180,000 to $200,000 as a realistic asking price, since I had bought the house and 18 acres for about $148,000 20 years earlier and the market was getting soft on the verge of the recession of 2008-9. (The 50 acres with the pond they thought could bring in $75,000 but I wasn't interested in selling that.)

I was reconciled to this but happened to stop by, on a lark, a fourth agent's office and showed him the land I was thinking of selling and keeping. He said he thought that he had a buyer in mind if I wanted to sell the 50 acres instead of the 18 acres and house. I said that was not my plan, but just for kicks, what did he think this fellow would pay for the 50 acre pond plot. He thought a minute and said, "I think he might pay as much as half a million for it, since he has a foundation with the sole purpose of conserving Deering land, and he has to spend a certain amount each year for that purpose".

I, playing Mr. Cool, while hiding my incredible astonishment at being possibly offered a half mill for a piece of land I had spent $50,000 on seven years earlier, said that this seemed like an almost fair price but that I really hadn't considered it. But I would show him the land to see if he would like to make an offer. I did, and he did, offering me $500,000 for the 50 acres as he had no interest in buying the adjacent 18 acres and house.

Once offered in a contract, I carefully and thoughtfully considered it for all of ten seconds before signing on the dotted line, expanding my investment portfolio considerably.

The second good fortune I had was that this cash entered my bank account when the market was at an all-time high in 2008, just before the 40% drop in stock market prices in 2009. Thinking the market was due for a drop because of the years-long frenzy in home speculation, I had left the money in cash for about six months, so when the market dropped (Dow Jones Index at 6,000 or 7,000, down from 15,000), I was able to enter the market and snap up decent stocks at discount prices, with both the $500,000 and some additional funds I had kept in cash awaiting the market fall.

A third piece of good fortune was when the local accountant I sought out (Susan Nottingham) said that because the 50 acres was adjacent to my home it could be considered as part of my home and thus, I would not have to pay the approximately $75,000 in capital gains taxes on the sale. Whoopee!

A final piece of good fortune was the following year when I negotiated the sale of the house and 18 acres for $212,000, and once again did not have to pay capital gains because Wendy had been living with me and thus the capital gains exclusion on a home occupied by a couple was not $500,000 but $1 million, saving another $15,000 or so in capital gains taxes. With this I moved back to the Virginia farm, gutted and restored it, built two additions, a 200 ft bulkhead, and a new sturdy dock. (Dad would be so proud, and astonished.) I continued investing in stocks, but conservatively, and have watched the Dow Jones average climb from a low of 6000 in 2009 up to 34,000 in 2021, taking my portfolio with it, with little action on my part.

At this time also, after watching our living expenses for several years on the farm, I began to shed the pauper's approach to saving and spending, realizing that I had enough money to keep myself and Wendy okay until the end of our days. I began to give more to charitable organizations. I began to treat myself and the family a little more generously; taking longer and more expensive trips; hiring help on the farm when I needed it rather than doing everything myself; and buying tools and some material things that make life easier, without agonizing over the cost so much. A real change from the penny pinching and saving which seemed to always mark my life.

Generosity vs Selfishness

Ever since I started working, I had given small sums to different charities. It wasn't much, usually $20-$50 mailed off to those organizations that I thought needed it most and would use it most effectively. Non-profits such as Doctors Without Borders, Human Rights Watch, Heifer International, Smile Train, etc. or organizations that gave me enjoyment, such as public radio and public TV. And there were local organizations who I thought were doing good, important work such as the Eastern Shore Coalition Against Domestic Violence (ESCADV), the Literacy Council, the local Food Bank, or organizations serving needy or minority populations (for both poverty and racism on the Shore were still strong). This charitable giving grew out of my empathizing with those in need.

Wendy went along and shared in the contributions to the organizations that I usually chose. For Wendy was a person who gave of herself directly rather than mainly monetarily to organizations she felt worthy. For example, she joined the boards of ESCADV and the Literacy Council. And became a member of the three-person local board of a chapter of an organization known as Dining for Women. This group raised donations once a month at a potluck dinner of local women which were sent off to the national organization to support projects to help impoverished women around the world. (Surprisingly, for its small size, at one point the local chapter of Dining for Women became the chapter contributing the most to this organization nationally.) Through the Literacy Council, Wendy also helped an adult student learn to read over a three-year period, meeting weekly for a few hours.

I also was on several local non-profit Boards. One in particular was fun … the Roseland Cinema and Entertainment Center (RCEC). This was a small group of volunteers who arranged to bring cultural events to the Shore, foreign films and performance films such as ballet and opera, and lecturers, and indoor and outdoor movies, which otherwise might not make it to the Shore. We arranged for most of these to be held in the Roseland movie theater, hence the name. Another board was the Academy for Lifetime Learning, a group of volunteers who organized a series of volunteer-led interesting courses or workshops in about 30 or 40 areas such as photography, knitting, travel, gardening, etc., whatever someone wanted to share with others. As mentioned earlier, I ran a workshop discussing ethical dilemmas, moral quandaries, and value conflicts.

But now that I was surer of the durability and sustainability of my wealth, I made larger donations to national and local organizations and Wendy, charitable at heart, and having recently inherited some money from her father, went along with these donations. And she had her own organizations such as ESCADV and Dining for Women that we gave money to as well. We gave some anonymously, as well as in our own names, and substantial amounts in the name of The Five Miles Farm, to honor Mom and Dad, who made it all possible for me, or in the name of Ben and Joy Nathanson, Wendy's Mom and Dad.

And we made personal anonymous gifts. Wendy would regularly ask ESCADV what they needed in terms of clothing or food and deliver it. One time on Christmas eve I saw a mother and father agonizing over whether to buy a $10 toy for their children. I pretended to find a $50 bill on the floor near them and asked them if they could use it as it wasn't mine. This worked so well that for about the past six Christmases I have taken $500 out of the bank in $50s and $20s and gone into Roses and Walmart looking for people on Christmas Eve who appeared able to use some extra money and give them a bill, pretending at times that I found it, and if that did not work (some would say that I should turn it in) I would just give it to them saying Merry Christmas and that it was money I did not need. Only once did I have a couple of women who overheard me giving the money to someone say "Oh, that's mine, I lost it a minute ago!" Needless to say, they did not get it.

I wondered what to do this year as the pandemic kept me out of stores. Wendy and I had just received the government COVID relief payments sent to everyone. Although we understood why these payments were needed in times of pandemic-driven unemployment, we did not really need the extra money, and wondered how to give this to those more in need. This was solved when one day I saw a long line of cars in line to pick up food at the Food Bank. I went to our bank, took out some money in large bills, and put one bill in each of 50 envelopes with a note "from a friend". Then I drove to the Food Bank one morning and gave away about 45 envelopes, one to each car of self-selected folks in need.

I came back in the afternoon to finish the last five, since there were only 45 cars in line that morning. Only to find that the Food Bank director asked to see me inside. Thinking that she was just going to thank me for such a nice gesture, I went in. Only to find her somewhat distraught, saying that I unfortunately had to stop, since all day long word had spread on the Shore about the Food Bank giving away money to everyone, and that folks were upset when they had to be told that this was not the case. So, I gave the remaining five envelopes to the staff and two cars outside with the warning that it was not from the Food Bank but from a friend and this was the last. This was clearly the case of unintended consequences, or "No good deed goes unpunished". Oh well.

Stymied in this effort, but with some of the Covid relief money still to give away, Wendy and I went to the Director of the Boys and Girls Club because Wendy thought that this person, as much as anyone, would know of families who would appreciate some extra money at Christmas. She was thrilled and said that she knew of many families in such need. Therefore, we gave her 15 more envelopes to distribute, with a larger bill in each, with a note from a "Friend", wishing them a Merry Christmas and thanking them for all they do to care for their family.

But the bottom line is that Wendy and I are giving to more charities each year and giving much more generously. And when I die I have instructed my lawyer to set aside some modest funds to endow an effort to address poverty, and inequality among races and ethnicities on the Shore.

But most of my effort over the past eight years has gone into finding funding for a new library, as previously discussed.

Religion and Spirituality

Religion may have played more of a role in my life that I think. I was raised as a Methodist, in the south, attending the United Methodist Church in Onancock. My mother and father, both quite shy socially, (Dad shy by nature and Mom shy class-wise), did not attend church, at least initially. On Sundays, they would drop me off in Onancock at the Methodist Church and my sister Sam off at the Baptist Church where most of her friends went. They would discreetly always pick us up on College Avenue across from the church. I learned the things you learn in a Christian church ... the life and teaching of Jesus, the miracles, the importance of faith, etc. I am certain that the teachings of Christ, because they meshed well with what a "good boy" believed, and how he acted, had a strong influence on my life. But I never bought into the son of God story, or the miracles... I was too much of a questioner, a realist, and even a scientist who needed explanations for things, to adopt things based upon faith.

However, without question, Christ's teachings about humility, treating people of all classes and stations well, helping those in need, and living by a set of selfless values that elevated a person, made a big impression on me. (Though not as big a motivator for attending church as sitting up front in the choir holding hands with Robin under our robes in front of the whole congregation.) For Sunday School was a social occasion for me, particularly Vacation Bible School, which was one of the few times during the summer when I had a lot of social contact with my peers each week, other than hitchhiking into town to play baseball some afternoons.

But I never gave much thought to my beliefs until I reached college and ideas began to challenge orthodoxy and resulted in my having to frame a belief system of my own. I also learned about the many equally valued and stultifying religions in the world, faithfully practiced by others. It was then that I had to decide exactly what religion, if any, I would live my life by. I chose none.

I do not find I need a higher power to guide me in the honorable and kind life I want to lead, having made those choices independent of any scripture. And yet a part of me understands the desire to believe. Another part of me thanks the fates for keeping Wendy or the children safe after a long trip and prompts me to ask that she or they be kept safe when leaving on that trip. Where does that come from? Who am I asking? I chalk it up to the fates as I do not believe in the power of prayer to a higher power, other than the power to achieve an effect on our own destiny through the process or act of believing, with no outside force responsible for that effect.

Thus, it must be mentioned that I do not believe in a heaven and hell or an afterlife, and certainly not one in which we are rewarded or punished for our way of living this life. It might be helpful if heaven and hell existed, as a reward or threat, to encourage responsible, socially ordered, respectful living here on earth and to discourage evil doing, but I don't see it.

It would also be nice to think that our consciousness might come back in some form of living plant or animal life, a la reincarnation, but I cannot see that either, and I don't believe it (after all, how did the first group of living things get here to be reincarnated time after time?) I think that therefore we must consciously choose how we live our life in ways we think are best for us, living in a society in which we all must exist. This implies weighing the consequences of a life of a criminal, a liar, a con artist, versus a life of service, respect for others, compliance with social laws and standards ... and all gradations in between. (This also is why I find my sympathies leaning towards those who by circumstance, talents, upbringing, or crises, find themselves unable to live the kind of successful, honorable life they would like, and are forced to live in poverty, scraping by as they can, sometimes leading to crime.)

I knew I truly was a person free to make choices for myself, free of the guilt caused by nonadherence to a set of rules set by a faith. This led to a need in my late 20s and 30s to make behavioral and life choices, at every instance, based upon the life I wanted to lead, the person I wanted to be, and who I wanted to be known as. This did not lead to a systematic code of conduct or ethics, which can be written down and followed. Rather it led to increasing comfort with the choices I made being in sync with the person I am. This meant not having to reflect too much on what to do in any situation, unless it was a close call in terms of rewards and consequences within the framework of the ethical life I chose.

Now this did not sit too well with my mother, who in her later years, say from 40 on, found a little church, the nearby Methodist Church in Cashville, which on a good Sunday had a congregation of 15-20, including the minister (who served three small churches each Sunday morning) and the choir. Mom became the organist and a regular attendee. Dad did not, at least initially. I think he was more of an independent thinker, and also shy socially, so he did not accompany Mom.

Until ... one Sunday when I was home for a holiday, I came

downstairs to find Mom crying, and quite loudly. Mom never cried. I occasionally went to church with Mom when I was home visiting. This was because I knew she wanted me to and because she asked me to. But I made her find out if it was one of those Sundays when communion was held because I did not want to embarrass her by being the only one who refused to walk down the aisle and take the body and blood of Jesus to eat. Didn't buy into that.

In any event her crying I learned, was because Dad refused to go with her to church. And because of her emotional distress (which I think had a lot to do with her being 50 and going through menopause), I began crying, and did something I regret doing to this day … I went out to the garage where Dad was building yet another boat, and still crying, yelled at him "Why don't you go to church with Mom?!"

After that he faithfully went to church every Sunday and they became big supporters of the church (if $25 each Sunday would be considered big support, which it was for that small church). The congregation was increased by one and Mom became the organist until her late '80s, when they replaced her in a big controversy (at least to Mom) with a machine that played the hymns. She began to lose contact with the church (in a bit of a huff) at that point.

I have come to lament my shaming of Dad in that instance and for that purpose.

Suffice it to say that I seem to have chosen to live a life following pretty closely the tenets of a religious life – a lot Christ-like, a little Buddhist, etc. -- as best I can. I worked it out in my own mind that my behavior had to be based on what I thought was the best way to live one's life. And, perhaps not surprisingly, many of the values that I chose to live by closely resemble those of my early religious teachings. This, without the trappings of Christianity or having to adhere to the more mystical beliefs associated with the religion, the miracles, the myth of the resurrection, the rituals. It seems to work ... for me.

Space, the Universe, and God

I stick this brief note in here because I have always been fascinated by the vastness, the mysteries, and the unknowability of the Universe, what it is, what it contains, and where, and if, it ends. And as mysterious, what is it IN? For nothing that we know here in our limited existence is not IN something else. Everything that we know has a boundary outside of which is something else.

In my short time on this earth, we have learned so much about space and the composition of the universe. Yet with each new discovery, old tenets must get tossed, and new theories emerge only to be tested by new discoveries. During my childhood, the magnitude of space astounded me, and I could never get my friends, with the exception of George Fosque and Ben Jaffee, to feel the same way as I did about the utter vastness, the awesome possibilities, and be humbled by our lack of understanding of the forces and entities "out there".

I bring this up in the context of my mortality because I think that the one thing I will miss most in not living into the future will be not being around to witness and understand our increasing knowledge of the origins and makeup of the Universe, and how this new knowledge and understanding changes our certainties about forces and concepts we have taken as absolutes. Where did this Universe come from? How did it develop? What is its end? I cannot conceive that there are no other living things "out there". I think there must be millions. Yet I cannot believe that the life forms that exist will have any resemblance to us, or that their anatomy, biochemistry or societal structures will be understood by us if found.

The vastness of the Universe, even as we now know it, caused me to question, and reject, the concept of a single God creating our world, watching our little earth, or even caring about what goes on in our lives as many seem to believe. How could he or she oversee the billions of galaxies, solar systems, and trillions of stars and planets spread across the billions of light years of space? It was inconceivable to me.

I also put the concept of a God who looked down on us all and knew our deeds and listened and answered our prayers in the context of what I was beginning to learn about the Universe. I could not reconcile the wonders and size of the Universe, and the billions of solar systems in as many galaxies, billions of light years apart, with the idea of a single maker who was omnipresent, or who even gave a damn about us earthlings. This latter juxtaposition of the Universe with a personal God, was what more than anything convinced me that the image of God as an all knowing and loving (or vengeful, depending upon what you read) personage, just wouldn't fly. I could entertain some force being responsible for bringing the universe into existence, but not an all seeing God answering our individual prayers. (A winning athlete thanking God for letting him win seems the height of absurdity and arrogance to me.)

Mortality

I don't think I have ever feared death. Now dying, that's another matter. I certainly don't look forward to the actual process of dying, which usually involves much discomfort, perhaps intense pain, lack of mobility and, the biggest dread of all – the possible inability to think or even communicate as the result of a stroke. Even dementia is not as threatening to me as a stroke, for with dementia you may not even be aware that you cannot think or communicate well, but with a stroke, you may desperately wish to communicate but be unable to. Aagh!

Approaching my 76th birthday I am much more aware of my mortality than ever. My last two years particularly have brought the realization home that I am aging rather quickly, as I cannot do the work, lift the weight, or even rise up from the floor, as effortlessly as I could a few short years ago. Arthritis is progressing, steadiness is faltering, stamina is diminished, and my blood is thickening due to a condition called hypercoagulation which makes me susceptible to blood clots and pulmonary embolisms, two of which have caused me to be hospitalized twice in the past two years. I do sense that age is creeping up on me more quickly than I had hoped. Perhaps this is why I am choosing to get up at 5 a.m. each morning to write this mini memoir … it's now or possibly never.

And as I see more and more of my friends and acquaintances die or sicken with cancer or other debilitating diseases, I see how short a period they are mourned. I see how little they are remembered, and how folks little realize or remember the legacy they have left for the world, even those who when alive, seemed to me to have lived a full life with substantial contributions. I wonder what legacy I will leave, if and how I will be remembered, and what lasting impact I have made. It's a conceit of course, to think that one should be remembered in any lasting way. But the wish is there, and leaving a legacy is important to me now. Hopefully, my nieces, nephews, stepchildren and grandchildren will remember me fondly. Maybe this book will help.

Anyway, I am feeling my mortality more acutely now, in this time of pandemic, when life, travel, friends, and adventures, must necessarily be put on hold, just as time for these things becomes shorter and shorter.

Thoughts on Issues of the Day...

I had planned to write, and actually had written, a reasonably long section on my thoughts on the major issues of today … inequity and inequality in the world, climate change, world trade, nationalism vs globalism, racism, the role of government, democracy vs autocracy and authoritarianism, you get the picture. But the more I fleshed out these issues and what I thought, I realized that this should go in a different kind of media, or book. So, I will leave this for later.

Finally ... Why "A Life Half-Lived?"

I've thought about this, and not in the context of time lived. I put it in the subtitle of this book because I think it especially important. I believe that many of us live less than full lives, and I do not mean in length of our lives. Not all of us, and not all the time, but many of us, and perhaps for too much of the time. For, in spite of the full-seeming lives we have led, I believe we could have done, and can do, much more to live up to our potential. And I think that the thing that limits us, that keeps us from being and doing all that we are capable of, from living fully, from being our authentic selves at every moment of our lives, is FEAR. This is possibly fear of several things at different times or situations. Fear of embarrassment, fear of being judged, fear of loving or of losing love, fear of failing, fear of succeeding, fear of being thought a fool, or being thought different, fear of risking, fear of dying ... all can keep us from living complete, authentic moment-to-moment lives, from making the difference in the world of which we truly are capable. I believe that we all too often censor ourselves because of these normal, human, but oh, so life-minimizing fears, and in so doing live partially-lived lives. For myself, I lived into my late 30s with these fears limiting me, before largely shedding them. And even now I must check myself to avoid letting them creep into, and limit, the way I live my life. (An example is the fear of what happens when this self-revelatory tome is published, which I've had to repeatedly overcome to include certain sections!)

There are, of course, some who seem to come closer to living full lives, who seem to go all out, who exist without these fears, who amaze us by their fearlessness, their willingness to wear purple, to defy convention, to speak and act boldly and with courage. And we wonder ... did they grow up with this fearlessness, or grow out of their fearfulness? For we may notice that the older we get, the more we are able to both recognize how our fears limit us, and to overcome those fears. And how liberating when we do! How intoxicating to live fully in the moment without those fears and self-censorship, to live up to our full potential and be the most complete human being of which we are capable ... to wear purple! To not fear the real or imagined consequences of acting as we would like or know we should. To recognize, address, and eventually overcome the particular fears which limit us from being fully alive and acting with courage.

Yes, it is scary, and often has consequences, but to not do so also has consequences ... physical, mental, and surely societal. For life is precious, and to live it knowing that you are not being the whole person you can be, to not do all you can do, to live with fear, even if mostly unconscious, is to sell it and yourself short. And I know we, and clearly I, must not do that, certainly in the time remaining to me. This I do believe and commit.

Thank you for that most precious of commodities: your time.

THE END

Addendum

Grandparents

Now a little about my grandparents Big Daddy (Allison J. Mathias), and Big Momma (Bessie McPherson Mathias), my mother's parents, and Pop Pop (Samuel D. Miles) and Mom Mom (Roxie Wessells Miles), Dad's parents.

Big Momma and Big Daddy

We lived with my grandparents on my mother's side for five years until 1951 when I was five. They were both a type of orphan. Big Daddy's mother and father were reportedly first cousins. His mother Jenny died not too long after Big Daddy's birth in 1892, and he was raised in Chicago by his father, Thomas Mathias, who was reportedly an alcoholic. The story is that young Big Daddy would at times have to go into the bars and retrieve his father to bring him home. When Big Daddy was eight, his father, or the authorities following Thomas Mathias' death, put a label in the eight-year old's buttonhole and sent him on the train from Chicago to New York to live with an aunt, May Morton, (evidently a common practice back then when a widowed man finds that he cannot take care of a child). Big Daddy had a sister, Olive, about whose early life little is known, though she later was known by all as living in rural New York state.

Big Momma's mother, Flora Drown, died in the 1890s when Bessie was three, of consumption, and her father, Wallace McPherson, took care of her with her older sister Frances and her brother, Roy. Wallace McPherson did not think he could raise her

Bessie McPherson Mathias
Big Momma

Bessie and Allison Mathias
Big Momma and Big Daddy

well, so he had another neighboring family, Harriett and Gene Whitlock, take her temporarily. She had a deformed hand (no thumb on one hand), and a limp from having hip dysplasia from birth. She was beautiful, and had a sweet, pure singing voice. Big Momma wrote a book, "Consider the Sparrow", which mirrored her life from 1893 to the 1960s in only slightly fictionalized form. Mom edited and completed the book and had it published in the 1980s after Big Momma's death.

Here are a few more tidbits I heard of their early history.

The story I was told was that Harriett Whitlock did not get along with Big Momma's father, Mr. McPherson, whom Big Momma adored, and after she took Big Momma in, she would not let him visit very often or take her back from them. The reason is unknown. The temporary arrangement became permanent. I'm told that later, near the end of his life, Wallace McPherson,

A page from Big Momma's 1917 ledger

Big Momma's father, came to live with us for a while on Kerr St. before he died. Harriett Whitlock, Big Momma's "adopted" mother, lived to be over one hundred years old.

I don't know much about Big Momma and Big Daddy's courtship, but Big Momma and Big Daddy met in Ellicottville,

NY. In 1913 Big Daddy was working for a neighbor on the Van Der Water dairy farm, selling products to a nearby creamery. Big Momma was teaching in a one-room school and living with a neighbor. Big Daddy was invited to supper at the neighbor's house, where he met Big Momma and it was the proverbial "love at first sight". They were married in 1913 in Aunt May Morton's parlor.

Because money was tight, Big Momma kept meticulous records of expenses and income in ledgers.

When the creamery shut down in 1921, they no longer had a sales outlet. Big Momma and Big Daddy thus moved from southwestern NY with their three children, Robert, Alice, and two-year old Helen, our mother, to the Eastern Shore at the urging of Big Daddy's uncle, John Stuart Mathias (Thomas's brother), a farmer, barrel maker, and general store owner in Greenbush, Virginia. On the Shore Big Daddy did all sorts of jobs - barrel making, carpentry (one of the builders of the Cape Charles School), gravedigger - you name it to keep body and soul together, and he probably did it. Big Daddy took whatever job he could to make do, working at one point for Charlie Russell in construction.

My Uncle Robert (Mom's older brother), who with his wife Peggy, had four children – Gayle, Stuart, Wade, and Phillip – once researched our Mathias family tree back to Wales, and noted that the original Thomas Mathias had emigrated to the U.S. in 1851. Robert's son Stuart, my cousin, who lives nearby, has a 2'x 3' auction poster, listing all the stock and crops to be auctioned on September 29, and 30, 1851, by Thomas Mathias who is "about leaving the country" for America. Another of Robert's sons, Wade, did additional genealogical work to trace our lineage back even further.

About leaving the country

Four Generations:
Grandpa McPherson, Bessie Mathias, Helen Miles, and Barbie Miles

Mom had an older sister as well, Alice Mathias, who had three children, Joyce, Josephine (Jo), and Steve, who became a song writer with several hits, including "She Believes in Me" sung by Kenny Rogers. Joyce married but died at age 50 from cancer. Jo returned to live on the Shore with her husband Kim Penland after he retired from his career in the oil business, which had them traveling around the world living in multiple countries. Jo has four children and nine grandchildren.

A brother of Thomas Mathias stayed in Wales and raised his family. The fantasy was that the family staying behind was living in "Keeston Castle" but when Robert visited Wales, he found the family living modestly on a small stone-walled farm with a simple farmhouse. I later visited those ancestors on their farm on a motorcycle trip to Europe in 1968. Genuinely nice people, of modest means, busily bringing in hay when I visited.

Big Momma and Big Daddy were good to us. Not too long after the stores were sold around 1950, they moved from the

Kerr Street house to "Tizit", (short for "This is it!") a house they had bought earlier in the forties with an orange and grapefruit grove in Mount Dora, Florida, not far from Orlando, which did not have the Disney complex at the time. Every winter they sent us a large crate of oranges and grapefruits on the train, which we enjoyed all winter. They also visited for a month or two every summer after we moved to the farm. Big Daddy would spend his time cutting brush along the road, which he loved to do, (probably where I got my love of doing this).

Big Momma loved playing the card game Canasta with all of us. This involved two decks of cards which resulted in large hands sometimes numbering 16 or 18 cards being held in our hands. The wonder was that Big Momma, with a deformed hand, could hold all the cards. She beat us regularly.

Big Momma also was an inveterate enterer of contests ... any kind, all kinds. Her favorites were contests requiring poetry or ditties for advertising products as she would write them and send them off all the time. We were amazed at how many she won, largely through her experience, which resulted in skill in knowing what the judges wanted based upon the product being hyped. She would win cash prizes, appliances (once a refrigerator), a few trips, and all sorts of small prizes, and must have entered three or four contests a week. Big Momma also kept several albums of pictures, poetry, prayers, and sayings, both hers and others. My mother, Helen, took this habit to extremes, and was the source of many of the pictures in this book. Big Momma helped around the house and gave Mom some companionship on the farm. I have perhaps 20 such albums of pictures and sayings I know not what to do with.

Big Daddy had some eccentricities. He liked to call all of us kids "George". Whether this was because he had trouble keeping our names straight is not known. He also loved glazed donuts for breakfast and had one or two every morning while visiting us in the summers. Big Daddy also would trade for a new car every year at the local Johnson's car dealership. He loved the smell and touch of a new car.

One trait that Big Momma and Big Daddy had was that whenever they decided to leave, after staying with us for a month or two on the farm in the summer, they would not tell anyone, just get up very early in the morning, about 3 or 4 o'clock, and just leave, very quietly, but with a note saying that they were "on the road". Big Daddy, born in 1892, died in 1969. Big Momma was bereft and lost, until Jo (Mom's niece, her sister Alice's daughter) and Jo's husband Kim Penland persuaded her to take her first airplane flight to stay with them for a month in England ... her "Impossible Dream" she said. Upon Big Momma's return she stayed with Mom and Dad at the Five Miles Farm for a month or so and returned to Florida where she died in 1976 at age 83.

Four Generations:
Big Sam Miles, Pop Pop Miles, Daddy, and Barbie Miles

Mom Mom and Barbie

Pop Pop and Barbie

Pop Pop, Mom Mom, Barbie, and me

Mom Mom and Pop Pop

Dad's parents were Clarence E. "Sam" Miles (Pop Pop) and Roxie Wessells Miles (Mom Mom). I don't remember much about Pop Pop, as he died in 1948 from Rocky Mountain Tick Fever at the age of 49, when I was three. He was a former railroad station master in Bloxom who became a poultry farmer, raising chickens in a small chicken house in Hopeton between Parksley and Bloxom. I do remember their house next to the chicken house, as my cousin Greg and I played there often.

Dad's brother Kenneth Miles also had a chicken operation for a while, and lived nearby with his wife Libby, and his sons Artie and Ted, both of whom remain on the Shore.

One night when I was very young, maybe five or six, I was spending the night at Pop Pop and Mom Mom's house, and they had pint pee jars in our rooms, so we did not have to go downstairs in the middle of the night. Sure enough, I had to go, and started peeing in the jar. Unfortunately, I filled that sucker and couldn't stop very easily and peed all over the place. Very embarrassing, but this book is about "episodes", and this was one I remembered.

Dad's father, Pop Pop, was the son of Samuel D. Miles or "Big Sam". Big Sam was a Chincoteague waterman who, the legend goes, "Could crush a clam in his bare hand."

I remember Mom Mom, Dad's mother, as being quite strict and we kids were a little afraid of her. I was not close to her, but my cousin Greg and his brother Harry (Dad's sister Sis and her husband, Wimpy Parks' children) were closer and spent more time with her, since they lived close to her in Bloxom, Virginia. I visited them often and Greg and I being about the same age, had many good times.

Mom and Pop Pop, and several other Miles generations, are both buried in the various Miles plots at the church in Modestown. The earliest Miles interred there was my great great grandfather Elijah Miles, born in 1827 and lived to the ripe old age of 97, dying in 1924, having had three wives and ten children. Wendy and I have arranged for markers in the newest Miles plot to be inscribed when we die. Though we will be cremated, it seems there should be some record of our life on this earth after leaving it.

I have inserted this addendum because I see in myself many of the characteristics of my grandparents and I thank them for my parents, as well as their time with us.

www.ingramcontent.com/pod-product-compliance
Lightning Source LLC
Chambersburg PA
CBHW042041240426
43667CB00047B/2938